THE DIALOGUE OF REASON

The Dialogue of Reason

An Analysis of Analytical Philosophy

L. JONATHAN COHEN

CLARENDON PRESS · OXFORD

1986

Oxford University Press, Walton Street, Oxford OX2 6DP

Oxford New York Toronto
Delhi Bombay Calcutta Madras Karachi
Kuala Lumpur Singapore Hong Kong Tokyo
Nairobi Dar es Salaam Cape Town
Melbourne Auckland
and associated companies in
Beirut Berlin Ibadan Nicosia

Oxford is a trade mark of Oxford University Press

Published in the United States
by Oxford University Press, New York

British Library Cataloguing in Publication Data

Cohen, L. Jonathan
The dialogue of reason: an analysis of
analytical philosophy.
1. Analysis (Philosophy)
I. Title
190   B808.5
ISBN 0-19-824905-5

Library of Congress Cataloging in Publication Data

Cohen, L. Jonathan (Lawrence Jonathan).
The dialogue of reason.
Includes index.
1. Analysis (Philosophy)—Addresses, essays, lectures.
I. Title.
B808.5.C55 1986   149'943   86-758
ISBN 0-19-824905-5

Typeset by Joshua Associates Limited, Oxford
Printed in Great Britain
at the University Printing House, Oxford
by David Stafford
Printer to the University

For Stephen, Daniel, Robin, and Juliet

Preface

PREPARATION of this book was made possible by my tenure of a British Academy Readership in the Humanities during 1982-4, and by a term's sabbatical leave from my college thereafter. Jonathan Adler supplied me with many perceptive comments on an earlier draft, and provoked me into making some drastic revisions of it. Ian Maclean enabled me to think how the various arguments of that draft might appear to many philosophers outside the analytical tradition, and I have tried to clarify the relevant passages accordingly. To both of these friends I owe a substantial debt of gratitude for the care with which they read the text and for the time they devoted to thinking about it. I only hope that the final version will not disappoint them too much. I am also grateful for the comments and criticisms offered by the Oxford University Press's reader, and by those attending various lectures, conferences, seminars, or classes (in about three dozen universities or institutes in Australia, China, Hungary, Italy, Netherlands, New Zealand, UK, USA, and USSR) at which I have read papers that included earlier drafts of parts of the book.

Almost all the text is published here for the first time. But some paragraphs of § 13 have appeared in Russian in *Voprosi Filosofii*, 2, 1980, pp. 143-56 and in Chinese in *Philosophical Problems of Natural Sciences*, 1, 1981, pp. 12-18. And some paragraphs of Chapter IV are about to appear in the published proceedings of the 7th International Congress for Logic, Methodology, and Philosophy of Science. I am grateful to the editors concerned for not objecting to my weaving this material into the text of the present book.

Pat Lloyd has typed and retyped and re-retyped my manuscript with the care, patience, and accuracy that characterize all her work.

Unless there are contextual reasons to suppose otherwise, the pronoun 'he' is to be understood in the text as meaning 'he or she', the pronoun 'him' as meaning 'him or her' and the pronoun 'his' as meaning 'his or her'.

The Queen's College   L.J.C.
Oxford
19 February 1985

Contents

I

Introduction: Analysis and Language

§ 1 WHAT HOLDS THE ANALYTICAL DIALOGUE TOGETHER– TENETS, METHODS, OR PROBLEMS?

Summary: Analytical philosophy deserves a better rationale than it has so far been given. Identifying it by the historical limits of participation in its dialogue, we need to elucidate what holds this dialogue together: tenets, methods, or problems?

PHILOSOPHY, as most philosophers would agree, aims at an explicit resolution of fundamental issues that would otherwise remain undiscussed. But this characterization, though it may roughly suffice to identify a familiar form of intellectual activity, is too vague to be philosophically illuminating. So among the fundamental issues that require philosophical resolution is the nature of philosophical enquiry itself. Of course excessive attention to this issue, as to any other methodological issue, may impede the progress of substantive enquiry. But from time to time philosophers undoubtedly owe their students, their critics, their colleagues, and themselves a relatively precise account–sometimes now called a 'metaphilosophy'–of the activity on which they take themselves to be engaged. Indeed, that activity stands just as much in need of a philsophical methodology, analysis, or rational reconstruction as does natural science or any other mode of intellectual enquiry. Philosophy is inherently self-critical.

But two very different kinds of metaphilosophy are possible– aggressive and defensive.

The aggressive option is chosen when a metaphilosopher pro-pounds reasons for finding fault with much or all of current philo-sophical practice within his intellectual community. Perhaps he also formulates a new programme and even takes some steps towards its execution. It is this aggressive option that has been exercised recently by anti-analytical philosophers like Rorty,[1] for example, and

---

[1] R. Rorty, *Philosophy and the Mirror of Nature*, Princeton: Princeton UP, 1980.

Kekes,[2] and in the past by such illustrious innovators as Kant and Wittgenstein.

The defensive option in metaphilosophy seeks instead to provide a rationale for some widely dominant philosophical practice within the relevant intellectual community. This is the option that will be pursued in the present book, with particular reference to analytical philosophy. Earlier in the century analytical philosophy was itself on the attack, shooting out its manifestos against a long-entrenched establishment. Now it is, in its turn, assaulted by mounting demands for alternative programmes. And against those assaults it deserves a better defence than it has so far been given.

An adequate apologia for analytical philosophy would achieve three closely interconnected objectives. Two of these lie in the judgement of the intellectual community at large, one in that of analytical philosophy itself. To satisfy external interest that apologia must both make coherent sense of the vast diversity of analytical activity that has actually developed and must also elucidate what kind of value that activity has. Chapters I and II of the present book aim to achieve this dual objective. But to satisfy internal interest an apologia must also achieve some non-trivial contribution towards a creative enhancement of analytical philosophy's self-awareness: it must show how the analysis of analytical philosophy is bound up with the resolution of some substantive issues, and that is what Chapters III and IV of the present book aim to show. Pursuit of the first two objectives without the third would risk an accusation–from the viewpoint of ordinary analytical philosophy–of being more concerned with form than with substance, or of allowing oneself to be satisfied with the description of what might be merely accidental features of all previous analytical philosophy, while to pursue the third alone would be just to dodge a large part of the case put forward by contemporary critics of analytical philosophy. But, if all three objectives are actually attainable, the apologia should have sufficient strength for its purpose. The case for radical change will turn out to be very much weaker than its champions suppose.

At first sight this kind of defensive metaphilosophy may seem excessively easy to get right. 'All you have to do', it will be said, 'is to restrict your list of recognized analytical philosophers so as to confine it to those whose work fits your rationale, and success is guaranteed. Anyone whose work does not fit your account can be rejected as not

<hr>

[2] J. Kekes, *The Nature of Philosophy*, Oxford: Blackwell, 1980.

being sufficiently analytical in his approach to the subject. Consequently, whatever the list of names you use to identify analytical philosophy, any success that you have in giving an account of it will be trivial.'

But fortunately this rather pessimistic prediction is unfounded, because the nature of the task, if seen in these terms, has been misconceived. The onward movement of philosophy is not to be thought of just as a sequence of authors and their writings, but as a continuing, many-sided dialogue. At any rate, that is how almost all philosophers themselves treat it, sometimes even at the cost of exaggerating their own ability to understand exactly what their predecessors were thinking.

Admittedly, it is possible for monologues to inform, edify, console, or entertain. But philosophy aims at persuasion, appeals to shared principles and invites criticism. It therefore takes place within the framework of a dialogue either in informal conversation, or in formal debate, or between imagined dramatis personae, or in successive publications, with one contributor taking over from another, through minutes, months, years, or even centuries. Indeed its overall progress, its periods of decline, its peaks of achievement, can be judged only in terms of changes in the quality of the dialogue and of individual contributions thereto.

People sometimes complain, as Kekes has recently done,[3] that philosophy, unlike science, exhibits no growing pyramid of consensus. There is no accumulation of philosophical knowledge, they say, and the main issues that Plato raised are still being discussed today. But it is in the nature of fundamental issues that they do not admit of universally acceptable solutions. Such solutions are possible only within an adequate framework of agreed premises or principles of inference, and controversy about fundamental issues arises where it does arise just because this kind of framework does not exist there. So the objective progress of philosophy has to be judged instead by appraisal of its merit as a dialogue between people who do not necessarily all share the same premises and principles. Its progress over time, or space, is to be seen in the embracing of new problems for discussion; in the more extensive matching of opposed theories; in the exposition and criticism of new arguments or the more rigorous discussion of old ones; in the more searching exploration of conceptual possibilities; in the more coherent, or more synoptic, development of

[3] Op. cit., pp. 4-5.

intellectual positions; in the strength of determination to leave no assumptions unquestioned–and so on. Conversely the occasional periods of decline in philosophy are marked by absence of challenge to widely accepted theories; by reduction in the variety of issues discussed; by the confounding of important distinctions that were once drawn; by lack of concern for powerful arguments that were once acknowledged; by failure to pursue a controversial principle far enough into its once recognized implications; or by suffocating silence.

More will be said later about this dialectical character of philosophical activity. What is relevant here is its impact on the preliminary delimitation of the field of enquiry. One cannot just pick out those philosophers whose work fits some preconceived paradigm, because what one has to be guided by is not a question-beggingly selective set of names but a relatively self-contained segment of dialogue. The boundaries of this segment are determined independently by the fact that much greater interchange of discussion and argument occurs and has occurred between some philosophers than between others, even though we may find many interesting circles of philosophical discussion and many subdialogues within more extensive ones. So any worthwhile rationale of philosophical enquiry must respect the effective limits of the particular dialogue to which it offers a contribution. It should not claim or expect cogency as an account of philosophical reasoning beyond those limits, but it has to cover the whole dialogue that is bounded by them.

How far, then, does the analytical dialogue extend? In its twentieth-century history the work of Frege in Germany, of Twardowski in Poland, and of Russell and Moore in Great Britain, has had a seminal effect, though earlier influences may be traced to men like Bolzano, Fries, Sidgwick, and Peirce. Substantial strands of continuity may also be detected through the work of Kant, Hume, Leibniz, and many others, right back to Socrates' initial search for definitions. From those sources a rich variety of interconnected philosophical discussion has developed in the post-1918 world. A full list of important and influential figures in the ensuring movement would have to include Wittgenstein, Schlick, Carnap, Popper, Ryle, Wisdom, Hempel, Reichenbach, von Wright, Quine, Austin, Strawson, Sellars, Goodman, Davidson, Hare, Rawls, Putnam, Kripke, Lakatos, Williams, Dummett, Hintikka, Parfit, and many others like them. Very considerable differences, in intellectual purpose or in substantive doctrine, separate many of these thinkers from one another. But their work, together with that of their associates, disciples, and critics, nevertheless constitutes a relatively well-bounded dialogue. Carnap, for example, interchanged many criticism with Popper and Quine, but few if any, with Husserl, Heidegger, Polanyi, or Derrida. And when serious discussions, or exchanges of criticism, *have* taken place between analytical philosophers and outsiders, these have tended not to constitute fruitful and continuing controversies, but occasional set piece affairs, where the participants meet once, as it were, and rather sterilely agree to differ, as at the conference at Royaumont in 1958.

So, despite a few overlaps, analytical philosophy is not difficult to distinguish broadly in these terms from other modern movements, like phenomenology, say, or existentialism, or from the large amount of philosophizing that has also gone on in the present century within frameworks deriving from other influential thinkers like Aquinas, Hegel, or Marx.

But the question that arises here about analytical philosophy is this. What holds it together? Is any one set of problems, methods, or tenets shared so widely that it operates, albeit perhaps implicitly or unconsciously, as a unifying force–a presupposition of communication–within the dialogue? Or is this apparent unity just a scattering of different similarities, like the system of facial resemblances within a family? Is it merely the product of a wide variety of networks of intellectual interests and practices that overlap one another at different points and do not share even a single all-pervading principle?

Those who are satisfied with an account in terms of family resemblance will presumably seek no further. Such an account is certainly tempting to many who are analytical philosophers themselves. When you are in a forest you may well see only the differences between the trees, not those between your own forest and others. But philosophers who support a family-resemblance account bear a heavy burden of proof. Such an account, if true, would be much more difficult to establish than a unitary explanation. No one could establish it just by pointing to the obvious differences between Wittgenstein's philosophy and Carnap's, say, or between Strawson's and Quine's. Nor could anyone establish it merely by displaying the actual overlaps of interests and practices in all their extensive detail. This kind of evidence might help to account for relative densities of critical interchange between different members of the analytical movement. But it would by no means exclude the possibility that some tacitly unifying theme pervades the whole movement. Obvious differences of topic, method, or substance could just result from different ways of pursuing this single theme: even a disease can take different forms in different circumstances. In order to exclude such a possibility altogether a space of mutually exclusive, and jointly exhaustive, unitary explanations would have to be demonstrated, and then each of these unitary explanations in turn would have to be shown inadequate to its task. But it is at least as difficult to demonstrate such a space of possible explanations for analytical philosophy as it is for some domain of natural-scientific theory. Characteristically, human enquiry proceeds instead, at these explanatory levels, by the invention and investigation of a new hypothesis as anomalies begin to threaten the one currently accepted or entertained. And that is how the argument of the present book will proceed. If the argument fails, the family-resemblance position will be strengthened, but it will not thereby be proved correct.

A substantially easier task would be just to make the development of modern analytical philosophy intelligible in historical terms. One could summarize the views of the most influential thinkers, specify their various originalities, and trace out the complicated patterns of source and influence. One could add appropriate references to the other cultural events and achievements which seem also to have affected analytical philosophy, or to have been affected by it, such as the mathematicization of logic (Boole, Frege, Russell), the rise of experimental psychology (Wundt, James, Watson, etc.), the overthrow of Newtonian mechanics (Einstein, Heisenberg, etc.), the invention of high-powered computers (Turing), or the revolution in grammatical theory (Chomsky). Such an account could not only do descriptive justice to the very wide variety of philosophical activity that has composed this dialogue; also, each new philosophical move, or each new turn in an old one, could be set in an illuminating context. The reader would be helped to understand what has gone on in much the same sense as a good book on the history of science helps him to understand seventeenth-century developments, say, in the theory of motion. What would thus be explained would be the occurrence of one or more temporal sequences of events in the intellectual history of the human race.

But that is not at all the type of explanation or understanding that the present book seeks to achieve. For there is also a characteristically philosophical question to be asked about the analytical movement, in abstraction from any consideration of its personal composition, of its temporal ordering, or of external influences that have affected it. What counts here is the content of what has been said, not the date or author of its utterance. Specifically, we may ask: on what assumptions about the nature of philosophical problems, methods, or doctrines can all, or very nearly all, the relevant strands of dialogue be regarded as sharing a distinctive philosophical objective? In a rather analogous way we can distinguish between a historical account of the early seventeenth-century achievements of Kepler and Galileo in the study of celestial or terrestrial motion, on the one side, and, on the other, the theoretical explanation of these discoveries by Newton when, in effect, he answered the scientific, non-historical question: on what assumptions about the nature of space, time, and matter can celestial and terrestrial mechanics be regarded as constituting different parts or consequences of a single scientific theory? No doubt Newton's question was scientific, not philosophical, and correspondingly his success in answering it was a vastly more startling and definitive achievement than any that a philosopher may attempt. But, despite this obvious disparity, the analogy may nevertheless serve to clarify just how much the main problem tackled in the present book differs from the questions that arise for historical accounts of the analytical movement. That difference should be further illustrated by the extent to which the proposed resolution of the problem touches at various points on substantive philosophical issues. The history of philosophy is just a branch of intellectual history in general, and obeys criteria of interest appropriate to this backward-looking perspective. But metaphilosophy, as already remarked, tends towards emptiness or banality unless it touches from time to time on some current issues in first-order philosophical discussion. So, on the way towards its conclusion, the present book will be found to say a good deal incidentally about thought, belief, judgement, and reasoning.

Again, it is worth remarking that at each level of reflection on a field of data the demands for deeper theoretical understanding press us to disregard certain kinds of differences as superficial or irrelevant in order to discover underlying unity. The success of this move at a lower level of reflection prompts us to essay it also at a higher one. Thus ice, water, and steam have to be conceived as the same kind of substance (though at different temperatures) in order that natural history may give way to chemical theory. Men like Dalton and Lavoisier in turn have to be conceived as sharing at least some common objectives in order that there may be room for the philosophy of science as well as for its history. So too, in a further twist of the spiral, Carnap and Wittgenstein have to be conceived as sharing some common intellectual purpose in order that the history of analytical philosophy may allow room for *its* philosophy.

For example, one answer to the philosophical problem about analytical philosophy is so familiar that to many it must appear a truism. The distinctive feature of the analytical movement, we have often been told, consists in its adherence to the methodological principle that philosophical problems are best approached as, or reduced to, problems about the linguistic expression of thought. Thus the nature of linguistic meaning becomes the central issue for philosophers to consider. It is regarded as the key that will unlock solutions of all the main problems in philosophy, because those problems are thought to be best treated as problems about meanings. This has been both the main burden of complaint among opponents of analytical philosophy, and also the commonest profession among its supporters. Indeed this dogma, restated recently by Dummett, is so well entrenched that many would suppose it incapable of being seriously challenged from within the analytical movement. Dummett writes:

Only with Frege was the proper object of philosophy finally established: namely, first, that the goal of philosophy is the analysis of the structure of *thought*; secondly, that the study of *thought* is to be sharply distinguished from the study of the psychological process of *thinking*; and, finally, that the only proper method for analysing thought consists in the analysis of *language*. . . . The acceptance of these three tenets is common to the entire analytical school.[4]

Was not Moore's most important contribution to that movement just his exceptionally painstaking enquiry into what could possibly be meant by the assertions of his neo-Hegelian contemporaries? Did not Frege, Russell, Lesniewski, and the early Wittgenstein all seek, in their various ways, to characterize the structure of a logically idealized language? Did not the Vienna Circle's verificationism amount to the imposition of limits on rationality via a criterion of meaningfulness? Is not all Carnap's work, and that of his disciples, focused on the logically articulate reconstruction of the language of science? Were not the later Wittgenstein, and Ryle, and Austin engaged with

---

[4] M. Dummett, *Truth and Other Enigmas*, London: Duckworth, 1978, p. 458.

problems that were supposed to arise from the variety of ways in which natural language operates as a mode of communication and self-expression? Does not even Quine's philosophy, for all his repudiation of the distinction between analytic and synthetic, represent a systematic obsession with the enigma of meaning?

To dispute such obvious attributions would certainly be ridiculous. But it does not follow that the linguistic thesis is therefore correct about the analytical movement as a whole. There may be substantial advantage to be gained–within philosophical, even if not within historical, enquiry–from seeing these linguistic issues as special cases of a more widely pervasive type of problem. Copernicus, as Newton showed us, was none the less studying phenomena of gravitational attraction when he and his contemporaries thought that he was studying the geometry of planetary motion.

In fact it will be argued in §§ 2-4 that there are strong reasons why the linguistic thesis has to be rejected. But this argument is not to be taken as a blanket criticism of all theories advanced under the auspices of the thesis. The argument is not opposed to the claim that important aspects of many traditional philosophical problems may be rewardingly treated as problems about meaning or meanings. Indeed, we may well have learnt much more from such treatment this century than from the efforts of those who have rejected it. What is at issue in the present book is not so much what philosophers in general should or should not be doing, but rather how analytical philosophers should conceive or describe what they are doing or have done. The book is not intended as an attack on analytical philosophy from some non-analytical standpoint, but as a way of reinforcing it from within by an updating of its sense of identity. In the earlier phase of the analytical movement a considerable variety of metaphilosophical theories about therapeutic analysis, conceptual clarification, linguistic geography, rational reconstruction, logical formalization, regimentation into canonical symbolism, etc. were actively discussed. These discussions tended gradually to fade out in the 1950s and early 1960s, giving way to an enormous expansion of substantive philosophical analysis. So now, with the products of this expansion before us, we are in a decidedly better position to discuss its implicit, underlying programme.

One can compare the change in our situation in this respect to the difference between the unavoidably programmatic standpoint of philosophers like Francis Bacon and René Descartes at the beginnings of modern science and the position of contemporary philosophers of science with three centuries of scientific progress to reflect on. Just as there is a much more informative basis now for the philosophical analysis of scientific enquiry, so too there is a much more informative basis now (though on an accelerated time-scale) for the philosophical analysis of philosophical analysis. Just as science came to be professionalized, over a period of three centuries, with the development of specialized societies, journals, accreditations, and endowments, so too analytical philosophy has gone through a similar process during the present century.

Of course, as already remarked, there were analytical strands in the work of many earlier philosophers (just as there was science before 1600). But these strands were generally tangled up there with various non-analytical themes. Some primitive psychology was often mixed in with the epistemology, some cosmology with the ontology, some theology with the metaphysics, some economics or anthropology with the political philosophy, and so on. Relatively pure examples of philosophical analysis are not easy to find before the present century (just as alchemy, astrology, religion, etc. were often mixed in with earlier scientific theory).

Hence it is scarcely less reasonable for metaphilosophers to look now for underlying principles of unity behind the superficial diversity and complex interconnectedness of analytical philosophy than it has been for nineteenth- and twentieth-century philosophers of science to follow Whewell in a search for underlying unity within the enormously wide range of enquiry that has come to be covered by the term 'natural science'. No doubt such philosophical searches can never succeed without imposing some degree of simplification and idealization on the untidy scatter of detail that is the historian's role to describe. But in this respect neither the philosopher of science nor the meta-philosopher is in a worse situation than is the scientist himself as he moves from natural history to physical theory.

What will emerge is that, in order to characterize analytical philosophy satisfactorily, we need first to shift attention away both from the substantive *doctrines* espoused in it (which at one time were predominantly positivist) and also from the *methods* of enquiry and exposition that are used in it (which are indeed often linguistic), and concentrate rather on unifying features of the *problems* with which its enquiries and expositions are engaged (§ 6). The contrast that is commonly, and rightly, drawn today is between analytical philosophy on the one side, and, on the other, philosophies preoccupied with

God, with dread, with consciousness, with personal belief, with deconstruction, or with politico-economic class struggle. So what is analytical philosophy preoccupied with? What are the characteristically pervasive features of the problems investigated by analytical philosophers? If those problems are not intrinsically about language, then what are they about? I shall develop the thesis (§ 6) that they are all, in one way or another, normative problems about reasons and reasoning, whether or not they profit from treatment in linguistic terms. So what inevitably come to the forefront of specifically *meta*philosophical discussion are problems about the nature of philosophical reasoning. If the key question in analytical philosophy is 'What is a reason for what?', the key question in analytical metaphilosophy is 'What kind of reasoning can support philosophical claims?' Within a discussion of this question new issues arise, new distinctions need to be drawn, and new paradoxes call for resolution (§§ 7-19). At the same time, if the problems of analytical philosophy are indeed problems about reasoning, we have to investigate whether the computational metaphor, which has come to dominate the experimental psychology of human reasoning, has any important metaphilosophical implications (§§ 20-4): should a computationalist thesis replace the linguistic one?

Practising philosophers sometimes find discussions about the nature of philosophy rather unsatisfying, because in such discussions familiar philosophical issues are normally referred to rather abstractly, or in outline, and are not discussed on their merits. Many scientists find philosophy of science unsatisfying for analogous reasons. It does not give them the kind of intellectual food that they have come to expect. But its problems nevertheless demand resolution. Similarly, the problems of metaphilosophy, which also need resolution, will not disappear because some philosophers have no taste for them. And in any case it will emerge in §§ 15-24 that concern with the nature of philosophical reasoning carries us inescapably into discussion of some important non-metaphilosophical issues.

Some philosophers are also likely to object to any theory that, while they thought of themselves as pursuing one objective (concerned with language), they were 'really' pursuing another (concerned with reasoning). In much the same way scientists may object to a theory that, while they thought of themselves as seeking to confirm their hypotheses, they were 'really' trying to falsify them. But antitheses such as these do not formulate the issue accurately. What is relevant here is just that substantive analytical philosophy has often occupied itself with a search for hitherto unnoticed presuppositions or implications, and so there is no reason why analytical metaphilosophy should not do likewise.

§ 2 SEMANTIC ASCENT AND SEMANTIC DESCENT

Summary. According to the most familiar doctrine analytical philosophy is held together by its engagement in linguistic analysis and the study of meaning. But this thesis runs into serious trouble in regard not only to many issues in ethics and political theory, but also to problems about knowledge, induction and ontology. A strategy of semantic ascent, as Quine called it, often has to be complemented by one of semantic descent.

A good theory, whether in philosophy or in science, is seldom worth sacrificing to a single anomaly, unless a better theory is already available. So it is scarcely surprising that the linguistic thesis about analytical philosophy has long remained standard doctrine. The only serious objection that could for long be raised against the thesis was that it excluded certain topics from the domain of analytical philosophy. And, since no interpretation of analytical philosophy was available that would convincingly embrace these topics, the linguistic thesis could plausibly be preserved by writing them off as unphilosophical. But, if analytical philosophy can now be prised apart from its linguistic false colours, that Procrustean manœuvre is no longer necessary.

These supposedly non-analytical topics constitute an important subcategory within the larger class of all those topics not amenable to the strategy that Quine has called 'semantic ascent'.[5] Semantic ascent is the shift, as Quine puts it, from talk of miles to talk of 'mile', from talking in certain terms to talking about them. By semantic ascent we may avoid difficulties that arise in talking about the existence or nature of certain alleged things, events, or processes by talking instead about the contexts in which it is appropriate to use their names. And in a sufficiently broad interpretation of the term 'context' here–an interpretation that includes logical, linguistic, evidential, and pragmatic relationships–it is clear that semantic ascent is a feature of methodologically authorized strategy that is shared by such otherwise

[5] W. V. O. Quine, *Word and Object*, Cambridge, Mass.: MIT Press, 1960, pp. 270-6.

disparate writers as Carnap, Wittgenstein, Ryle, Quine, Austin, Davidson, and many others. It certain embraces not only most of Quine's own practice (despite his rejection of the analytic-synthetic distinction) but also Carnap's preference for philosophy in the 'formal' model of speech, as distinct from the 'material' one,[6] Wittgenstein's 'battle against bewitchment of our intelligence by means of language',[7] Ryle's 'logical geography',[8] Austin's enquiries into English word-uses and speech-acts,[9] Davidson's programme for truth-conditional semantics,[10] and much else besides.

Of course, Quine does not claim that semantic ascent and philosophical enquiry ought to be coextensive. He points out that, just as observation of objects may be relevant to philosophical issues, so too semantic ascent can sometimes be useful for non-philosophical purposes. Einstein's departure from classical conceptions of absolute time and length, for example, is 'too radical to be efficiently debated' by physicists 'at the level of object talk unaided by semantic ascent'.[11] But the trouble with the linguistic thesis is not that not all semantic ascent is philosophical, but that not all philosophy profits from semantic ascent or from use of the various linguistically oriented techniques (Carnapian, Rylean, Wittgensteinian, Davidsonian, etc.) that semantic ascent makes possible. Certain problems traditionally discussed by philosophers cannot be wholly resolved in such a way: the reverse strategy, which I shall call 'semantic descent', is often more appropriate there. If we are querying the use of a given term in a particular context, we shall often get nearer the underlying issue by talking instead about whatever it is that the term purports to name or denote, or about that to which the term applies.

Moreover a choice between these different orientations of analysis may be available at more than one level. Thus one can distinguish between analysing the concept of 'meaning', analysing the meanings of important terms like 'knowledge', and analysing the structure of important kinds of knowledge such as historical knowledge. So any ascription of semantic ascent or semantic descent to a philosopher's

[6] R. Carnap, *The Logical Syntax of Language* (trans. A. Smeaton), London: Kegan Paul, Trench, Trubner, 1937, pp. 288-315.
[7] L. Wittgenstein, *Philosophical Investigations*, Oxford: Blackwell, 1953, p. 47e.
[8] G. Ryle, *The Concept of Mind*, London: Hutchinson, 1949, p. 15.
[9] J. L. Austin, 'A Plea for Excuses', *Proceedings of the Aristotelian Society*, 57, 1957, pp. 1-30.
[10] D. Davidson, *Inquiries into Truth and Interpretation*, Oxford: OUP, 1984.
[11] Op. cit., p. 272.

argument must always be understood as being made relative to an implicit or explicit specification of the problem that he is tackling.

The problems that have been commonly cited as resistant to solution by semantic ascent are all concerned with moral, political, or aesthetic values. The philosophy of language seems to have only limited relevance here. With the aid of an appropriate conception of linguistic analysis one can discuss, for example, whether the linguistic function of indicative sentences in which ethical terms occur is to utter commands (Carnap), to express or evoke emotions (Ayer), or to imply universal prescriptions (Hare),[12] or whether instead the linguistic meanings of such sentences should be distinguished from the speech-acts performed by uttering them (Searle).[13] One can discuss the relations between 'ought' and 'is' (Searle), between 'ought' and 'can' (Montefiore), between 'ought' and 'may' (von Wright), between 'ought' and 'good' (Hare), or between 'ought' and 'obligatory' (Brandt).[14] Or again, in regard to legal terminology, one can discuss the relations between 'right', 'privilege', 'power', and 'immunity' (Hohfeld) or the merits of contextual definition as against definition by genus and difference (Hart).[15] Or one can discuss the uses of expressions like 'freedom', 'authority', and 'the State' in political controversy (Weldon).[16]

But linguistic discussions such as these touch only the linguistic or conceptual framework within which questions about social values should be debated. They do not answer any of that vast range of questions which concern the general principles on which moral, legal, and political decisions should be based. If anyone wishes to discuss what kinds of duty, freedom, or privilege deserve respect, he has to engage in semantic descent. If anyone wishes to discuss the underlying issues about the nature of law that influence definitions of

---

[12] R. Carnap, *Philosophy and Logical Syntax*, London: Kegan Paul, Trench, Trubner, 1935, p. 24; A. J. Ayer, *Language, Truth and Logic*, London: Gollancz, 2nd edn., 1946, p. 107; R. M. Hare, *The Language of Morals*, Oxford: OUP, pp. 177-9.

[13] J. Searle, 'Meaning and Speech Acts', *The Philosophical Review*, 71, 1962, p. 423.

[14] J. Searle, *Speech Acts: An Essay in the Philosophy of Language*, Cambridge: CUP, 1969, pp. 175-98; A. Montefiore, '"Ought" and "Can"', *The Philosophical Quarterly*, 8, 1958, pp. 24-40; G. H. von Wright, 'An Essay in Deontic Logic and the General Theory of Action', *Acta Philosophica Fennica*, 21, 1968, pp. 6-36; Hare, op. cit., pp. 18-197; R. B. Brandt, 'The Concepts of Obligation and Duty', *Mind*, 73, 1964, pp. 374-93.

[15] W. N. Hohfeld, *Fundamental Legal Conceptions* (ed. W. W. Cook), New Haven, Conn.: Yale UP, 1920; H. L. A. Hart, *Definition and Theory in Jurisprudence*, Oxford: OUP, 1953.

[16] T. D. Weldon, *The Vocabulary of Politics*, London: Penguin, 1953, pp. 45-75.

fundamental legal terms–Do judges legislate? Must a legal rule conform to pre-legal standards of natural justice? etc.–he has to probe below the purely linguistic level. He has to discuss duty, for example, not 'duty'.[17]

So what can defenders of the linguistic thesis say about the title of those non-linguistic questions to a place in analytical philosophy?

At one time it would have been plausible to claim that philosophers who concerned themselves with such substantive issues were operating rather on the periphery of the analytical dialogue. Moore, for example, certainly felt nothing incongruous about passing on from his critique of naturalistic definition to the claim that an analysis of personal affections and aesthetic enjoyments would reveal them to include all the greatest, and by far the greatest, imaginable goods.[18] What was to be analysed here, on Moore's view, was not a meaning or linguistic function but a complex organic unity of emotion and cognition. But Moore, it might have been said, was too early and too archaic a figure in the analytical movement for his concern with non-linguistic issues alongside linguistic ones to be significant. Similarly, Popper's championship of the open society might have been discounted in this connection because he has often explicitly dissociated himself from the linguistic treatment of philosophical issues.[19]

Such a defence of the linguistic thesis, however, is no longer available. The validity of utilitarianism, for example, is no longer challenged–as Moore challenged it[20]–on the ground that Mill's principle of utility is either a trivial tautology or a faulty statement about the meaning of a word. Instead it is attacked by arguments involving semantic descent. The argument may now be that utilitarianism picks up too little of the world's moral luggage (B. Williams): too many issues are left undecided by it.[21] Or, instead, the principles of justice may be traced back to what would be the outcome of an original social contract if people made one (Rawls), rules of social co-operation and ideals of moral excellence may be grounded on a need to escape

---

[17] See L. J. Cohen, 'Theory and Definition in Jurisprudence', *Proceedings of the Aristotelian Society*, supp. vol. 24, 1955, pp. 213-38.

[18] G. E. Moore, *Principia Ethica*, Cambridge: CUP, 1903, p. 189.

[19] K. R. Popper, *The Open Society and its Enemies*, London: Routledge and Kegan Paul, 1945; cf. id., *Conjectures and Refutations: The Growth of Scientific Knowledge*, London: Routledge and Kegan Paul, 1963, pp. 17, 293, 346.

[20] Op. cit., pp. 9-17 and p. 108.

[21] B. Williams, 'A Critique of Utilitarianism', in J. J. C. Smart and B. Williams, *Utilitarianism: for and against*, Cambridge: CUP, 1973, p. 173.

through the horns of the Prisoner's Dilemma (Margalit), or legitimacy may be denied to any State activity that goes beyond the provision of minimal protection (Nozick).[22] In an earlier generation Weldon argued that 'when verbal confusions are tidied up most of the questions of traditional political philosophy are not unanswerable because all of them are confused formulations of purely empirical difficulties'.[23] But the difficulties with which, more recently, Williams, Rawls, Margalit, and Nozick have been occupied are normative, not empirical, ones.

Of course, there is a different tack that defenders of the linguistic thesis might at one time have taken. They could have pointed out that, rather than exclude normative problems from analytical philosophy, some analytical philosophers have invented a special category of meaning to embrace them. Thus Stevenson assigned two kinds of meaning to terms of praise or condemnation like 'good' and 'bad'.[24] Occurrences of such words were supposed to be capable of having both an evaluative and a descriptive meaning. The evaluative meaning was held to be the same in all contexts, the descriptive to vary with the context, as in 'good novel', 'good gardener', 'good carburettor', 'good person', 'good action', etc. In this way questions about whether a specified kind of human behaviour is good or bad were open to being construed as questions of meaning–specifically, as questions about the descriptive meaning, in appropriate contexts, of 'good' and 'bad'. And answers to such questions could then be called 'persuasive definitions'.[25] In short, problems of substantive ethics could apparently be resolved by semantic ascent.

This measure briefly concealed a rather awkward restrictiveness in the linguistic thesis. But it was too obvious a play on the word 'meaning' to be popular doctrine for long. We learn the qualities of a good carburettor from an engineer, not from a dictionary, and the engineer discovers them by experimental research on appropriate machines, not by a survey of native-speakers' practices. Nor need we fail to understand one another at any point when disagreeing about the qualities that a good novel should have. So in contemporary ethics what is held to be at issue is not what is or should be the meaning of 'good' or 'right', but what things are good or right. And articles about

[22] J. Rawls, *A Theory of Justice*, Oxford: OUP, 1972; E. Margalit, *The Emergence of Norms*, Oxford: OUP, 1977; R. Nozick, *Anarchy, State and Utopia*, Oxford: Blackwell, 1974.   [23] Op. cit., p. 192.
[24] C. L. Stevenson, *Ethics and Language*, New Haven, Conn.: Yale UP, 1944, pp. 206 ff.
[25] Ibid., p. 210.

abortion, animal rights, euthanasia, famine relief, feminism, test-tube babies, torture, etc. appear in great numbers in professional journals that also publish articles about referential opacity, relative identity, or substitutional quantification. So the editors and editorial boards of those journals must be supposed to have a conception of philosophical enquiry that embraces some forms of semantic descent as well as of ascent.

Obviously there is nothing instrinsically peripheral or marginal about all this recent work, even though some of it may descend to a level of particularity at which familiar philosophical issues are no longer directly evident. So the linguistic thesis can now be rescued only by insistence that substantive ethics and substantive political theory–not to mention analogous studies of problems about art, education, etc.–form a category of intellectual enquiry that is as different from analytical philosophy of values as substantive science is from analytical philosophy of science. Analytical philosophy, it must then be said, is concerned to analyse moral or scientific concepts, not to use them in arguments for or against specific moral principles or scientific theories. If the practice of analytical philosophy and the practice of ethical or political theory have become rather more intertwined in recent years, this is to be put down to a shift in the dominant interests of the persons or groups involved, rather than regarded as a revealing manifestation of deep and fundamental connections that were always implicit in the intellectual procedures employed. The fact that some analysts moonlight as moralists is of no more significance than the fact that some of them moonlight as scientists.

At first sight this seems a temptingly plausible account of the situation. But on closer scrutiny the plausibility disappears–for at least four reasons.

Consider first the supposed analogy between scientific theories and statements of moral principles as co-ordinate topics for philosophical analysis. The trouble is that in another important respect substantive ethics and the statement of moral principles are co-ordinate with the analysis of moral concepts rather than with science and scientific theory. Fundamental ethical differences–about the nature of justice, say, or the value of life–are like certain disagreements in conceptual analysis in that they resist available procedures for conclusive intellectual determination to a greater extent than fundamental scientific differences do. No doubt this is largely because both substantive ethics and conceptual analysis find it difficult to avoid appealing, at certain crucial points, to the far from unanimous tribunals of intuition, common sense, or general acceptance (about which more will be said in §§ 8-19), while science respects instead the normally united tribunal of experience. But the upshot is that ethical enquiry, with its strategy of semantic descent, is not so easily prised apart from its association with philosophical enquiries that require semantic ascent.

Secondly, you must reckon with the fact that this association goes right back to the beginnings of European philosophy. It is already apparent in the writings of Plato and Aristotle. In Plato's *Republic* the Socratic quest for definitions is integral to the enquiry into how people ought to live. And you cannot put down the persistence of this association to a mere accident of cultural tradition unless you can explain why it nevertheless still continues so strongly to resist the centrifugal forces that have operated on other branches of intellectual enquiry like psychology, economics, or cosmology, that were once associated with philosophy. There is a real problem here for the linguistic thesis.

Thirdly, in some of its aspects even the problem of meaning, which according to the linguistic thesis is centrally important, may need treatment by semantic descent. A question highly relevant to the resolution of that problem is 'How is linguistic communication possible?' And the question may well be answered, as by David Lewis,[26] with a theory about the kind of tacit conventions that would underwrite the assignment of truth-conditions to linguistic signals. So here there is an undeniable analogy with the kind of semantic descent that takes place in some kinds of political theory when an answer is sought for the question 'How is political obligation possible?', since a tacit social contract may be supposed to underwrite the assignment of pre-legal rights and duties to citizens.

Fourthly, the attempt to treat ethics as being co-ordinate with science, *vis-à-vis* analytical philosophy, begs a highly important question. It assumes that the analytical philosophy of science is concerned only with conceptual analysis and with the logically sophisticated reconstruction of scientific theory. But science is very much more than an activity with words, so the philosophy of science cannot be concerned only with the analysis of its linguistic manifes-

[26] D. K. Lewis, *Convention: A Philosophical Study*, Cambridge, Mass.: Harvard UP, 1969.

tations. For example, the experimental testing of hypotheses affords an important subject-matter for philosophical investigation, as Bacon, Whewell, Herschell, Mill, and many others realized. So one can compare discussion of the principles that should regulate the conduct of such tests with discussion of the principles that should regulate people's conduct towards one another. And, just as any worthwhile discussion of principles that should regulate the conduct of experimental tests must be closely tied in with analyses of the concept of evidential support, the structure of a scientific theory, etc., so too any worthwhile discussion of the principles that should regulate people's conduct towards one another must be closely tied in with analyses of the concept of responsibility, the structure of moral judgement, etc. In both fields of enquiry semantic descent and semantic ascent complement one another. When Popper insists that questions about the meanings of words are quite unimportant for the philosophy of science, he is looking only at one side of a coin, of which only the other side was looked at by Carnap.

Indeed, what has now emerged is that the linguistic thesis about analytical philosophy is faced with more than just one kind of anomaly. The need for semantic descent, on appropriate occasions, is not peculiar to ethics and social theory. It is quite pervasive also in epistemology and philosophy of science. (No one should be surprised, therefore, that the philosopher—Wittgenstein—who probably did most to encourage the conception of analytical philosophy as being confined to the critique of language came to concentrate most of his attention on other problems than those that belong to ethics or to the philosophy of science.)

Consider knowledge itself. A good deal of recent controversy about this topic has been concerned with the analysis of the concept (or, if you like, with the characterization of the meaning of the word 'knowledge' and its equivalents in other languages) in terms of a set of conditions that are severally necessary and jointly sufficient for a person to be said to know that such-and-such is the case. The traditional account, with an ancestry traceable to Plato's *Theaetetus*, is supposed to be that statements of the form '*x* knows that *p*' are true if and only if *x* has a justified true belief that *p*. Gettier proposed paradoxes about the presence of 'justified' in this analysis, Radford about that of 'belief', and so on.[27] Austin at one time—not his finest

---

[27] E. Gettier, Jr., 'Is Justified True Belief Knowledge?' *Analysis*, 23:6, 1963, pp. 121-3; C. Radford, 'Knowledge—By Examples', *Analysis*, 27:1, 1966, pp. 1-11.

hour–even suggested that the crucial topic to be studied was the speech-act of giving one's word that is performed by uttering sentences beginning with the first-person present indicative of the verb 'to know' and is comparable to the speech-act performed by uttering sentences beginning with 'I promise'.[28] But this literature will not take us far if instead we ask ourselves about the nature of various important cases or kinds of knowledge, i.e. if we concern ourselves with certain items that happen to fall under the description 'knowledge' rather than with the implications of that description or the conditions for applying it. We may become occupied, for example, with the structure of experimental knowledge and its differences from that of historical knowledge. And then any awareness we may have of what these words–'experimental', 'historical', and 'knowledge'–mean serves only to direct our attention to the subject-matter of our enquiry: we cannot derive our answers therefrom. We want to construct appropriately idealized accounts of how experimentalists and historians conduct their enquiries and justify their conclusions, and of what they may at best achieve, not appropriately idealized accounts of how the words 'experimental' and 'historical' should be used and of what that use may at best achieve. A man may well know the meaning of the word 'experimental' without knowing any rules of experimental method. He may also know the meaning of the word 'evidence', without knowing how to measure the relevant probabilities. So linguistic analyses of the concept of evidence (like Achinstein's[29]) are inherently inadequate to resolve the epistemological problem about evidence. Or again, we need to investigate the content of mathematical knowledge even in order to determine whether a causal analysis of the concept of knowledge (like Goldman's[30]) is admissible. *If* what mathematicians know includes the properties of certain abstract entities, *then* it cannot be a necessary condition for knowledge that what is known be causally related to the knower's state of mind: abstract entities do not have causal properties.

The same point may also be illustrated by a brief discussion[31] of the

---

[28] J. L. Austin, 'Other Minds', in A. Flew (ed.), *Logic and Language* (2nd series), Oxford: Blackwell, 1955, pp. 142-7.

[29] P. Achinstein, *The Nature of Explanation*, New York: OUP, 1983, p. 336.

[30] A. Goldman, 'A Causal Theory of Knowing', *Journal of Philosophy*, 64, 1967, pp. 357-72.

[31] For a longer one see L. Jonathan Cohen, 'The Problem of Natural Laws', in D. H. Mellor (ed.), *Prospects for Pragmatism: Essays in Memory of F. P. Ramsey*, Cambridge: CUP, 1980, pp. 211-28.

difference between the results of pursuing the strategy of semantic ascent in relation to the much-vexed problem of natural laws (and the counterfactual conditionals derivable from them) and the results of pursuing the strategy of semantic descent there.

When pursuing the former strategy philosophers seem unable to provide a relevant analysis that is not either question-begging or obviously wrong. Solutions that analyse a law as a generalization holding across some chosen set of possible words tend to make assumptions in the specification of this set that use some part of the vocabulary which is up for clarification (like Stalnaker's stipulation that there are no differences between the actual world and any of the chosen worlds except those that are 'required', implicitly or explicitly, by the antecedent of any counterfactual conditional derivable from the law[32]). Solutions that eschew modalities altogether either make questionable factual assumptions, like Quine's assumption of infinite divisibility, which is required to support his suggestion that any statement about a natural kind could and should be reduced to a statement about the class of those objects that are similar to one another in virtue of certain matching parts.[33] Or, like Ramsey's pragmatism,[34] they fail to elucidate why axiomatized representations of actually occurring conjunctions should be supposed to give us knowledge about the truth of unactualized conditionals. And solutions that analyse natural laws as generalizations deducible within a system of scientific theory fail to allow for our readiness to derive counter-factuals from certain generalizations that are not so deducible, as when the tried and tested therapeutic efficacy of a particular drug has not yet been given any biochemical explanation.[35]

On the other hand a strategy of semantic descent leads us to ask, not what it means to call knowledge of a uniformity 'knowledge of a natural law' rather than 'knowledge of an accidental uniformity', but rather how this difference between kinds of knowledge is possible. Accordingly, we now enquire what the difference is between the mode

[32] R. C. Stalnaker, 'A Theory of Conditionals', in N. Rescher (ed.), *Studies in Logical Theory*, (American Philosophical Quarterly Monograph, 2), Oxford: Blackwell, 1968, pp. 98-112.

[33] W. V. O. Quine, *Ontological Relativity and Other Essays*, New York: Columbia UP, 1969, pp. 114-38.

[34] F. P. Ramsey, *Foundations: Essays in Philosophy, Logic, Mathematics and Economics* (ed. D. H. Mellor), London: Routledge and Kegan Paul, 1978, p. 149.

[35] L. Jonathan Cohen, *The Diversity of Meaning*, London: Methuen, 2nd edn., 1966, pp. 303-11.

of enquiry that leads at best to knowledge of a natural law and the one that leads at best to knowledge of an accidental uniformity. We have to look at the difference between how the former kind of conclusion is justified and how the latter is: the difference between the two kinds of conclusion themselves is not what resolves the philosophical problem, but merely what sets it. We can then see that in establishing, or trying to establish, a law of nature we use eliminative induction. In principle, we try out our hypothesis in experiments that exercise suitable controls on potentially relevant circumstances, or we explore the range of its explanatory and predictive power. Because we thus learn (or try to learn) that something holds for such-and-such sorts of circumstances, not just for such-and-such individuals, our finding (or putative finding) applies just as well to unactualized cases, in those circumstances, as to actualized ones. And so far as it does hold in this way across all possible cases our finding may be regarded as a law. Accidentally true generalizations, however, are established by enumerative induction; and so, since all the actual cases have then to be considered in turn as individuals, no inferences about unactualized cases are legitimated. In this way the distinction between natural laws and accidental truths as conclusions of our reasonings can be explained in terms of the difference between eliminative and enumerative methods, respectively, in the structure of those reasonings. But such an explanation is made possible only by pursuing the strategy of semantic descent rather than that of semantic ascent.

Note too, a striking difference between the kind of examples normally cited by a philosopher who thinks of the problem of knowledge as a problem that calls for semantic ascent and those normally cited instead by a philosopher who thinks of it primarily as a problem for semantic descent. The former kind of example tends to be rather marginal or far-fetched, because it is intended to check out the limits or frontiers of our concepts. It is intended to test whether certain conditions, which happen to be present in some prototypical cases, are really necessary, or really sufficient, for the application of the term under analysis. So, on questions about the connection between knowledge and belief, we are asked to bear in mind what we should say about neurotic examinees who think they're guessing but aren't (Radford) or about the possibility of scientists' producing highly sophisticated forms of hallucinatory belief (Unger).[36] But those philosophers whose epistemology relies rather on semantic descent

---

[36] Radford, op. cit., pp. 2-7; P. Unger, *Ignorance*, Oxford: OUP, 1975, pp. 7-8.

are inclined to choose quite central examples, because these have an unassailable title to be invoked as paradigmatic instances of what is under examination. Thus Newtonian mechanics or Einstein's theory of relativity are cited again and again by Popper as examples of scientific knowledge, and I have elsewhere cited Newton's investigation of the spectrum of light and von Frisch's work on bees' sensitivity to colour as particularly elegant and illuminating specimens of experimental reasoning.[37] In short, semantic descent leads the epistemologist down into the actual history of mainstream science, while semantic ascent tends to lead him upwards into an imaginary world of freaks, speculation, and science fiction.

Many philosophical problems, like that of knowledge, require both semantic ascent and semantic descent for their resolution. But in certain cases one of the two strategies is more pertinent than the other. Thus attempts to solve the problem of induction solely by semantic ascent (Strawson, Edwards, Ayer) are doomed to disregard the heart of that problem.[38] We are told that arguments for a generalization that are based on an appropriate number or variety of its instances must be inductively valid because that is what 'inductively valid' means. (Compare Stevenson's view about the descriptive meaning of 'good'.) But just what are the criteria of appropriateness here? These too, in all their relevant specificity, have to be part of the a priori discoverable meaning of 'inductive validity', if the problem of induction is to be solved by semantic ascent. But to make them part of the a priori discoverable meaning of 'inductive validity' leaves no room for having to consult the laboratory judgements of reputable scientists in order to help sustain an account of the principles of controlled experiment. And even when, by an exercise of semantic descent, we have been able to construct such an account, we are still left with the question: what gives inductions authorized by those principles a title to rationality? Without an answer to that question we cannot even begin to meet Hume's sceptical challenge. No doubt Hume begged the question in favour of his scepticism by assuming (at least in the relevant

---

[37] K. R. Popper, *The Logic of Scientific Discovery*, London: Hutchinson, 1959, pp. 19, 22, 50, 81, etc.; L. Jonathan Cohen, *The Probable and the Provable*, Oxford: OUP, 1977, pp. 147 and 129-31.

[38] P. F. Strawson, *Introduction to Logical Theory*, London: Methuen, 1952, pp. 256-7; P. Edwards, 'Bertrand Russell's Doubts about Induction', in A. Flew (ed.), *Logic and Language*, Oxford: Blackwell, 1951, pp. 68-9; A. J. Ayer, *British Empirical Philosophers*, London: Routledge and Kegan Paul, 1952, pp. 26-7.

passages[39]) that all rational inference is deductive. But it is equally question-begging for some of his opponents just to assume, through their exercise of semantic ascent, that inductive inference is rational also. What is needed, in order to meet at least a part of Hume's challenge, is a characterization of rationality that is independent of the meaning of 'inductively valid' or 'inductively supported' but is nevertheless so constructed that inductively valid or inductively supported inference turns out to be rational.[40] That mode of inference must be shown to fall within the denotation of 'rational', rather than be linked to it by a network of alleged semantic implications.

A related point may be made about Carnapian confirmation-theory. Carnap held at one time that assessments of how much a given statement of evidence supports a specified scientific hypothesis were analytic and a priori for any particular confirmation-function.[41] That is to say, an agreed evaluation of this support might in principle always be achieved by the strategy of semantic ascent. But such a view runs counter to the fact that scientists are often forced by new evidence to revise their assessment of how much a given set of experimental results supports a specified hypothesis. Perhaps the results were not controlled for a certain variable, the relevance of which has only now been discovered–like pregnancy in the original safety tests for thalidomide: in that case the old results gave less support than was supposed at the time. In order to accommodate this kind of possibility in science we have to set up our philosophical reconstruction of inductive assessment in such a way that inductive support is treated as being itself an empirically confirmable or disconfirmable relation, not a semantically derivable one.[42] So again it is the strategy of semantic descent, not ascent, that has a crucial role in epistemology, once an initial clarification of the concept of inductive support has been achieved.

Nor are epistemology, ethics, and social theory the only branches of philosophy in which semantic descent has an important part to play. Ontology is another.

Admittedly, Carnap held that the only legitimate ontological

---

[39] D. Hume, *A Treatise of Human Nature*, London: J. Noon, 1739, bk. 1, pt. 3, § 14.

[40] Such a characterization is attempted in L. Jonathan Cohen, 'How Far is Induction Rationally Justifiable?', in P. Weingartner and H. Czermack (eds.), *Epistemology and Philosophy of Science*, Vienna: Hölder-Pichler-Tempsky, 1983, pp. 245-53.

[41] R. Carnap, *Logical Foundations of Probability*, Chicago: Chicago UP, 1950, p. 181.

[42] As in L. Jonathan Cohen, *The Implications of Induction*, London: Methuen, 1970, pp. 35-59, and id., *The Probable and the Provable*, pp. 129-66.

questions–questions about the existence of, say, numbers, propositions, or physical object–were 'pseudo-objects' sentences, in the sense
that, despite superficial appearances to the contrary, they were not
really about objects at all but only about the linguistic framework in
which it might be appropriate to discuss them.[43] He insisted that his
own phenomenalistic system, *Der logische Aufbau der Welt*, had no
ontological implications beyond this.[44] But it can hardly be accepted
that the actual nature of a thing is irrelevant to the correct choice of
terminology for discussing it. Certainly Galileo's telescope helped to
determine that the celestial world belongs to the same category of
reality as the sublunary one and that the basic questions which arise
about planets are those also relevant to other material structures, not
those relevant to immaterial ones or to intelligences. So the situation
is more appropriately represented by Quine's insistence that, even if
semantic ascent is necessary for the fruitful formulation of ontological
questions, yet the resolution of such questions is interconnected with
other issues for which semantic ascent is inappropriate. Even if you
succeed in establishing translation rules from physical-object sentences to sense-datum ones the question whether sense-data exist
would still arise.[45] Compare Kim's view that our belief in the
reducibility of one theory to another often derives from belief that the
properties described in the former theory are in fact supervenient on
those described in the latter instead of its being the case that belief in
supervenience always derives from belief in reducibility.[46] Not
surprisingly, therefore, some analytical philosophers now even take
up a position which is directly antithetical to Carnap's. Wolterstorff,
for example, has claimed that his ontology of 'predicables' is a
description of the most general structure of what there is, not of the
most general structure of that conceptual scheme of ours which we
apply to what there is.[47] Indeed, if we look back to Russell's logical
atomism in 1924, we can see him too writing about the analysis of
reality into simples, in opposition to Bradley's metaphysical holism.
In Russell's view at that time semantic ascent was not essential,

[43] *The Logical Syntax of Language*, pp. 284-6; 'Empiricism, Semantics and Ontology',
Revue internationale de philosophie, 4, 1950, pp. 20-40.
[44] 'Intellectual Autobiography', in P. Schlipp (ed.), *The Philosophy of Rudolf Carnap*, La
Salle, Ill.: Open Court, 1963, pp. 18-19.
[45] *Word and Object*, pp. 265 and 274-6.
[46] J. Kim, 'Supervenience and Nomological Incommensurables', *American Philosophical Quarterly*, 15, 1978, p. 154.
[47] N. Wolterstorff, *On Universals: An Essay in Ontology*, Chicago: Chicago UP, 1970,
p. xii.

analysis was of fact, not meaning, and his decision in favour of pluralism was taken 'on empirical grounds'.[48]

Perhaps it will be objected, on behalf of the linguistic thesis, that ontologists like Wolterstorff are just not to be regarded as part of the analytical movement. But, even if we ignore Russell's broad use of the term 'analysis', it still seems relatively arbitrary to exclude Wolterstorff from the analytical movement if Quine is included, since his position is no further from Quine's in one direction than Carnap's is in the other. For Carnap all legitimate ontological questions are purely linguistic ones, for Wolterstorff none are, and for Quine there just are no purely linguistic questions at all. Certainly Wolterstorff does not argue with any less regard for the usual logical proprieties than do Carnap or Quine. So, in terms of the kind of argument that he is offering, and also implicitly willing to listen to, he is eligible for admission to the same philosophical dialogue.

§ 3 THE REPLACEMENT OF DISAGREEMENTS ABOUT METHOD BY DISAGREEMENTS ABOUT SUBSTANCE

Summary. At one time analytical philosophers claimed possession of a method that would achieve conclusive resolutions for all philosophical disagreements. But though they were often intolerant of each other's views about the nature of this method they were in broad agreement about most issues of substance. Later analytical philosophers have been much less concerned about methodological issues and much more inclined to disagree about issues of substance, even where they were practising semantic ascent. A purely linguistic account of analytical philosophy cannot explain this disagreement.

So far I have been arguing that semantic ascent is not a necessary feature of analytical philosophy: many important issues require, and have obtained, treatment by semantic descent instead. But even where semantic ascent is the appropriate strategy to use, it may not suffice to ground a resolution of the issue. Other sources of premises or other principles of method may be needed as well. The crucial, underlying problems are rarely, if ever, just semantic. At any rate, unless this is so, several developments within the field of language-oriented analysis are hard to understand.

---

[48] B. Russell, 'Logical Atomism', reprinted in B. Russell, *Logic and Knowledge* (ed. R. C. March), London: Allen and Unwin, 1956, pp. 323-43.

The leaders of the analytical movement in the immediately post-1945 period, i.e. the generation of Wittegenstein, Carnap, and Ryle, often disagreed strongly about the correct methodology for semantic ascent in philosophy. Should logical formalisms be employed, or not? Is the main object to assign crucial words and phrases in existing languages to their correct conceptual categories, or to construct new languages that will do the same work as existing ones but less problematically? Should philosophers put forward theses at all, or just battle against linguistic bewitchment? Can the study of English, or French, resolve philosophical problems, or do those problems transcend the idioms of particular natural languages? Indeed, because these analytical philosophers all tended, implicitly or explicitly, to agree with Schlick's programmatic claim in 1930 to be provided with 'the means of settling all so-called philosophical disputes', in an absolutely final and ultimate manner',[49] their serious disagreements could only be about the nature of this means–i.e. could only be methodological rather than substantive. Any serious disagreement of a substantive nature would have tended to discredit the claim to have within their collective grasp a conclusive method of settling all philosophical disputes. So the analytical philosophy of the later 1940s exhibited, on the whole, an ideological consensus in which it seemed reasonable to hold that 'there is nothing in the nature of philosophy to warrant the existence of conflicting philosophical parties or "schools"',[50] as a highly influential book of Ayer's had put it in 1936. The analytical philosophers of that time, few as they were, tended to oppose belief in Cartesian dualism, to be positivist rather than religionist and phenomenalist rather than realist, to favour logicist accounts of mathematics and non-statement-making accounts of moral judgements, and so on. But they did not think of their adherence to these views as in any way compromising their claim to be above the ordinary mêlée of conflicting schools. Indeed, some of them even used the term 'philosophers' to refer only to those allegedly confused thinkers from whom they wished to distance themselves, with the implication that the analytical method was so different from traditional philosophical methods that its practitioners should not be expected to pass under the same professional label.

During the last thirty-five years, however, analytical philosophers

---

[49] M. Schlick, *Philosophical Papers* (ed. H. Mulder *et al*). Vol. 2, Dordrecht: Reidel, 1979, p. 171.
[50] *Language, Truth and Logic*, London: Gollancz, 1st edn., 1936, p. 230.

have increased enormously in numbers and have come to disagree much more widely on matters of substance; and, perhaps because they are readier to expect some such disagreement as inevitable, they are much more tolerant on matters of methodology and are no longer inclined to use the term 'philosophers' pejoratively. This development was foreshadowed by what happened in the philosophy of mathematics. Just as Russell's great logicist enterprise acted as the original paradigm for Vienna Circle analysis, so too the development of alternative programmes for the reconstruction of mathematics (Brouwer and Hilbert) prefigured the post-Vienna phase of diversification in the analytical movement.[51] Russell had aimed at the reduction of number-theoretical concepts to logical ones and the derivation of arithmetical truths from logical laws. And when the straightforward thrust of the original project came to be blocked by problems about completeness, about the axiom of infinity, and about the status of type-hierarchies, it became apparent that linguistic analysis alone could not provide a conclusive answer to the question: what is the basis of arithmetical reasoning? At the same time the continued promotion of formalist and intuitionist projects alongside the logicist one suggested that traditional controversies between nominalism, conceptualism, and realism were still very much alive.

It took some time for these developments to have any general impact. In 1946 Ayer was still endorsing the view that all arithmetical truths are provably analytic, fifteen years after Gödel's published proof (of the incompleteness of arithmetic) had shown it to be untenable and even Russell didn't know of Gödel's proof until 1949.[52] But with the resumption and expansion of academic studies after the Second World War the floodgates of controversy soon burst wide open. And this surge of controversy did not by any means derive entirely from differences in direction of enquiry, as in the issue (discussed in § 2 above) between semantic ascent and semantic descent, but also from differences in the conclusions arrived at by different practitioners of semantic ascent. Much of the tumult raged *within* the world of linguistic analysis. In 1950 Russell again took the first major blow. His theory of definite descriptions, authoritatively

---

[51] For the history of these developments see W. and M. Kneale, *The Development of Logic*, Oxford: OUP, 1962, pp. 672-88.

[52] *Language, Truth and Logic*, 2nd edn., 1946, p. 77-82; and M. Polyani, *Personal Knowledge: Towards a Post-Critical Philosophy*, London, Routledge and Kegan Paul, 1958, p. 118. Cf. K. Gödel, 'Über formal unentscheidbare Sätze der Principia Mathematica und verwundter Systeme', *Monatshefte für Mathematik und Physik*, 38, 1931, pp. 173-98.

held out hitherto as a model of what a philosophical analysis should be like,[53] was powerfully criticized by Strawson, who offered a rival account.[54] Strawson eschewed any formalization. But though his methodology for philosophy was thus very different from Russell's, the disagreement that he emphasized was one of substance, not method. Russell, he argued, was wrong about how the word 'the' functions. And soon there was no longer any orthodoxy discernible. Philosophical dialogue has a natural tendency to generate opposing theories, and this tendency now reasserted itself. Atomist theories of people's beliefs (Carnap) were opposed by holistic ones (Quine); conventionalist elucidations of necessity (Ayer) were opposed by essentialist ones (Kripke); truth-functional criteria of deducibility (Gentzen) or modal ones (Lewis and Langford) were opposed by relevance criteria (Anderson and Belnap); arguments for atheism (Mackie) were opposed by arguments for theism (Plantinga); intentional theories of meaning (Grice) were opposed by truth-conditional ones (Davidson); bodily continuity, as a criterion of personal identity (Williams), was opposed by psychological inter-connectedness (Parfit); phenomenalist reconstructions of scientific theory (Goodman) were opposed by arguments for realism (Sellars); and so on.[55]

Despite all this there are admittedly some philosophers who still echo Schlick's programmatic optimism, albeit in a more sophisticated form. Thus Quine thinks that the strategy for semantic ascent 'carries' the discussion into a domain where both parties are better agreed on the objects (viz., words) and on the main terms concerning them'.[56]

---

[53] e.g. *Language, Truth and Logic*, 2nd edn., 1946, pp. 60-62; cf. pp. 22-4.

[54] P. F. Strawson, 'On Referring', *Mind*, 59, 1950, pp. 320-44.

[55] R. Carnap, *Meaning and Necessity: A Study in Semantics and Modal Logic*, Chicago: Chicago UP, 1947, pp. 53-5; Quine, *Word and Object*, pp. 68-79; Ayer, *Language, Truth and Logic*, 2nd edn., 1946, p. 133; S. Kripke, 'Naming and Necessity', in D. Davidson and G. Harman (eds), *Semantics of Natural Language*, Dordrecht: Reidel, 1972, pp. 253-355; G. Gentzen, 'Untersuchungen über das logische Schliessen', *Mathematische Zeitschrift*, 39, 1934, pp. 176-210 and 405-31; C. I. Lewis and C. H. Langford, *Symbolic Logic*, New York: Dover, 1932; A. R. Anderson and N. D. Belnap, Jr., *Entailment: The Logic of Relevance and Necessity*, Princeton, NJ: Princeton UP, 1975; J. L. Mackie, 'Evil and Omnipotence', *Mind*, 64, 1955, pp. 200-12; A. Plantinga, *The Nature of Necessity*, Oxford: OUP, 1974, pp. 213-17; H. P. Grice, 'Meaning', *The Philosophical Review*, 66, 1957, pp. 377-88; Davidson, *Inquiry into Truth and Interpretation*; B. Williams, *Problems of the Self*, Cambridge: CUP, 1973, pp. 1-25; D. Parfit, 'Personal Identity', *The Philosophical Review*, 80, 1971, pp. 3-27; N. Goodman, *The Structure of Appearance*, Cambridge, Mass.: Harvard UP, 1951; W. Sellars, *Science, Perception and Reality*, London: Routledge and Kegan Paul, 1963, pp. 106-26.   [56] *Word and Object*, p. 272.

Similarly some philosophers, even after decades of increasingly wide-ranging controversy, still believe that the search for a correct philosophy of language, as 'the foundation for all the rest of philosophy', can be brought to a successful conclusion within a finite period of time. For example, in support of that belief Dummett has claimed that there is at least one 'agreed final conclusion' in philosophy, namely Frege's quantifier-and-variable analysis for the logic of generalization.[57] But even this claim is untenable: it conflicts with Sommers's elaborate development of an alternative analysis for generalization in natural language, based on the subject-and-predicate tradition of Aristotle and Leibniz.[58]

Again, some critics of analytical philosophy have supposed that most of its themes are already worked out. For example, Rorty[59] has claimed that analytical philosophy 'has little more to do'. But, as its literature shows, the actual dialogue of analytical philosophers disappoints all expectations of finality and finds no shortage of new problems, new arguments, and new solutions.

In sum, the method of semantic ascent has now apparently lent itself, in one way or another, to the exposition of a vast variety of conflicting philosophical doctrines, without any of the emerging consensus that distinguishes the progress of science and was originally expected from logico-linguistic philosophy. If all that was at stake was the existing structure of language and the nature of its component elements, the sheer factuality of the problem might have been expected to ensure eventual agreement. Indeed, as we have just seen, that was Quine's explicit expectation for the strategy. But, since clearly recognizable analogues of traditional disputes keep breaking out again within the dialogue of linguistic analysis, it looks as though some of the underlying issues cannot be linguistic at all, and so something must be at stake other than what can be revealed by talk about the method of semantic ascent. Considerations outside language have to be found for favouring some linguistic analyses over others.

Indeed from a historical point of view language has been extensively influenced by the various political, religious, scientific, and cultural forces that play on it. At any one time, therefore, when we look at linguistic usage philosophically, premises about political, religious,

[57] Dummett, op. cit., p. 454.
[58] F. Sommers, *The Logic of Natural Language*, Oxford: OUP, 1982.
[59] Op. cit., p. 173.

scientific, or cultural values may be relevant to questions about which implications of a word we should select as normal and which as deviant: 'person' is one good example, 'substance' another.[60] Thus philosophers sometimes seek to support their attitude towards abortion by invoking a semantical criterion whereby a human foetus turns out to be, or not to be, a person. But, when the certainty of this semantical criterion is seen to be disputable, it becomes more plausible to accept that people may refine their concept of a person so as to be consistent with their attitude towards abortion. Above all the expectation of an eventual consensus seems radically flawed. So far from there being nothing in the nature of philosophy to warrant the existence of conflicting philosophical parties or 'schools', it has rather to be insisted that no account of analytical philosophy–even in its apparently linguistic form–can be adequate which does not explain what there is in its nature to warrant the existence of conflicting parties or schools.

A related point is this. If philosophical issues hang on the actual nature of language, it would be reasonable to suppose that philosophical utterances running counter to the nature of language are a kind of nonsense. So, within the Vienna Circle, charges of meaninglessness were quite common in informal discussion, especially in the mouths of Schlick, Carnap, and Waismann.[61] It was not just that, by virtue of an argument about how meanings are taught, positivistic doctrines were ascribed a secure foundation in linguistic fact and metaphysical theories were rejected as nonsense because empirically unverifiable.[62] Even positivistic colleagues could be accused of uttering meaningless sentences by a philosopher who was sufficiently convinced that his own views were the correct ones. After all, if you believe, as Ayer once did,[63] that all important philosophical propositions are analytic truths and that analytic truths are linguistic tautologies, then you must hold that any denial of your own philosophical thesis is a kind of nonsense, like something that is logically self-contradictory.

But as early as 1927 at least one member of the Vienna Circle, Karl Menger, had denied cognitive value to any philosophy that insists on a

---

[60] Cohen, *The Diversity of Meaning*, pp. 102-3.
[61] K. Menger, *Selected Papers in Logic and Foundations, Didactics, Economics*, Dordrecht: Reidel, 1979, p. 14.
[62] Schlick, op. cit., pp. 457-81.
[63] *Language, Truth and Logic*, 2nd edn., 1946, pp. 26 and 78-9.

particular version of constructive mathematics and rejects results not obtainable within such a version as meaningless. Menger contended that this kind of dogmatism should be relegated 'from logic and mathematics to the biography of the proponent'.[64] Later, in 1934, Carnap came to express a similar attitude in his 'Principle of Tolerance'.[65] 'It is not our business', the Principle claimed, 'to set up prohibitions, but to arrive at conventions.' Carnap concluded: 'In logic there are no morals. Everyone is at liberty to build up his own logic, i.e. his own form of language, as he wishes. All that is required of him is that if he wishes to discuss it, he must state his methods clearly, and give syntatical rules instead of philosophical arguments.' And clearly this position was a kind of half-way house where, purportedly in the light of the example set by mathematicians, Carnap was tolerant of alternative logical systems though reluctant, as yet, to support any of them with arguments for fear of relapsing into a position of intolerance.

But the reluctance was unnecessary. Philosophers can discuss the merits and demerits of different artificial languages in relation to particular tasks without implying that all such languages but one contain nonsense. Carnap himself, for example, later entered into considerable controversy about the value of one kind of inductive logic as against another. He discussed the nature of the reasons that may be given for accepting this or that particular axiom of inductive logic, and he appealed to 'the actual procedure of physicists' in order to determine the structure of the universal laws to which such a logic might apply.[66] And in general the many controversies that have raged in analytical philosophy during the past thirty-five years or so have been conducted without any reversions to the older practice of accusing opponents' utterances of meaninglessness. Tacitly at least, though for the most part not explicitly, almost everyone[67] has accepted that language lends itself to the expression, and intelligible communication, of an indefinitely wide variety of philosophical theses and arguments. Its nature is far too flexible to determine unique outcomes for philosophical investigations. So, since such unique

[64] Op. cit., p. 11.
[65] *The Logical Syntax of Language*, pp. 51-2.
[66] R. Carnap, 'Replies and Expositions', in P. Schilpp (ed.), *The Philosophy of Rudolf Carnap*, pp. 977-8 and 987.
[67] A rare exception is H. E. Kyburg, Jr., 'Scientific and Philosophical Argument', in J. H. Fetzer (ed.), *Principles of Philosophical Reasoning*, Totowa, NJ: Rowman and Allanheld, 1984, p. 149.

outcomes are constantly claimed to be arguable, other premisses–non-linguistic ones–must be looked for. Semantic ascent cannot suffice.

Further support for this conclusion comes from an interesting shift in attitude that tends to take place eventually among those social or political groups which at the outset are strongly opposed to logico-linguistic analysis on political, religious, or metaphysical grounds. Thus modern formal logic was once associated in many people's minds not only with Russell's truth-functionalism and extensionalism but also with his anti-Hegelianism, with his opposition to natural theology, and even with his unconventional opinions on ethical issues. Similarly, linguistic method in philosophy, so far as it exploited formal-logical techniques, was associated with the anti-metaphysical stance of the Vienna Circle. So the reception of modern formal logic into educational curricula has been rather a slow affair. For example, it was not firmly established in Scotland until the mid-1950s, perhaps because Hegelianism remained influential in Scotland for several years after the Second World War (whereas it was much less evident then in England). And in the 1970s formal logic was still not as yet firmly established in philosophical curricula in either Greece or Spain, perhaps because of the military dictatorships that had been in power there. Modern formal logic was also widely suspect in Roman Catholic circles in the immediate post-1945 period until the work of Bochenski and other Dominicans helped to give it respectability. It encountered much hostility from philosophers in the USSR until the 1960s, and recently it was still out of favour in Chile (except among mathematicians). But it is easy to understand these facts in the light of what has already been said about the insufficiency of semantic ascent to determine unique philosophical solutions. Apparently people first mistakenly suppose–as the work of Russell and the Vienna Circle may well lead anyone to suppose–that by using techniques of logico-linguistic analysis a philosopher is inevitably committed to holding certain substantive, positivist doctrines. But, when they come to see that this is not the case and are willing to live with the consequences, they relax opposition to the contemporary methodology of semantic ascent and even begin to use it themselves. Positivist conclusions, they see, require other premisses than those afforded by semantic ascent. (Wisdom's 1945 paper[68] on the analysis of theistic language was an

---

[68] J. Wisdom, 'Gods', *Proceedings of the Aristotelian Society*, 45, 1945, pp. 185-206.

important pathfinder here, because it illustrated how analysis might come to terms with religionism.)

Perhaps someone will object that, if our theory of meaning as it stands is not powerful enough to resolve the central conceptual issues of analytical philosophy, then instead of concluding that those issues need more than just semantic ascent for their resolution we should rather conclude that our theory of meaning needs to be widened or deepened until it can indeed encompass the relevant issues. An adequate theory of meaning, it might be said, will carry with it a resolution of such other issues as the disputes between atomists and holists, between conventionalists and essentialists, between phenomenalists and realists, and so on. Well, perhaps a theory of meaning might indeed be constructed to do all this. But so much the worse for it. One indispensable requirement for a theory of meaning is that it should explain the possibility of linguistic communication between people. Now, where there is properly reasoned controversy or dialogue, there must be communication: in order to be able to argue against an opposing doctrine or an opposing argument on its merits, one needs to be able to understand it. So a satisfactory theory of meaning ought to be able to explain the possibility of communication and mutual comprehension between philosophers holding widely opposed opinions. But, so far as a theory of meaning implies a particular philosophical thesis to be unacceptable, this requirement cannot be satisfied. Such a theory of meaning has either reverted to the old Vienna Circle futility of crying 'meaningless' when opposing doctrines is heard, or at the very least it purports to embroil its opponents in a tangle of incoherence whereby they cannot talk even about the meanings of their own theses without inconsistency, since on a supposedly proper analysis of what they thus assert they are presupposing the falsity of those theses. In short, theories of meaning should be maximally unassuming and unambitious on philosophically controversial issues if they are to explain as much as possible of the successful communication that actually takes place. It follows that the linguistic account of analytical philosophy cannot be defended by the claim that an adequate theory of meaning would resolve all the controversies now blocking the way to any consensus of the kind that the linguistic thesis has always promised. The analytical theory of language needs to concentrate on its proper tasks, which exclude the pursuit of such imperialist aspirations.

§ 4 THOUGHT, MEANING, AND VERIFICATION

Summary. The doctrine that the process of thought is not distinct from its linguistic expression, and the doctrine that the meanings of statements are taught by giving instructions about their verification, combined to support the positivist phase of analytic philosophy. But the latter doctrine has to be discarded if we are to take account of how meanings are assigned or adjusted by an appropriate use of analogy. The former doctrine blocks the path of psychological enquiry and is not needed as a rationale for the strategy of semantic ascent.

Although we can see now that semantic ascent is neither a necessary feature of all analytical philsophy (§ 2) nor sufficient to determine unique resolutions of any important philosophical problems (§ 3), we need to ask just where the earlier, positivist champions of analytical philosophy went wrong, in order to be sure that the linguistic thesis has no foundation in the theory of language.

The positivist phase of analytical philosophy was based on two doctrines about language. If positivist limits to the thinkable are to be sustained, both these doctrines have to be upheld. One doctrine is that all thought consists in the mental processing of linguistic forms. 'The process of thought', as Ayer once put the point,[69] 'is not distinct from the expression of it.' The other doctrine is that to be taught the meaning of a sentence we need to learn what observations would verify the statements that it makes and what would falsify them. Thus, according to Schlick, 'whenever we ask about a sentence "What does it mean?" we want a description of the conditions under which the sentence will form a *true* proposition and of those which will make it *false*'. That was, for example, how Einstein thought it proper to answer the question 'What do we mean when we speak of two events at distant places happening simultaneously?'[70] And when the two doctrines are conjoined they entail that we cannot think about anything that is intrinsically unobservable. God, moral rights, and physical particles are all inconceivable.

This linguistic positivism was not open to the stock objections raised against Hume's empiricism. In Hume's view 'all our simple ideas in their first appearance are deriv'd from simple expressions,

---

[69] A. J. Ayer, *Thinking and Meaning*, London: H. K. Lewis, 1947, p. 25.
[70] Schlick, pp. 457-59.

which are correspondent to them, and which they exactly represent'.[71]
From this premiss Hume drew his positivistic conclusions about what
we must be thinking when we think about causation, about our minds,
and so on: namely, causation is just constant conjunction, the mind is
just a collection of interrelated momentary experiences, etc. But the
trouble with Hume's theory that thoughts ('ideas') copy experience
was its inability to account for several important elements in everyday
thinking. For example, we can neither picture logical operations in
our minds nor hum them in our heads. Nor could the copy theory
readily accommodate different levels of specificity, as when we
distinguish between the thought of a tree, of an oak, or of an oak in
leaf. Nor could it differentiate thoughts about the past from thoughts
about the future. And clearly the doctrine that the process of thought
is not distinct from its linguistic expression could make light work of
all these difficulties, since all discussable differences of thought must
be expressible in correspondingly different words or phrases. Moreover, when the verificationist doctrine was subjoined the foundations
were laid for an empiricist philosophy that was just as restrictive as
Hume's in regard to causation, mind, etc.

But this positivist phase of analytical philosophy was too paradoxical to last, and its verificationist doctrine was obviously the
weaker of its two main premisses. Those philosophers who identified
all demonstrations of a statement's meaning with instructions for its
verification or falsification were ignoring the role of analogy in the
assignment and comprehension of a wide range of meanings. In
natural science certainly, *pace* Schlick, Einstein's question about
'simultaneity' is not the only kind of semantic issue that arises.
Another relevant issue is, for example, how to define the names of
newly postulated submicroscopic entities in analogical terms. Certain
kinds of physical particles may be thought of as resembling more
familiar, middle-sized objects in having parameters of mass, spin,
charge, velocity, etc., but as differing from them by not having
parameters of colour, temperature, etc.[72] Moreover, if analogical
models can determine meanings for the terminology of theoretical science, they can do this also for the vocabulary of religion, as both modern and medieval theologians have recognized.[73] 'God' may be said to
mean someone resembling humans in being a person, but differing in

[71] Op. cit., bk. 1, pt. 1, § 1.
[72] M. Hesse, *Forces and Fields*, London: Nelson, 1961, p. 24.
[73] J. F. Ross, *Portraying Analogy*, Cambridge: CUP, 1981, pp. 161-71.

not being subject to biological processes, or to limitations of power, etc. So the view that all thinking is an operation with language does not make traditional theism unintelligible, as Ayer once held it to be.[74] The truth or falsity of sufficiently precise theological claims remains just as much a matter for intelligible discussion as does the truth or falsity of, say, nineteenth-century atomism. That is why we can understand arguments, like those of Plantinga or Mackie, that the existence of an omniscient, omnipotent, and benevolent being is, or is not, compatible with the world as we know it. Indeed, there is now experimental evidence to support the view that people can learn to name even everyday kinds of objects correctly by drawing analogies with previously observed instances or with mentally constructed prototypes.[75] So analogical reasoning may enter into semantic learning at quite an early stage.

Nor can one repudiate the use of analogy as a way of determining meanings without running into serious difficulties in elucidating the familiar comprehensibility of metaphor. Metaphorical meaning seems always to depend on an analogy of some kind:[76] if the clouds this evening are said to be made of pure gold, it is because they have the colour–even though not the other properties–of pure gold. It follows that, unless you are willing to accept the very serious impoverishment of language that would result from excluding the creative force of metaphor, you cannot exclude analogical determinations of meaning. And, if analogical determinations of meaning are admissible, so too are the linguistic usages characteristically favoured by theists.

What was thus wrong with Ayer's project for a verificationist criterion of meaningfulness was not just that it ran foul of the ingenious paradoxes constructed by Church, Hempel, and Scheffler.[77] Such paradoxes have nothing to do essentially with observational verifiability, and affect any attempt to define an appropriately homogeneous category of theory in terms of a certain category of

---

[74] *Language, Truth and Logic*, 2nd edn., 1946, p. 116.

[75] See the papers in E. Rosch and B. B. Lloyd (eds.), *Cognition and Categorization*, Hillsdale, NJ: Erlbaum, 1978, and the discussion in G. Cohen, *The Psychology of Cognition*, London: Academic Press, 2nd edn., 1983, pp. 81-9.

[76] Ross, op. cit., pp. 109-19.

[77] A. Church, review of A. J. Ayer's, *Language, Truth and Logic*, 2nd edn., *Journal of Symbolic Logic*, 14, 1949, pp. 52-3; C. G. Hempel, 'Problems and Changes in the Empiricist Criterion of Meaning', *Revue internationale de philosophie*, 4, 1950, p. 50; I. Scheffler, 'Prospects of a Modest Empiricism', *Review of Metaphysics*, 10, 1957, pp. 383-400 and 602-25.

singular statements plus the usual vocabulary of deductive logic.[78] So
they tell us nothing specific about the nature of meaning. Nor was
Ayer's project rendered harmless by acceptance of its inapplicability
to non-statement-making utterances–i.e. to commands, recommen-
dations, prayers, greetings, etc. Even when applied only to statements,
a verificationist criterion was still dangerously potent. It forced a
phenomenalist, or at least anti-realist, interpretation on to scientific
theories and disallowed any theological discussion. The core of the
trouble was rather that Schlick's and Ayer's verificationism turned its
back altogether on the possibility of any word's acquiring, or adjusting, its meaning by analogy. Consequently, if the project was on the
right lines, what science could claim to exist was permanently limited
by the pretensions of empiricism, whereas with the help of appropriate
analogies, scientific theory can continue to expand the horizons of
ontology–as it is commonly supposed to have done for the past three
or four centuries.

For reasons such as these, the more recent phase of analytical
philosophy has rightly been more receptive to realist philosophies of
science (Maxwell, Sellars, Smart[79]). The verificationist doctrine, in all
its many versions, has been widely, though by no means universally,
rejected. Hence that doctrine, despite its centrality in the earlier
period, obviously cannot be taken as a defining feature of analytical
philosophy. But what about the doctrine that the process of thought is
not distinct from its linguistic expression? If this doctrine had to be
accepted it would provide a perspicuous rationale for the strategy of
semantic ascent. Even though the methods of linguistic analysis are
neither necessary for the treatment of all major philosophical
problems (§ 2) nor sufficient for the unique resolution of any (§ 3), yet
every problem about the analysis of a *thought* would be equatable with
some problem about the analysis of a sentence, statement, or other
linguistic entity.

For most purposes it would do no harm to accept such an equation,
since it allows us to analyse any statable thought. But, although the
hypothesis that all thinking is an operation with language does not

[78] See L. Jonathan Cohen, 'Is a Criterion of Verifiability Possible?', in P. A. French,
T. E. Uehling, Jr., and H. K. Wettstein (eds.), *Studies in Epistemology*, (Midwest Studies
in Philosophy, 5), Minneapolis: Minnesota UP, 1980, pp. 351-2.

[79] G. Maxwell, 'The Ontological Status of Theoretical Entities', in H. Feigl and G.
Maxwell (eds.), *Minnesota Studies in the Philosophy of Science*, 3, Minneapolis: Minnesota
UP, 1962, pp. 3-27; Sellars, op. cit., pp. 106-26; and J. J. C. Smart, *Philosophy and Scientific
Realism*, London: Routledge and Kegan Paul, 1963, pp. 16-49.

itself set any readily specifiable limits to *what* people can think about, it does set quite definite limits in regard to *who* can think. Language is a very flexible instrument for those able to exploit its potential. But, if it is the only instrument of thought, then neither human infants nor wild adult chimpanzees can think at all. Thus Ayer tells us that young children do not elaborate 'a common-sense theory of the physical world' on their own: 'they are taught a language which already embodies it, and whatever may be logically possible, it is factually improbable that they would arrive at it otherwise'.[80] Correspondingly non-human animals are often said to lack rationality in virtue of their lacking language: if they are languageless they cannot have factual knowledge and so they cannot have reasons. For example, Bennett argues that linguistic behaviour is the only behaviour 'which obeys rules correlating performances with empirical states of affairs', and hence that linguistic capacity is necessary for rationality.[81] Again, Davidson argues that no creature can have a belief unless it has the concept of a belief, because it could not otherwise understand the possibility of being mistaken, and that no creature can acquire the concept of a belief except through its role in the interpretation of other creatures' utterances. From these two premisses he concludes that no creature can have a belief unless it is a member of a speech-community.[82] And Hacking's 'answer to the question of why language matters to philosophy now' is that, because of the role played in our scientific culture by language, 'sentences ... serve as the interface between the knowing subject and what is known'.[83]

However, despite the arguments of these philosophers, there are a lot of data from psychological experiments that support the possibility of non-linguistic thought. Whatever may be the case about other concepts, some of those required for the common-sense view of the physical world seem to be elaborated by animals and infants on their own and do not have to be acquired through the medium of language-learning. For example, some non-human primates are said to behave, in appropriate circumstances, just as if they expect to recover food from a closed container several hours after they saw it put there. That is, they are said to behave as if they assume objects to be capable of

[80] A. J. Ayer, *The Central Questions of Philosophy*, London: Weidenfeld and Nicholson, 1973, p. 106.
[81] J. Bennett, *Rationality: An Essay towards an Analysis*, London: Routledge and Kegan Paul, 1964, p. 88.
[82] *Inquiries into Truth and Interpretation*, p. 170.
[83] I. Hacking, *Why Does Language Matter to Philosophy?*, Cambridge: CUP, 1973, p. 187.

existing independently of their own experience. Again, there is said to be clear evidence that one-month-old human infants will show a visual preference for an object previously explored in the mouth but not seen, and several other cross-modal associations between sensory properties have been demonstrated. There is evidence that infants perceive the unity and boundaries of objects by detecting the spatial arrangement of their surfaces, not by analysing colours and textures. There is evidence that infants in the first year of life are sensitive to relations of contact and non-contact between objects, and can represent these relations for a cognitively effective period of time. They apparently turn to look where their mother has turned to look, as if there were a common object to be seen. They seem to perceive visual space in a three-dimensional way, and despite considerable perspectival changes in forms and apparent size, caused by rotation or movement in depth, infants apparently know that form and size of objects remain invariant under these circumstances. They apparently know which perspectival transformations of regular patterns are a cue to depth. Even at thirty weeks they apparently know which side of a photographed, tilted, rectangular window is the nearest one.[84]

If psychologists are correct to interpret these data as evidence of thought, then, so far from its being factually improbable, as Ayer claimed, that children can arrive at the common-sense conception of the physical world without being taught a language, it is factually probable that they do arrive at it without this. What is more, they seem to exhibit rationality in their responses to pre-linguistic experiments (e.g. by responding appropriately to changes in perspective), and they give strong indications in many of these experiments that they have beliefs about objects (e.g. about invariance in size and shape). Indeed,

---

[84] For useful surveys of the literature see O. L. Tinklepaugh, 'An Experimental Study of Representative Factors in Monkeys', *Journal of Comparative Psychology*, a8, 1928, pp. 197-202; and P. Van Geert, 'Attributing Knowledege to Children', in B. de Gelder (ed.), *Knowledge and Representation*, London: Routledge and Kegan Paul, 1982, pp. 194-209; cf. A. M. Leslie, 'Discursive Representation in Infancy', ibid., pp. 60-93; and E. S. Spelke, 'Perceptual Knowledge of Objects in Infancy', in J. Mehler *et al.* (eds.), *Perspectives on Mental Representation: Experimental and Theoretical Studies of Cognitive Processes and Capacities*, Hillsdale, NJ.: Erlbaum, 1982, pp. 409-30; G. Butterworth, 'Structure of the Mind in Human Infancy', in *Advances in Infancy Research*, vol. 2, Norwood, NJ: Ablex, 1983, pp. 1-29; id., 'Object Permanence and Identity in Piaget's Theory of Infant Cognition', in G. Butterworth (ed.), *Infancy and Epistemology*, Hassocks: Harvester Press, 1981, pp. 137-69.

there is now a lot of evidence that, *pace* Hacking, natural language is not the fundamental form in which even adults are best described as storing and processing information, as will emerge in § 20 below from discussion of the computational metaphor in modern cognitive psychology.

But, even if all such claims are inadequately supported by the experimental data or establish the existence of non-linguistic thinking only at a very primitive level, at least the issue is an intelligible one. The arguments of philosophers like Bennett and Davidson–arguments that exclude such possibilities a priori–are blocking conceptual paths that need to be kept open if the relevant empirical enquiries are to be promoted. It is this point, not the present results of the enquiries themselves, that counts most strongly against the linguistic thesis. The clear implication is that analytical philosophers ought not to base any part of their metaphilosophy on the doctrine that equates the process of thought with its linguistic expression. Though this a priori doctrine allows us to analyse any statable thought, it has undesirable consequences for the progress of experimental psychology. And we do not need the doctrine. Even without recourse to it we can still explain, and justify, the role of semantic ascent in analytical philosophy, as will be shown in § 6 below.

§ 5 NATURALIZED EPISTEMOLOGY VERSUS NORMATIVE EPISTEMOLOGY

Summary. It would not be correct to characterize the distinctive aim of analytical philosophy as the pursuit of intellectual clarification. Nor can we characterize it, in Quine's terms, as 'a limning of the most general traits of reality', mainly because this ignores the normative element in epistemology.

What should succeed the linguistic account of analytical philosophy? We might dally for the moment with the suggestion that analytical philosophy is essentially a system of prophylactics against, and antidotes for, intellectual confusions. It exists, we may be told, to promote clarity of thought and unravel conceptual log-jams. After all, Wittgenstein's original claim in 1922 was that 'the object of philosophy is the logical clarification of thought' and that 'the result of philosophy is not a number of "philosophical propositions", but to make propositions clear',[85] and Schlick echoed this claim in his programmatic paper of 1930 'The Future of Philosophy'.[86]

Undeniably most (though nowadays, unfortunately, not all) analytical philosophers attach a high value to clarity of exposition. Unlike Hegelians or Heideggerians, they deliberately eschew tortuous syntax, elliptical exposition, and the replacement of plain statement by enigmatic hints, rhetorical paradoxes, or woolly metaphor. But analytical philosophers are also claimed to aim at creating clarity in the minds of their readers, and here it is not clear how the relevant concept of clarity should itself be clarified. If the clarity to be created by analytical philosophy is just a clarity about use and meaning which is to be achieved by the strategy of semantic ascent, then the arguments against the linguistic thesis will apply also against the clarity thesis. If, instead, the kind of clarification desired is not restricted to that attainable by the strategy of semantic ascent, then the target of this clarificatory enterprise needs to be specified and its specification is the core problem for metaphilosophy. We need to know just what it is that good analytical philosophy makes people clearer about. Either way, therefore, the clarity thesis fails. But we should, of course, expect an adequate account of analytical philosophy to explain why intellectual clarification could have appeared as so important an objective to many of its practitioners, just as such an account should also explain why many of them might have thought it appropriate to concentrate on a strategy of semantic ascent.

Nor is there much point in the claim that analytical philosophy issues in an activity of clarification rather than in a sequence of clarificatory propositions. For in either case a sequence of sentences has to be uttered and understood, and a question therefore arises about the nature of what has thus been said. Whatever the characteristic effect of analytical philosophy on a hearer or reader, this effect is certainly supposed to be exerted via the meanings of its sentences rather than via, say, their metre or rhyme. Indeed, there is still no shortage of volunteers to publish exegeses for the texts of philosophers who have described themselves as being engaged in an activity of clarification rather than in the production of clarificatory propositions. Above all, that description still leaves open the question: what is it that analytical philosophy characteristically seeks to clarify?

---

[85] L. Wittgenstein, *Tractatus Logico-Philosophicus*, London: Kegan Paul, Trench, Trubner, 1922, p. 77 (para. 4.112).

[86] Op. cit., p. 172.

It might perhaps appear more promising to insist that the study of meanings is not fundamentally separable from the study of fact, because this looks like reconciling the linguistic account with the need for semantic descent as well as ascent. Thus Quine, who introduced the term 'semantic ascent' into the literature of analytical philosophy, has himself written that 'the quest of a simplest, clearest overall pattern of canonical notation is not to be distinguished from a quest of ultimate categories, a limning of the most general traits of reality'.[87] Once the distinction between analytic and synthetic propositions is shown to be untenable, so too is the distinction between linguistic and factual components in our system of beliefs. We are left, therefore, with the need to use some highly unspecific terms, like 'reality', for what is represented by this system. Indeed, that term must also cover the system itself, since the task of studying the system is consigned by Quine to psychological science.[88] So Quine does not take philosophical *problems* to be essentially linguistic in nature, even though he does take the right philosophical *method* to operate mainly via a strategy of semantic ascent. On the question of problems, what has here been called the 'linguistic thesis' about analytical philosophy must give way, in Quine's view, to what one can best call the 'reality thesis', namely the thesis that the dominant aim of analytical philosophy is to limn the most general traits of reality.

However, there are at least three strong objections to this view.

The first is that it either takes no account at all of philosophical ethics or identifies that branch of philosophy with the psychology of moral judgement and moral decision. But the problems of philosophical ethics will not just disappear, and if we try to treat them as problems about psychological processes we lose the possibility of drawing any distinction between reality as it is and reality as it ought ethically to be. Or, if the distinction drawn is between reality as it is and reality as this or that thinker in fact prefers it, then there is no room for disagreement between you and me about how reality ought to be: I must accept the fact that you prefer it to have such-and-such features, while you must accept the fact that I prefer it to have others.

The second objection is that the common-sense distinction between linguistic and factual components in our system of beliefs should not be too cavalierly dismissed. There is certainly no difficulty about how, in a rough and ready way, we can enter the charmed circle

---

[87] *Word and Object*, p. 161.
[88] *Ontological Relativity and Other Essays*, p. 82.

of vocabulary within which the terms 'analytic' and 'synthetic' belong. We enter it, as we enter so many other lexical circles, by ostension: the idea of analyticity is very easily conveyed to philosophy students by means of examples, just as basic terms for family relationships are taught to children. But anything that is thus offered as an example of analyticity, or of syntheticity, should be taken to be a belief, a statement, a proposition, or a sentence in a particular context, not just a sentence *tout court* or a grammatically well-formed string of words. Since a sentence—consider 'Water is H_2O', for example—can then have both analytic occurrences in formulating some human beliefs and synthetic ones in formulating others, it becomes possible to reconcile the view that the analytic-synthetic distinction is sometimes worthwhile with the view that no *sentence* is irredeemably analytic or irredeemably synthetic.

Thirdly, and perhaps most seriously, Quine's epistemology fails to pay sufficient attention to the fact that within anyone's system of beliefs the most important relationship that one belief or conjunction of beliefs can be thought to bear to another is that of being some kind of a reason or justification for it. Our predictions, explanations, inferences, arguments, and deliberations are all grounded in this structure of relationships. It is also what allows us sometimes to think of ourselves as having knowledge and not just true belief. So the exercise of intelligence requires not just the possession of a well-attested set of beliefs, but also the conscious or unconscious possession of a set of norms or principles for determining whether or not a given set of beliefs is well-attested. We can think of some of these as rules of sentential well-formedness, some as decision-procedures for consistency or deducibility, some as criteria of proof or measures of probability, some as rules for ensuring that observations are veridical, some as precepts of experimental method for investigating or assessing causality, some as strategies for acquiring and processing statistics, some as guidelines for idealization, simplification, and systematization in theory-construction, and so on. But they are all norms, not factual beliefs, and a philosopher who is concerned only to limn the most general features of reality will miss that aspect of them altogether. For it will not do to say that he will come across them as facts about his own and other people's sets of accepted sentences. What the epistemologist has to investigate is not how beliefs come in practice to be thought well-attested. He is concerned instead with how beliefs *ought* to attain that status and what criteria they *ought* to satisfy (even though he has always to bear in mind that–here as elsewhere–'ought' implies 'can' and so factual beliefs about what is mentally or physically possible may legitimately constrain our cognitive norms). In short, Quine's naturalized epistemology is a task for psychologists, sociologists, and historians of ideas. But the kind of epistemology that philosphers need to pursue is unnaturalizable, because it is concerned to prescribe and evaluate universal norms, not to describe, predict, or explain the multiple variations of actual human practice.

Indeed, wherever norms are involved there is always an internal as well as an external point of view. Legal positivists, for example, like Holmes,[89] may choose to take the external point of view of a sociologist (or historian or company adviser) and identify the bearing of the law on a particular case with what the court will in fact decide it to be. But that point of view is quite inappropriate for the advocate who is trying to persuade a judge what he ought to decide, or for the judge himself who is trying to deliberate about this. Analogously, however much progress is made by psychologists, sociologists, or historians in discovering how beliefs are *in fact* formed, there must always be questions also–from the internal point of view–about how they *should* be formed. So, however much some philosophers may want to naturalize epistemology, there will always be a demand for the unnaturalized variety.

Perhaps it will be objected that the facts which can replace norms here are not so much psychological facts about how people think, but usefully learnable facts about how this or that purpose may be achieved. For example, a rule or principle that is expressed normatively as 'Whenever you want x, do y' can always be changed into the assertoric form 'Anyone who wants x will be satisfied best by doing y' or 'Wherever y is done, x results.'

But somewhere or other, in a fully explicit intellectual system, there must still be a norm which prescribes or permits action on the basis of whichever of such assertoric sentences is appropriate to the situation. So in that kind of context these sentences carry an ineliminable normative import. Indeed, so too do any assertoric conditional sentences that are used in articulating a person's corpus of belief, since each of these may be invoked as validating a corresponding rule of inference. Even quite specific assertions like 'If it rains this

[89] O. W. Holmes, 'The Path of the Law', *Harvard Law Review*, 10, 1897, pp. 457 and 476.

afternoon, the march will be cancelled', have permissive inferential rules as correlates, like 'From an occurrence of rain this afternoon, infer the cancellation of the march.' Moreover, in accordance with your current point of view you can take either the asserted conditionals or the norms as primary. You can either read off the norms from the assertions or the assertions from the norms.

More exactly, the situation is this. If you want to use assertoric forms as much as possible in articulating a standing system of belief, then you also need to include at least one primary norm in the system, to prescribe or permit action on the basis of any appropriate assertion. If, instead, you want to use norms as much as possible in your articulation, then you need at least one norm to authorize reading off conditional assertions from the others. But you don't have to go all the way in either direction. Rather it is justifiable to think of the more general principles as being primarily regulative, since that is how they would mostly enter into human reasoning. To believe or assert them as facts (and perhaps as facts that are relatively immune to empirical challenge) is appropriate only for those philosophers who are determined to formulate metaphysical theses. For them reality itself is simple, say, or economical. But others will be satisfied instead to include relative simplicity or economy–appropriately defined–among the grounds for preferring one scientific theory to another. Similarly, it is justifiable to think of the more specific principles as being primarily factual, since that is how they, with their vulnerability to adverse experience, would mostly enter into human reasoning. It seems rather wasteful to set up a rule that is going to operate on relatively few occasions. Finally, a very large number of principles–especially causal laws and other natural-scientific generalizations–may be needed to an equal extent in both roles. In order to report discoveries, or to constitute premises for further scientific conclusions, they function as assertions: when they provide the know-how for industrial production, or for anything else that involves prediction or retrodiction, they function as rules.

Accordingly, Quine's 'reality thesis' does not assist us much towards providing an alternative, non-linguistic account of analytical philosophy. Indeed, its failure to recognize the importance of the normative dimension in epistemology leads it to share a major defect with the linguistic thesis. Since it does not recognize that our intellectual reactions to events depend on the epistemological norms that we happen to include in our system, and on the priorities that we allocate to them, it tends to assume, as the linguistic thesis also does, that analytical philosophers, like natural scientists, should be expected to converge towards consensus in respect of any problems they investigate: knowledge of facts, like knowledge of meanings, admits, if attained, of no alternative conclusions. But, as argued in § 3, this is just the opposite of what actually happens now in analytical philosophy. On a wide range of issues it is divergence, rather than convergence, that has increased during the last thirty years, just as divergence has in the past always been in evidence over the long term in philosophy. And what is needed is an account in non-linguistic terms that will make sense of this divergence.

II

Analysis and Reasoning

§ 6 ANALYSIS AS REASONING ABOUT REASONING

Summary. Analytical philosophy is occupied, at an appropriately general level, and in a great variety of ways, with the reasoned discussion of what can be a reason for what. As such it is a strand in the total history of western philosophy from Socrates onwards rather than just a modern movement. It also tends to promote certain social and cultural values, though without the intellectual impoverishment that results from taking the aim of philosophy as being 'to give meaning and purpose to life'.

WHAT has emerged in §§ 2-3 is that linguistic accounts of analytical philosophy point to techniques that may assist in resolving some of its problems but not all. So the general nature of analytical philosophy cannot be characterized in terms of such accounts. Nor does the psychology of the thinking process seem capable (§ 4) of providing any decisive guidance for metaphilosophy. Where analytical enquiry is concerned with human thought, it is the content of that thought, not the process, that occupies attention.

But on what issues about this content does analytical philosophy explicitly or implicitly concentrate its attention? If we examine seriatim the problems that actually puzzle analytical philosophers we shall find that the problems of analytical philosophy are all normative problems connected in various ways with rationality of judgement, rationality of attitude, rationality of procedure, or rationality of action. Analytical philosophy seeks a reasoned resolution of such problems, and it fills a gap that naturalized epistemology is in principle incapable of filling (§ 5). Not that it ever hypostatizes rationality in the high, Hegelian manner. No analytical philosopher would proclaim, for example, that 'Reason is both substance and infinite power, in itself the infinite material of all natural and spiritual life as well as the infinite form, the actualization of itself as content.'[1] Analytical

---

[1] G. W. F. Hegel, *Reason in History* (trans. R. S. Hartman), Indianapolis: Bobbs Merrill, 1953, p. 11.

philosophy occupies itself instead, implicitly or explicitly, with the humbler task of reasoning, at an appropriate level of generality, about how good a reason what can be for what. Some direct or indirect involvement in this task is the most specific common feature that pervades every significant contribution to the dialogue identified in § 1.

One main source of such problems is constituted by sceptical challenges to accepted tenets of rationality. Thus Thrasymachus, as a character in Plato's dialogue, raised the question: is there any reason to be altruistic? And Pyrrho, Montaigne, Hume, Popper, and Quine, for example, have all been influential through raising similar challenges to accepted patterns of reasoning. Is there any reason for a person ever to trust his senses, or to credit the existence of some other minds like his own, or to believe that some objects, or temporal relations, exist independently of his own experience? Can observed events support the truth of predictions about as yet unobserved ones? Can we ever justify one way of translating the words of a foreign language rather than another? Such questions as these, though deceptively simple in their initial formulation, are notorious for having often provoked lengthy and complex philosophical enquiries. Some philosophers—most recently Nozick[2]—formulate such questions as requests for explanations of how something is possible: for example, how is knowledge possible, given that at any time we may be dreaming? But the explanation that is thus required is, nevertheless, one that will show the adequacy of relevant reasons to refute sceptical doubts.

Another kind of stimulus to analytical philosophy arises from paradoxes, where mutually inconsistent conclusions seem equally plausible. We seem to have certain innate or culturally built-in principles of reasoning that can be shown by clever and imaginative thinkers to conflict with one another, even though the situations in which inconsistency actually arises are not common enough to cause trouble in everyday life. The problem of free-will, Zeno's paradoxes of motion, Eubulides' paradox of self-reference, the Prisoner's Dilemma, Russell's set-theoretical antinomy, Hempel's paradoxes of confirmation, Kyburg's lottery paradox, and Newcomb's paradox about choice are all familiar examples. An act is arguably free, and yet also causally determined. An arrow obviously moves, and yet is arguably stationary. A self-falsifying proposition is arguably true, and yet also false. The apparently most rational choice of each of two

---

[2] R. Nozick, *Philosophical Explanations*, Oxford: OUP, 1981, pp. 8-13.

prisoners is nevertheless not the choice that produces the best available result. And so on. Because self-contradictory conclusions are irrational these paradoxes demand resolution. The standard response is to seek appropriately revised systems of reasoning (about action, motion, truth-value, time, choice, probability, etc.) that are themselves evidently immune to paradox, but are describable within a framework that explains or elucidates how the antinomies are generated. Alternatively, an attempt is made to show how, within some appropriate paraconsistent system, the irrationality that is apparently manifested by the contradictions in question may be controlled, confined, or eliminated.[3]

A third source is the tension between a mind's awareness of itself as a subjective universe of consciousness and its awareness of the world as an objectively existing reality. This tension gives rise to many problems about time and space; about how body and mind are related; about the structure of mental life; and about the nature of personal identity over differences in temporal and spatial location. And the dominant aim of analytical philosophy here is to investigate how we can reason coherently on such issues. What validates inferences from bodily states to mental ones, or vice versa? Is reason always the slave of the passions? On what assumptions of continuity do a person's hopes or fears about future events depend? And so on.

A fourth source of problems about rationality lies in the study of meanings and messages. For example, to describe a word's various meanings or functions is to list the characteristic reasons for its use, whether these reasons emerge as satisfaction-conditions, relevant evidence, rhetorical force, logical structure, implications, incompatibilities, categorial assignments, or an assembly of examples and analogies. An expression that there is never any reason of any kind to utter is an expression that has no sense. Correspondingly, to analyse a *concept* linguistically is first to identify the concept by specifying a word-meaning in some such way and then, in some other such way, to refine that meaning.[4] So conceptual analysis typically relates one kind of reason for using a certain word to another. Thus Russell identified the function of 'the' in definite descriptions by his example 'The author of Waverley was Scotch', and offered an analysis of it in terms of that

---

[3] See, for example, N. Rescher and R. Brandom, *The Logic of Inconsistency*, Oxford: Blackwell, pp. 34-42.
[4] L. Jonathan Cohen, *The Diversity of Meaning*, London: Methuen, 2nd edn., 1966, pp. 21 and 95-127.

sentence's implications and logical structure.[5] Hare identified an evaluative meaning of 'good' by pointing to the similarities and differences between 'good' and 'red', and he then offered an analysis of it in terms of its rhetorical force.[6] And to know the message normally conveyed by a given sentence one needs to know the typical reasons for uttering it, such as its meaning, the speech-acts that it can achieve in appropriate contexts, the implications or presuppositions of its utterance, and so on. Indeed the linguistic form of analytical philosophy, though it has been pursued in so many different ways, may be viewed in general as the study of rationality in and about language-use. What Ryle once called 'talk about talk', and Quine 'semantic ascent', is a part, but only a part, of reasoning about reasons.

A fifth source of problems about rationality lies in the foundations of deductive logic, in the relations between logic and language, and in the logics of tense, modality, inductive support, etc. Are words and sentences the ultimate units of logical analysis? Does logical truth depend on linguistic convention? Could different logics apply to different languages or different uses of language? Since logic studies the most general principles of reasoning, analytical philosophy cannot avoid close interest in the status and content of logical theory.

A sixth family of problems is supplied by mathematics. For example, what is the nature of mathematical proof? What are its limits? What ontology, if any, does it assume? What kinds of reasons can there be for modifying its premisses? What justifies the application of mathematical theorems to the solution of problems about reality?

A seventh problem-area is constituted by the natural sciences along with economics, sociology, psychology, linguistics, history, and other intellectual disciplines. What is the justification for pursuing such-and-such a science? What are its characteristic modes of heuristic and of expository reasoning, and how do they compare with those of other sciences? How do its technical terms function? Does acceptance of its findings constitute a reason for adopting this or that ontology? Can it give us reasons why things happen as they do, or only descriptions of how things happen? How does statistical theory, or any other branch of mathematics, assist its reasoning? And how is it connected with

---

[5] B. Russell, *Introduction to Mathematical Philosophy*, London: Allen and Unwin, 1920, pp. 176-8.

[6] R. M. Hare, *The Language of Morals*, Oxford: OUP, 1952, pp. 111-36.

other sciences? Can it support or explain, or be supported or explained by, them?

An eighth group of problems arises about the rationale for people's actions, decisions, or attitudes, for cultural patterns, or for social and political institutions of various kinds. What are the foundations of human ideals, moral rules, educational values, professional standards, or commercial ethics? Some issues here are relatively specific and topical, like the morality of nuclear war or test-tube babies: others are much more general, like the rationality of altruism or the opposition between a utilitarian and a contractarian theory of justice, or between a consequentialist and a deontological theory of moral duty. And, though incidental questions are bound to arise about the conceptual structure of decision, intention, action, responsibility, co-operation, law, etc., the seminal issues may always be seen as arising in the context of deliberation or justification. It is they that give importance to the other questions. The question 'What makes (or should make) a rule or principle a legal one?' is important, for example, because it may affect the validity of philosophical arguments about what kinds of laws should be passed, about how the courts should decide cases in which the law is doubtful, or about whether civil disobedience is ever justified.

Each of these groups of problems overlaps or interconnects with others, and at least two other groups of problems also fit the proposed account of analytical philosophy. One of these is about the justification or non-justification of beliefs in the existence of miracles, divine providence, immortal souls, etc. The other is about the reasons for identifying an object as a work of art, or for ascribing greater aesthetic merit to one text or musical composition than to another. And, no doubt, many more groups of problems could also be listed here. Some popular issues in analytical philosophy may seem on superficial consideration to be of a different nature. But, on closer inspection, they can be shown to owe their popularity to their connections with that tangled web of procedures and principles, assumptions and methods, that constitute human rationality.

Certainly we can easily see in these terms why the pursuit of clarity could appear to some as the dominant purpose of analytical philosophy. To appreciate how good or bad a reason one type of proposition is for another a philospher's readers need to have a sufficiently clear conception of both types of propositions and of the nature of their relationship. But clarity here is just a necessary part of the means to a presupposed end, not a sufficient end in itself. Or again, some general thesis–say, a verificationist account of meaning–may help to explain why each of a series of analyses of particular concepts comes off. The status of those analyses is thus clarified, and the experience vocalizable by 'Now I see clearly why . . .' is certainly integral to the pragmatic dimension of explanation in such cases. But this connection between explanation and the achievement of mental clarity in relevant respects is not unique to philosophical explanation. It belongs just as much to scientific explanation also. And the difference between these two types of explanation is more clearly delineated in terms of their repective subject-matter than in terms of the mental states respectively associated with them. How could we tell a philosophical explanation from a scientific one just by its raw feel?

Truth, however, might seem a more promising candidate for the role of an independent issue. To be interested in reasons, it might be said, requires us to examine a set of relations between propositions, whereas to be interested in truth requires us to examine a value that a proposition may have in itself. But why is truth an important philosophical issue? The answer is surely twofold. First, the concept of truth has a key use in the intuitive characterization of deducibility. We require a deduction to preserve truth: if the premisses are true, the conclusion must also be true. So the concept of truth is too central to the study of reasoning to be left unanalysed. Secondly, true beliefs are what we normally take to be in our interest to have, not false ones. Truth is the primary object of intellectual enquiry. So the truth of a proposition, if it is relevant to our concerns, is the best reason we can normally have for accepting it into our stock of stored information. In other words, truth is a general category of reason in this regard, much as justice is–when the justice of an act is considered a reason for doing it. Consequently, no investigation of actual and possible patterns of reasoning would be complete without an exercise in semantic descent to examine the nature of those categories of reasons–i.e. without asking what truth must be if it is to constitute so valued a reason for accepting a proposition, and what justice must be if it is to constitute so valued a reason for performing an act.

Perhaps the objector would now rejoin that, since so many different kinds of thing can function as reasons for other things, the proposed account of analytical philosophy would endow it with too large and indiscriminate a field of interest.

Admittedly the problem of determining relevant borderlines is compounded when the strategy of semantic descent is acknowledged to be co-ordinate with that of semantic ascent. But by no means every question that is directly or indirectly about reasons, justification, or rationality is a question in analytical philosophy. The particular reason why you went to London yesterday is of no interest to philosophers, except perhaps as an instance of a certain category of reason–e.g. beliefs or purposes. If it had been someone else, going somewhere else, for another purpose, the example might have done just as well. The philosophical question might be 'What makes a belief a reason for doing something?' but not 'Why did you go to London yesterday?' Similarly the reason for the prevalence of malaria in a hot and swampy country is not philosophically important, but the general nature of causal explanation (or of truth) is. Very many questions about reasons that arise quite normally in the everyday conduct of private and public life, or in the prosecution of scientific enquiry, are thus far too specific or limited in their scope to be suitable issues for philosophical examination.

Of course, the relevant frontier between excessive specificity and adequate generality can only be determined rather roughly and provisionally in a particular problem-area at a particular date, and generally shares a considerable stretch of no man's land with other disciplines. In contemporary cognitive science, for example, many theoretical interests are shared by philosophers with psychologists, linguists, computer scientists, or neurophysiologists. Indeed, it was only in the earlier period of modern analytical philosophy, when a method of resolving all genuinely philosophical problems was supposed to be available (§ 3), that–correspondingly–the frontier between philosophical and non-philosophical problems was held to be sharply defined and easily recognizable. As confidence in the existence of a single, all-powerful technique has waned, so too has belief in the existence of such a determinate frontier. But powerful intellectual pressures combine to ensure that a frontier of some kind always re-emerges, even if in relation to any other discipline it consists rather of a belt of shared territory–gradually shading off on either side–than of a line that starkly demarcates two mutually exclusive territories.

One often noted source of pressure here is the tendency for a segment of philosophical enquiry to hive off as a separate discipline when sufficient numbers of people share a distinct and limited field of problems, have no immediate desire to move beyond these problems, and also agree about most relevant methodological issues. An intellectual specialization of this kind used only to be recognizable by historical hindsight, because its emergence was not marked at the time by any organizational splintering of social groups. But in the modern world the existence of such a specialized consensus is very soon reflected in the existence of distinct academic institutions (journals, departments, research allocations, etc.). So, in the last three centuries, the level of generality or abstraction at which characteristically philosophical issues are seen to arise in a particular problem-area has been maintained by the gradual transformation of certain more specialized enquiries into the separate disciplines of cosmology, economics, linguistics, psychology, etc. And what has been left to philosophy are the ultimate, and therefore irredeemably controversial, issues that the special sciences, within the shelter of their consensual frameworks, have contrived to by-pass.

There is also, working in the same direction, an equally important, but perhaps not so often remarked, pressure from within philosophy to retain its synoptic potential. Many philosophers still feel that they ought, in principle, to be able to get sufficiently acquainted with every branch of analytical philosophy for them to be capable of discerning relevant analogies, or of hypothesizing general principles, that can be carried over from one branch to another as the subject progresses. Thus, for example, the idea of alternative possible worlds may be imported from the context of Leibnizian theodicy into the semantics of modal logic (Kripke) or into the analytical philosophy of art (Wolterstorff).[7] At the same time it would be generally agreed that a foundational principle should not be adopted in one branch of philosophy if it might lead to major difficulties elsewhere. Thus a philosophical theory of probability must cover not only the general judgements of probability that are made about games of chance, or in the natural or social sciences, but also the singular judgements that are made in determining particular matters of fact in courts of law. But synoptic views are possible only to the extent that concern with detail is pruned back. So the synoptic ideal tends to reinforce existence of some kind of frontier between topics of philosophical and non-philosophical interest within the study of reasons.

---

[7] S. Kripke, 'A Completeness Theorem in Modal Logic', *Journal of Symbolic Logic*, 24, 1959, pp. 1-14, and 'Semantical Considerations on Modal Logics', *Acta Philosophica Fennica*, 16, 1963, pp. 83-94; N. Wolterstorff, *Works and Worlds of Art*, Oxford: OUP, 1980, pp. 106-247.

What is claimed here, therefore, is that the unifying force in analytical philosophy is its engagement with the reasoned investigation of reasons at that level of generality (varying in accordance with the subject-matter) where no conclusions can be taken as universally granted. Not that this investigation, whether conservatively or reformatively oriented, has been a widely declared aim in the present century, or an acknowledged masterplan. But it nevertheless turns out to be the objective that has in effect been systematically fostered and promoted by analytical philosophers. The importance of this objective is the underlying, though unrecognized, presupposition of the movement. Indeed, it is this that also ties modern analytical philosophy into the classical mainstream. Whatever other themes exercised Plato, Aristotle, Aquinas, Hume, Kant, and even Hegel, they all at times sought reasoned solutions for problems about rationality. And it was primarily in virtue of this continuity that Moore, Schlick, Carnap, Wittgenstein, and Ryle could claim to be discussing many of the same issues as their classical predecessors. For, in all analytical philosophy, the main direction of interest is towards problems about the concepts and arguments involved in certain issues, rather than towards problems about the truth or falsity of certain factual conclusions. What has analytical interest is the question 'How, if at all, may we argue about the existence, or non-existence of God?' rather than the question 'Does God exist?', just as it is the Davidsonian question 'How may we reason about human action?' rather than some more Sartreian question like 'Why do we feel nausea at the contingency of objects, and anguish in the predicament of choice?'

Of course, it is only so far as philosophical movements are to be characterized by the nature of the problems they seek to resolve, that analytical philosophy may be regarded as a continuous strand in the development of Western philosophy from its beginnings in Socratic dialogue. Continuity of method, as distinct from continuity of problem, was explicitly repudiated by Carnap, Wittgenstein, Ryle, and many other modern analytical philosophers, when they introduced their logical or linguistic techniques as revolutionary innovations. But, as we have already suggested in §§ 2-3, the problems constantly overflow such techniques, and a characterization of analytical philosophy in terms of method or doctrine has to give way to one in terms of problems.

One particularly good example of this emerges from examination of the controversy between Popper and Carnap about the nature of the relationship between experimental data and scientific theory.[8] The question between them, as it might appear to an impartial third-party, was whether scientists researching an issue characteristically aim at the most improbable hypothesis that will survive rigorous experimental tests, or rather at the hypothesis that will authorize predictions with the highest available probability on the evidence of the experimental data. In this controversy the professed methodological disagreement between the two participants was, rather strikingly, ignored. Apparently neither side thought it relevant to the matter in hand that, according to Popper, the philosophy of science has nothing to do with the study of language, whereas according to Carnap it actually consists in the logical reconstruction of the language of science. If they had thought this difference relevant, they might have concluded that they must be arguing at cross-purposes. But they didn't draw this conclusion, and what made it possible for them thus to ignore their antithetical difference in professed methodology was that in practice (*pace* Carnap[9]) both sides were clearly concerned with the same underlying problem, namely how to characterize the reasoning that best relates theory-appraisal to experimental data.

Similarly many critics and commentators have discussed the private language issue that was raised by Wittgenstein in some of his later writings.[10] But these discussions rarely pay any attention to Wittgenstein's professed methodology. Indeed, it might be rather boring just to discuss whether or not what Wittgenstein wrote on the subject of private language does in fact have the therapeutic value at which he professed to be aiming. Fairly obviously it doesn't, because so many philosophers go on discussing the subject. So what these philosophers look to instead, when they treat Wittgenstein here as a participant in the analytical dialogue, is the content of his relevant remarks. They treat him as if he were arguing a specific answer to some such question as: how is it possible to reason about meanings?

Not that techniques of ordinary language analysis, or of logical reconstruction, have in any way exhausted their utility. Rather, the

---

[8] See the discussion in P. A. Schlipp (ed.), *The Philosophy of Rudolf Carnap*, La Salle, Ill: Open Court, 1963, pp. 213-26 and 995-8.

[9] Contrast how Carnap describes his view ibid. with what he actually wrote in *Logical Foundations of Probability*, Chicago: Chicago UP, 1950, pp. 1-2.

[10] e.g. the symposium 'Can there be a Private Language?' of A. J. Ayer and R. Rhees, in *Aristotelian Society Proceedings*, supp. vol. 28, 1954, pp. 63-94; P. F. Strawson, 'Critical Notice of L. Wittgenstein's *Philosophical Investigations*', *Mind*, 63, 1954, pp. 70-99; and S. A. Kripke, *Wittgenstein on Rules and Private Language*, Oxford: Blackwell, 1982.

role of language in conscious ratiocination and interpersonal communication guarantees the continuing value of semantic ascent as a philosophical strategy, even if there is no justification for the excessively far-reaching claims that used to be made on its behalf. We should at least get to know the various linguistic frameworks within which so much of our reasoning is evidently conducted, and we should even evaluate alternatives to them. We must certainly exploit their relative palpability, whenever we wish to discuss the nature of the reasonings for which we use them. In short, we should use the strategy of semantic ascent wherever it is appropriate. But we have to look through such linguistic techniques to the underlying problems–which are all problems about reasoning–if we are to determine the deeper purposes and presuppositions of analytical philosophy. Indeed in many problem-areas these linguistic techniques will not even be applicable and semantic descent will be unavoidable.

It also needs to be borne in mind that, just so far as the problems of analytical philosophy are problems about reasoning, analytical metaphilosophy must take a special interest in problems about philosophical reasoning. So analytical philosophy cannot avoid having a rather closer, more self-conscious concern with issues in philosophical methodology than have those schools of philosophy that are not especially occupied with problems about reasoning, like Marxism or existentialism.

Admittedly, the earlier generation of modern analytical philosophers tended to claim a more comprehensive continuity of topic with traditional philosophy. The method that such a philosopher championed was usually supposed by him to resolve *all* philosophical problems, not just problems about reasoning. He could not think of non-analytical philosophy as concerned, at least on some occasions, with issues in which he had no professional interest, because his methodology embraced a theory about all, or almost all, philosophy pursued by other methods than his own. He attributed the genesis of such philosophy (see §§ 2-4 above) to 'bewitchment of our intelligence by means of language', to 'category mistakes', to the use of the 'material' mode of speech where the 'formal' would have been more appropriate, or to some other such source of systematic error. So, if we now take modern analytical philosophy to be continuous with much of earlier philosophy only in respect of a certain highly important and readily specifiable range of problems, namely basic normative issues about reasoning, we certainly imply a more tolerant attitude towards some kinds of non-analytic philosophy. We imply that, though claims to have a panacea for all philosophical disquiets were certainly made at one time by some modern analytical philosophers, such claims are not essential to analytical philosophy as it is best understood. The task for analytical philosophy is to apply appropriate methods for the resolution of normative problems about reasoning–as in normative epistemology, for instance, or normative ethics. It is not to deal with every issue that a librarian has ever catalogued as philosophical. Even within this narrower and more determinate field there is plenty of room for controversy, it appears, and plenty of room too for introducing new issues or putting a new gloss on old ones (see § 14 below).

Rorty has claimed that the notion of philosophy as an autonomous discipline, distinct from and sitting in judgement upon both religion and science, is of mid-nineteenth-century origin and arose from the preoccupation of modern philosophers with the theory of knowledge.[11] And, if this claim is correct, analytical philosophy could certainly not be said to share its distinctive central theme–the study of rationality in science, religion, and elsewhere–with the classical mainstream. But Rorty's claim does not fit the historical facts. On the one hand, the notion of philosophy as an architectonic discipline is at least as old as Plato's account of what he called 'dialectic' in his *Republic*. On the other hand, some leading analytical philosophers–most notably Russell, Quine, and Popper–have tended to emphasize features of continuity between science and philosophy rather than to insist on the autonomy, independence, or higher-order status of philosophy.[12] Nor is it true, as Rorty has also claimed, that modern philosophers have been preoccupied with the theory of knowledge.[13] This description certainly does not fit Spinoza's *Ethics*, for example. And Hume devoted only one of the three books of his *Treatise* to the study of human understanding: the other two were concerned with emotion, action, and morality. Moreover, for Hobbes, Locke, and Rousseau it was certainly the role of reason that was crucial in human society, not that of knowledge. Even for Bacon the jurisprudence of

---

[11] R. Rorty, *Philosophy and the Mirror of Nature*, Oxford: Blackwell, 1980, pp. 131 ff.
[12] e.g. B. Russell, *History of Western Philosophy*, London: Allen and Unwin, 1946, p. 864; W. V. O. Quine, *Word and Object*, Cambridge, Mass.: MIT Press, 1960, p. 161; and K. R. Popper, *Objective Knowledge: An Evolutionary Approach*, Oxford: OUP, 1972, p. 34.
[13] Loc. cit.

common law was co-ordinate with the science of nature as a field for inductive reasoning.[14]

Moreover, once the unifying theme of analytical philosophy is recognized, the direction of its socio-political influence is apparent. This influence is mediated through higher education, through drama and literature, through the more responsible sections of the media, and through the prevailing climate of ideas. By its systematic exploration of reasons and reasoning, analytical philosophy helps to consolidate the intellectual infrastructure that is needed for systems of social organization within which disputes are reflected in argument and counter-argument, rather than in the use or threat of violence. By virtue of its preoccupation with rationality it promotes awareness that the intellectual merit of a person's opinion does not hinge on his membership of a particular party, priesthood, or hermetic tradition. And, with its interest in picking out ultimate issues for discussion, it tends to undermine any support for the view that certain accepted principles, prerogatives, or presumptions are intrinsically immune to rational criticism and reappraisal. No tenets are sacrosanct for it. Even the widespread positivism of the 1920s and 1930s has to be seen (as in § 3 above) as a passing fashion among analytical philosophers rather than as an intrinsic commitment. Their characteristic common task is best described as being just to clarify, evaluate, improve, or redesign the various rational frameworks within which people can determine the optimal solutions of their personal, social, cultural, technical, or scientific problems.

Admittedly, even in the study of science, there is room for careful enquiry into the non-rational aspects of human judgement. But it does not follow from this, as Polanyi apparently thought it did,[15] that we can afford to dispense with analysis of the rational aspects. Again, we may sometimes achieve benefits by behaving violently, irrationally, or arbitrarily for the moment. But that fact may then be seen as justifying our current behaviour. We may also do well to study the influence of prejudice, passion, or instinct upon individual judgements and collective decisions, and to make appropriate allowances for this influence. But that is itself a reason for carrying out a certain type of study, and for acting on its findings. In sum, the fact that people often

[14] P. H. Kocher, 'Francis Bacon on the Science of Jurisprudence', *Journal of the History of Ideas*, 18, 1957, pp. 3-26.
[15] M. Polanyi, *Personal Knowledge: Towards a Post-Critical Philosophy*, London: Routledge and Kegan Paul, 1958.

act irrationally, and sometimes do so profitably, does not in any way limit the scope, or count against the value, of analytical philosophy. It still deserves respect as a cultural movement that makes for tolerance, universal suffrage, ethical pluralism, non-violent resolution of disputes, and freedom of intellectual enterprise, and is in turn promoted by them. Doctrinaire tyrannies certainly have good reason to ban it.

This is not to say that political or cultural values should always animate the discussions, or guide the conclusions, of analytical philosophers. Philosophical reasoning takes a wide variety of forms which will be discussed in §§ 7-12 below. Indeed philosophy would be greatly impoverished if it were confined, as Kekes has recently proposed that it should be, to justifying 'world views' or to giving 'meaning and purpose' to life.[16] With such a restriction in operation many intellectually important issues would tend to get ignored. Who would bother themselves about logical paradoxes, about rival interpretations of the probability calculus, about the nature of mathematical proof, or about how proper names function? Hence, just as it can be harmful to subordinate scientific research to the needs of technology, because, as Bacon put the point, 'experiments of light' come before 'experiments of fruit',[17] so too it can be counter-productive to design the programme of philosophical enquiry with an eye to the social benefits that this enquiry may achieve.

However, an analytical philosopher should certainly be aware of the overall cultural effect to which his own work can hardly help making some slight contribution, even if his conscious aim is not at all to promote that effect but merely to resolve some intellectual puzzles. He will not then run the risk of being even momentarily impressed by the claims of other philosophies to superior social relevance. Nor should he underestimate the importance of the current input from analytical philosophy into the discussion of problems about human reasoning with psychologists, with linguists, with computer scientists, with economists, with decision-theorists, with lawyers, with clinicians, with theologians or with other specialists. Inter-disciplinary journals, like *The Behavioural and Brain Sciences* or *Philosophy and Public Affairs*, afford ample evidence of this fruitful co-operation. Kekes has claimed,[18] echoing an earlier remark of Gellner's about modern

---

[16] J. Kekes, *The Nature of Philosophy*, Oxford: Blackwell, 1980, p. xi.
[17] F. Bacon, *Novum Organum*, 1620, bk. 1, para. 70.
[18] Op. cit., p. 4.

American philosophy,[19] that 'the disappearance of philosophers would make no difference to the intellectual life of our society'. But those who make such claims can hardly have reflected on the matter with sufficient intellectual seriousness or sense of social responsibility. Both political and academic facts belie them. If the normative study of reasoning did not already exist, it would need to be invented.

§ 7 DIFFERENCES BETWEEN CATEGORICAL AND
HYPOTHETICAL, AND BETWEEN DEDUCTIVE AND
INDUCTIVE, MODES OF PHILOSOPHICAL REASONING

Summary. In analytical philosophy both categorical and hypothetical modes of reasoning are possible, according as the argument is claimed to rest on acknowledged truisms or on hypothetical assumptions. Moreover either mode of reasoning may take either a deductive or an inductive form. But, in order to make this evident, we need to elucidate how induction can operate in relation to issues that are not matters of observable fact or experimental enquiry.

Statements about the nature of philosophy run a well-known risk of refuting themselves. If, for example, the proposition 'There are no metaphysical truths' is true, it looks like being itself a metaphysical truth and therefore evidence of its own falsity. Analogously, even though the statement that analytical philosophy is concerned with the structure of rationality seems otherwise well-supported, it would nevertheless run the risk of self-refutation if intended as being itself a thesis within analytical philosophy, since it states the problem that analytical philosophy sets out to tackle but says nothing about the kinds of reasoning that may be employed in the solution of that problem. If the philosophy of science is focused on problems about scientific reasoning, and ethics on problems about the justification of actions, then an appropriately focused metaphilosophical enquiry should have an analogous direction of interest. It should lead into the treatment of problems about philosophical reasoning. It should raise the question: how is the reasoned study of rationality possible?

We need first to note here that the reasoned study of rationality has two possible modes of procedure in relation to a given problem.

---

[19] E. Gellner, *The Devil in Contemporary Philosophy*, London: Routledge and Kegan Paul, 1974, pp. 37-8.

One mode aims at proof. It seeks to justify some categorical conclusion with a certainty that is as strong as acceptable premisses allow. For example, it may seek a kind of reflective equilibrium, as in Rawls' theory of justice,[20] where considered principles, adequately rich in content, are to be rendered coherent with one another by whatever qualifications, rejections or supplementations are found to be necessary and justifiable. Another example of adopting such a categorical procedure is provided by those analytical philosophers who have claimed to find a single coherent conceptual structure in some particular area of natural language, like Ryle's logical geography of the concepts that we use in thinking about mental activity.[21]

Admittedly, analytical philosophers have sometimes denied the possibility of establishing categorical conclusions on certain issues that they are, nevertheless, willing to discuss. For example, Ayer once said that it is not within the province of philosophy to justify our common-sense beliefs.[22] But this depends on what is to count as a justification. We should certainly weaken the philosophical case for thinking any of our supposedly common-sense principles incorrect if we could show that they are all mutually consistent; and we provide reasons for thinking some of them correct wherever we are able to show that some of them corroborate one another.

Again, Waismann made an even stronger claim–that philosophical arguments are insufficiently rigorous to prove anything. In Waismann's view the function of a philosophical argument is just to display an insight or communicate a new intellectual vision.[23] But this thesis is incoherent. Philosophical reasoning does not normally have the rigour or certainty of mathematical proof. But neither does experimental, or forensic, proof. If philosophical reasoning could not be evaluated by its own standards (which will shortly be discussed) it would be of no help even for Waismann's purposes. Good philosophical reasoning has to be distinguished from bad, even if only because weak, circular, or otherwise invalid arguments are unlikely to display interesting insights or communicate new intellectual visions. Nor can a philosopher dispense with proofs and rely solely on examples, as Waismann thought possible,[24] without generating unnecessary opportunities for commentators to dispute about the point

[20] J. Rawls, *A Theory of Justice*, Oxford: OUP, 1971, pp. 20-1.
[21] G. Ryle, *The Concept of Mind*, London: Hutchinson, 1949, p. 8.
[22] A. J. Ayer, *Language, Truth and Logic*, London: Gollancz, 2nd edn., 1946, p. 25.
[23] F. Waismann, 'How I see Philosophy', in H. D. Lewis (ed.), *Contemporary British Philosophy*, London: Allen and Unwin, 1956, p. 471.   [24] Ibid., p. 482.

of this or that example. It's a rare example that cannot illustrate more than one principle.

The other mode of procedure in analytical philosophy seeks to display implications rather than state proofs. It aims to start from hypothetical assumptions and to point out that, *if* a certain view is held, *then* such-and-such conclusions follow or become plausible. Collingwood[25] denied that philosophers ever argued like this. But it was certainly the procedure that Carnap canonized for philosophical logic with his principle of tolerance (see § 3 above), and it is often how the strengths and weaknesses of different philosophical positions—realism versus anti-realism, say, or nominalism versus essentialism—are compared. Its use tends also to stress the importance that analytical philosophers characteristically attach to philosophical arguments as distinct from philosophical conclusions. If they always needed to come to *conclusions*, the hypothetical mode of procedure would be unacceptable. And this mode of procedure is especially well adapted to the needs of philosophical dialogue, where the implications of a thesis may need to be teased out in order to make those who might adopt it aware of what commitments they would thus be accepting. Moreover, the possibility of this hypothetical mode of procedure explains why it is not a serious criticism of semantic ascent in analytical philosophy that people can make words mean what they want them to mean, and so a particular linguistic form is never tied irrevocably to a particular implication. For we can always argue hypothetically that, *if* a word has a certain meaning, *then* it must have such-and-such an implication.

The categorical mode of procedure is obviously congenial to philosophers who like positive conclusions. The hypothetical mode tends to attract those who prefer to be more guarded and non-committal, especially when there has long been more than one kind of categorical conclusion that people are known to support in a particular problem-area. Even then, the hypothetical arguer will tend to avoid outlandish assumptions, as if there were no point at all in putting forward his argument unless at least some people might be inclined to accept its assumptions. But both modes of procedure are often used by the same author within a single discussion, with some issues being treated categorically and others hypothetically. Or, maybe, he will first put forward a thesis categorically, but revert to the hypothetical mode of

[25] R. G. Collingwood, *An Essay on Philosophical Method*, Oxford: OUP, 1983, pp. 121-36.

procedure if his premisses are challenged. Or he will put forward an argument hypothetically and some of his readers will find the argument's assumptions sufficiently acceptable to be ready to adopt its conclusions categorically.

It is also perhaps worth noting that the distinction drawn here between categorical and hypothetical modes of procedure in philosophical reasoning is a methodological one, and not the same as that drawn recently by Unger between 'categorical' and 'conditional' problems.[26] Thus, for Unger, the question whether or not determinism is correct poses a 'categorical' problem, while the question whether or not determinism is compatible with free-will poses a 'conditional' one. But, according to the distinction drawn here, both problems can be treated either in a categorical or in a hypothetical manner. We can argue whether determinism is demonstrable from incontrovertible premisses, or just whether it is valid in the context of certain assumptions about the unity of science, say, or about physical theory, or about rational theology. Equally we can argue both whether compatibilism is demonstrable from incontrovertible premisses, or whether it is valid in the context of certain assumptions about, say, computationalist claims in cognitive psychology.

Of course, any piece of hypothetical reasoning may be said to imply a categorically arguable assertion—namely the assertion that the conclusion of the reasoning follows from its stated assumptions. But this fact does not destroy the difference between a philosopher's discussing a given problem as if he accepts certain premisses from which a resolution of the problem can be shown to follow, and his discussing it as if a resolution can be derived only with the aid of some premisses to which he does not wish to pledge himself.

An at least equally important but rather less obvious difference is that between deductive and inductive patterns of philosophical argument. This distinction cuts across that between categorical and hypothetical modes of procedure and is more deeply rooted. We cannot so readily convert a deductive into an inductive argument, or vice-versa, and the difference between the two will turn out to have fairly far-reaching implications in the resolution of philosophical problems.

A great deal of reasoning in modern analytical philosophy, as also in classical philosophy, has undoubtedly been deductive in character, whether proceeding from categorically asserted or presupposed

[26] P. Unger, *Philosophical Relativity*, Minneapolis: Minnesota UP, 1984, pp. 63-4.

premisses, or from hypothetically assumed ones. Descartes's proof of an external world was certainly of this form, and Spinoza's *Ethics* was explicitly cast in a deductive mould. Any transcendental argument–any argument from the very possibility of sensory experience, say, or of interpersonal communication–must also have a deductive form when all its premisses are made explicit. So too must be any argument of the kind that Ryle held in high esteem,[27] whereby a proposition is shown to be untenable because of the intolerably paradoxical conclusion–a self-contradiction, perhaps, or an absurdity, or an infinite regress–that flows from it. So too must be any argument that admits of formalization within a system of postulates and proof-rules, as when Carnap[28] derived the supposed properties of confirmation-functions in this way. Nor, of course, need the rules of inference operative in philosophical deductions be purely logical ones, such as *modus ponendo ponens*, *modus tollendo tollens*, etc. In fact, any accepted generalization may function as a rule of inference in appropriate contexts, as already remarked in § 5. Such an inference can always be transformed into some logically canonical pattern by treating the operative generalization as a tacit, presupposed premiss.

Nevertheless, it is not correct to say, as Passmore has said, that 'philosophical reasoning, if it is to be valid at all, must be deductive in its formal structure'.[29] A great deal of reasoning in modern analytical philosophy is inductive, not deductive.

I do not mean that it is based on experiment or observation. Both terms–'deductive' and 'inductive'–are used here to describe a type of inferability, without reference to the subject-matter of inference. In deductive reasoning our conclusion must be true if the premisses are true. Through inductive reasoning–of the kind that is relevant here–we may acquire some level of justified confidence in a generalization if we accept reasons for supposing that the generalization holds good in certain varieties of instance. Now deduction undoubtedly operates on propositions about numbers, legal obligations, social virtues, moral worth, or aesthetic merit as well as on propositions about observable facts. Of course, it was once assumed that admitting the existence of evaluative *propositions* was tantamount to admitting the existence of non-natural attributes or relations. And empiricist prejudice against non-natural attributes or relations has a strong foundation in the ideal

[27] Op. cit., p. 8.
[28] *Logical Foundations of Probability*, pp. 315-26.
[29] J. Passmore, *Philosophical Reasoning*, London: Duckworth, 1961, p. 6.

of ontological parsimony. But even empiricists do not have to hold, because of this prejudice, that the inferential liaisons of evaluative utterances in the indicative mood cannot be reconstructed in classical logic. Your (or my) moral code can assign truth-values to such utterances without commitment to any ontological extravagance, so that all the ordinary laws of truth-functional logic may be seen to go through for evaluative propositions just as well as for factual ones; and all the laws of quantification theory will hold good for evaluative predicates, like 'good' and 'bad', as well as for descriptive ones like 'red' and 'square'. Accordingly, just as propositional and predicate logic are thus indifferent to the subject-matter of the deductive inferences that they enable us to analyse, so too the general structure of inductive reasoning may be conceived as being applicable to any kind of subject-matter within which the existence of non-accidental uniformities, or approximate uniformities, is presupposed.

Unfortunately some of the best-known writers on induction have failed to see this. J. S. Mill,[30] for example, set up his inductive logic as a system of rules for drawing conclusions from experiments. Induction, in his view, is occupied solely with the establishment of correlations or cause-and-effect relationships between events: the only relevant uniformities are laws of nature. Similarly Carnap, Hintikka, and their followers propose measures for inductive confirmation that treat it solely as a relation of probabilification between two descriptive propositions.[31] One proposition E confirms another H in accordance with the ratio of the range of possible worlds in which $H\&E$ is true to the range of possible worlds in which E is true.

But Francis Bacon, who pioneered the study of inductive reasoning in modern philosophy, was quite explicit in his insistence[32] that this pattern of reasoning, just like syllogistic reasoning, was applicable in ethics and jurisprudence as well as in natural science. Indeed his planned restatement of English law involved the inductive establishment of legal rules or 'maxims' on the basis of common law judgements in individual cases, just as much as his plans for the advancement of science involved the inductive establishment of causal laws on the basis of observed individual events. In the one case,

---

[30] J. S. Mill, *A System of Logic Ratiocinative and Inductive*, London: Longman/Green, 1896, bk. 3.

[31] *Logical Foundations of Probability*, pp. 279-92; J. Hintikka, 'A Two-Dimensional Continuum of Inductive Methods', in J. Hintikka and P. Suppes (eds.), *Aspects of Inductive Logic*, Amsterdam: North-Holland, 1966, pp. 113-32.

[32] Op. cit., bk. 1, aphorism 127. Cf. Kocher, op. cit.

natural justice required that in a legal system like cases should be treated alike; in the other, nature itself required that in a scientific theory like causes should be attributed like effects. In the one case, the jurist got nearer and nearer to God's moral law as he mounted the pyramid of more and more comprehensive legal maxims; in the other, the scientist got nearer and nearer to God's laws of nature. In both cases the same elimination of alternative hypotheses by falsifying instances; the same need for what we should now call 'controls'; the same increase of certainty with evidentially tenable increase of generality; the same requirement that generalizations should not only cover known instances but also lead to new knowledge, were operative. And it is quite possible to develop this seminal idea in a more sophisticated form. For example, Bacon never discussed the constraints that one statement of inductive support may impose on another. Yet we need to know how the support for a conjunction is affected by the support for its conjuncts; how the support for H is affected by the support for its negation; how the support for H affects the support for its logical consequences; and so on. When the principles governing these constraints are articulated with an appropriate degree of rigour, it turns out that they too apply to inductions about what ought to be done just as well as to inductions about what actually happens,[33] so long as we consider that form of induction which pays attention to relevant variations in kinds of instances rather than just to multiplicity of instances.

In general, the position is that a subject-matter is implied to admit of such inductive reasoning if non-accidental uniformities, or approximate uniformities, are thought capable of existing in it. And this condition holds good in at least seven different areas. It holds in every field of scientific investigation in which causal laws are supposed to operate; in every jurisdiction in which correct judicial decisions are locked into a system of conformity with precedent or statute; in every grammar-bound language; in mathematics; in every ethics that respects the golden rule; in every human skill (industrial, administrative, diagnostic, therapeutic, chess-playing, etc.) that is susceptible, via an exercise in expert systems analysis, to simulation by computer program; and in every domain of semantical, epistemological, or metaphysical enquiry in which underlying principles of correct reasoning are at issue. Moreover, every statement of such a uniformity, whether

[33] L. Jonathan Cohen, *The Implications of Induction*, London: Methuen, 1970, pp. 155-82.

factual or normative, has some explanatory value in relation to its subject-matter, just because of the uniformity's non-accidental character. But it would be wrong to suppose, as is sometimes suggested, that induction can be usefully defined as inference to the best explanation. The fact is that inductive support is a matter of degree, not of absolute achievement. Moreover, even the currently best-supported hypothesis may provide an explanation that is defective in other respects. Support is only one consideration, though a very important one, with regard to the acceptance of an explanation. Another is conceptual economy, for example, or resemblence to some already accepted paradigm.

Perhaps someone will object that reasoning from common law precedents cannot be inductive because a single precedent may sometimes be cited as giving strong support to a general rule. But even in natural science, on suitable occasions, a single experiment may be cited as giving strong support to a general hypothesis. The commonplace rule against basing induction on a single case is a useful warning to the rash, but it could be dangerously obstructive to the expert. That was why Mill posed the question 'Why is a single instance, in some cases, sufficient for a complete induction, while in others myriads of concurring instances, without a single exception known or presumed, go such a very little way towards establishing an universal proposition?'[34] A fuller answer to this insightful question is available elsewhere.[35] Here it will be sufficient to note that the variety of instances required to give a particular level of support to a generalization is bound to vary inversely with the extent to which the scope of the generalization has been explicitly, or implicitly, restricted by relevant qualifications. If the generalization is in any case not intended to apply to circumstances C, then there is no need or even room for testing whether the presence or absence of C will falsify it. Accordingly, the wider the restrictions that we impose on its application, the fewer the tests that are needed, so far as we know (or may assume that we know) what kinds of circumstances are relevant–i.e. are potential falsifiers– for generalizations of that kind. And where we do not know this (and may not assume that we know it) such restrictions on the application of a generalization can be given in the form of an indeterminate prefix 'Normally . . .' or 'Other things being equal . . .', which then acquires a

---

[34] Op. cit., 1896 edn., bk. 3, ch. III, § 3, p. 206.
[35] Cohen, *Implications of Induction*, pp. 142-53.

strength of significance[36] in proportion to the paucity of the evidence. In particular, that is commonly how one or two appeals to the reader's moral conscience, in appropriately selected examples, may suffice to support some generalization about what it is right or wrong to do.

Note too that, if the inductive standing of a generalization can be maintained or even enhanced (in the face of otherwise adverse evidence) by restrictions of scope, or by the introduction of relevant qualifications, we can treat these, if we wish to, as alterations to the meaning of the generalization rather than to its verbal formulation. Indeed, we may often learn more by investigating in what sense a statement is true than by assuming some fixed sense for it and then investigating whether it is true. Certainly, much legal reasoning is often said to be concerned to establish the correct meanings of legal rules rather than to establish their truth or validity, which is taken for granted.[37] The courts need to determine what kinds of relationship are, or should be, covered by terms like 'ownership', 'possession', etc., in the rules of law in which they occur. Similarly, many analytical philosophers have said that they are not out to challenge any of the propositions that common sense upholds, but only to analyse the meanings of certain key terms in them (such as 'cause', 'physical object', etc.).

It is also in this context that we can understand what is going on when philosophers argue by analogy. When Plato argued that a ruler's function *qua* ruler is to aim at the benefit of his subjects, just as a shepherd's function *qua* shepherd is to aim at the benefit of his flock,[38] he was implicitly using the example of a shepherd in order to provide inductive support for a generalization from which he could derive a conclusion about a ruler. If the relevant circumstances of the two types of case are sufficiently alike, then a single example can provide substantial support for an appropriate generalization, just as a single precedent may provide substantial support for the implicit rule of common law under which judgement is awarded in a novel case of the same general kind. Correspondingly, both in philosophy and in law, an argument by analogy may be weakened or refuted by the demonstration of relevant differences between the two types of case: the

---

[36] L. Jonathan Cohen, *The Probable and the Provable*, Oxford: OUP, 1977, pp. 134-85.

[37] e.g. O. C. Jensen, *The Nature of Legal Argument*, Oxford: Blackwell, 1957, p. 28; and E. H. Levi, 'An Introduction to Legal Reasoning', *University of Chicago Law Review*, 15, 1948, p. 502. Cf. Cohen, *The Implications of Induction*, pp. 165-6.

[38] *Republic*, 345 D.

generalization that is inductively supported is not then the same as that from which the desired conclusion is derivable. For example, to shake the present argument you would need to demonstrate a *relevant* disanalogy between philosophy and common law jurisprudence.

In experimental reasoning the data for inductive inference are the observed experimental results, whether these observations occur before, or after, anyone thinks up a hypothesis that they check. Typically a putative effect is found to co-occur with its putative cause in such-and-such a relevant variety of particular instances, and not to occur in a matching variety of cases when the putative cause is absent. The strength of the inductive conclusion is then to be assessed in terms of the thoroughness of the test: the greater the relevant variety of circumstances manipulated, the more thorough the elimination of alternative hypotheses. What corresponds to this where inductive reasoning is not concerned with problems about causes and matters of fact? In jurisprudence reported judicial decisions constitute the corresponding data, though it is not always easy to extract the precise principle in accordance with which the decision should be taken to have been made. Just as the operation of hidden variables may make it difficult to interpret an experimental result correctly, so too the presence of certain relevant factors in a legal case may not be noticed by some of those who analyse it. But at least the court's award of judgement to the plaintiff, or to the defendant, has an institutionally recognized validity (unless successfully appealed). That the particular plaintiff, or defendant, has such-and-such a legal right in virtue of certain specifiable events or relationships is now a legal datum to which various acts of acknowledgement may give public effect. But what comparable data are available to the philosopher as brute facts to support inductive generalizations? The deductivist may urge that it is just because there are no such data, that philosophy, as distinct from natural science or jurisprudence, is a wholly deductive enquiry. So we shall obviously need to consider quite carefully what kinds of premisses are available to analytical philosophers for their inductive arguments–and, indeed, also what kinds of premisses are available to them for their deductive arguments–if we are to elucidate how such arguments can on occasion be categorical rather than just hypothetical.

Of course, it is always possible to treat an inductive argument as a piece of deductive reasoning by imputing tacit additional premisses about the extent to which data of such-and-such a kind support hypotheses of the kind at issue. But this banal possibility does not affect the point of the distinction that I am drawing. Metaphilosophers who exploit it must still distinguish between those patterns of deductive reasoning that rely on such premisses and those that do not, and the substance of everything that is said in §§ 7-14 about philosophical induction will still need to be said, albeit in different and less perspicuous terms.

§ 8 THE ROLE OF INTUITIONS

Summary. In order to understand how categorical philosophical reasoning operates, one has to clarify the nature of the data available to it. These data are given by intuitions about what should be inferred, judged or meant in such-and-such a context. After the Second World War appeals to intuition became common in analytical philosophy, though not in the sense in which Schlick derided them. But we need to differentiate between such appeals, as Sidgwick did, according as they are concerned with particular cases, general propositions, or fundamental principles.

In order to appreciate the ways in which deduction and induction actually operate in categorical philosophical reasoning, it is necessary to examine closely what is going on when contemporary analytical philosophers appeal to what they sometimes–but not always–call 'intuition'. This term is used by many of them, and will be used here by me, in a sense that is different from the one traditional in philosophy. And clarification of the usage is essential for present purposes. We have to reckon with the fact that philosophical analyses are very often based on premisses that derive from tacit or acknowledged intuitions, in this sense, about what counts as a reason for what. For example, it may be held intuitively evident that the inclusion of statements in such-and-such a relationship to one another or to the world at large counts as a reason for calling some given string of sentences an 'explanation', and this intuition may then function as a premiss that justifies, or helps to justify, some proposed analysis of explanation.

Those readers who find themselves unwilling to accept something like the following account of intuition and its function in analytical philosophy need to ask themselves what alternative source of philo- sophical premisses they would propose. Or would they wish to confine analytical philosophy to the hypothetical mode of procedure?

Bergson, Husserl,[39] and other metaphysically oriented contemporaries of the Vienna Circle used the term 'intuition' differently. They used it in its traditional sense to denote some rather superior mode of acquiring knowledge, like Plato's 'eye of the soul'[40] or Spinoza's 'intuitive science'.[41] Though they thought of this special faculty in a variety of different ways, they all supposed it to be the characteristic method of self-enlightenment that philosophers could school themselves to practise. Not surprisingly, therefore, the members of the Vienna Circle tended originally to refrain from using the term 'intuition' or its derivatives to name any source of data that they were prepared to respect. For example, Schlick[42] argued that knowledge basically involves a relation or comparison between two constituent factors, as when we discover a new property of some familiar substance or identify the species of a particular bird by its colour and shape, whereas intuition, as in Husserl's intuitions of essences, is just a mode of experiencing within which no relation or comparison need be present. 'So long as an object is not compared, or in some way incorporated into a conceptual system, it is not known. By intuition a thing is only given to us, not apprehended.'[43] So Schlick called the phrase 'intuitive knowledge' a contradiction in terms, and he insisted that appeals to intuition had no legitimate role in philosophy.

Later Ross[44] used the term 'intuition' in a way that, at least at first sight, was not open to Schlick's strictures. In Ross's usage a genuine intuition is still incapable of error: if some person's intuition is that p, it follows necessarily that p is true–self-evidently true. But Ross thought of the intuitively knowable rightness of fulfilling a promise as indeed a feature of the fundamental nature of the universe. In his view a proposition asserting such an action to be right was ascribing a non-physical attribute to it. Ethical propositions of this kind are thus supposed to be vehicles of synthetic a priori knowledge that is grasped by the intuitions of mature thinkers. Nevertheless, this new intuitionism,

---

[39] H. Bergson, *Introduction à la métaphysique*, Paris: A. Bourgeois, Cahiers de la quinzaine, 1903, *passim*; E. Husserl, 'Philosophie als strenge Wissenschaft', *Logos*, 1, 1911, pp. 289-341.

[40] *Republic*, 533 D, cf. 514-22.

[41] *Ethics*, pt. 2, prop. 40, n. 2.

[42] M. Schlick, 'Gibt es intuitive Erkenntnis?' *Vierteljahrschrift für wissenschaftliche Philosophie und Soziologie*, 1913, pp. 472-88, (trans. P. Heath) in Schlick, *Philosophical Papers* (ed. H. L. Mulder *et. al.*, vol. 1, Dordrecht: Reidel, 1979, pp. 141-52.

[43] Ibid., p. 146.

[44] W. D. Ross, *The Right and the Good*, Oxford: OUP, 1930.

though at first sight not open to Schlick's objection, was no more popular with analytical philosophers than the older one was. Strawson, for example, argued that terms like 'right' and 'good' do not function in the way that Ross or Prichard supposed: they do not, after all, ascribe relations or attributes, so there is no subject-matter—no knowledge—for ethical intuition to grasp.[45]

But the term 'intuition' does not always connote either the apprehension of essences or a mode of awareness that operates on a characteristic subject-matter and relates a knower to objects, as seeing or touching does. Instead, among analytical philosophers, the term can connote the having of a certain attitude to specified propositions. In this sense 'His intuition is that p' does not imply the truth of p, and even the assertion of 'My intuition is that p' does not commit the speaker to having reflectively accepted that p. An intuition that p is now just an immediate, unreflective, and untutored inclination, without argument or inference, to judge that p (and that anyone who faces the same issue ought also to judge that p), where the judgement that p is of a kind that is in principle not checkable by sensory perception or by accepted methods of calculation.

Nothing positive is implied thereby about the specific nature of p's content, where p is the intuited proposition. Certainly p need not be concerned with non-natural facts or essences. But also, though the judgement that p is obviously classifiable as a priori (because not checkable by sensory perception), it need not be analytic because it need not be concerned at all with a problem about meaning: it could be concerned with a problem about what ought, or ought not, to be done; about what may, or may not, be inferred; about the nature of knowledge; and so on. Nor does the term 'intuition', in this sense, connote a form of introspection, since intuitions of the relevant kind may be implicit in spoken judgements without any need, as there sometimes is, for the speaker to search the data of his consciousness. Nor, as I said, need p even be true, though a person's utterance, in this sense, of 'My intuition is that p' does imply that at the moment *he* is inclined to believe it true that p. So in analytical philosophy the term 'intuition' does not now describe any form of cognitive act, whether superior or inferior to sensory perception. Such intuitions are not a form of knowledge of any kind, since 'He knows that p' always implies the truth of p whereas 'His intuition is that p' does not. Nevertheless, an intuition that p, in this sense, is not cited as a mere hunch that is

[45] P. F. Strawson, 'Ethical Intuitionism', *Philosophy*, 24, 1949, pp. 23-33.

subsequently to be checked by sensory perception, or by accepted methods of calculation, and discarded if it fails to meet this test. Rather, it is an inclination of mind that is taken to originate from the existence of a system of tacitly acknowledged rules for making judgements about relevant topics. That is how intuition can come to suggest what is a reason for what. And that is its title to be cited as a source of prima-facie data that any relevant philosophical reasoning should take into account. Because each intuition may be presumed to originate from such a system of rules, it is prima-facie evidence as to their content.

An intuition of this kind should be immediate and unreflective, in the sense that it should not be the outcome of considered thought. If intuition is to provide the ultimate premises of philosophical argument, those premises should not themselves be the conclusions of further reasoning. If they were such conclusions, then the real premises of philosophical argument would remain unstated. A critic may be tempted here first to echo Rawls's claim that ideally a moral philosopher begins by adjusting his considered judgements about relevant issues into reflective equilibrium,[46] and then to object, therefore, that an analytical philosopher's starting-points are considered judgements, not immediate and unreasoned ones. But this analysis of philosophical reasoning does not push to the heart of the matter. When we scrutinize a considered judgement as a candidate for entry into reflective equilibrium, we have to reconstruct the considering that it may be presumed to have undergone. Only thus can we determine the size of its debt to relevant rather than irrelevant considerations, and thence ascertain the extent of the intellectual sacrifice that would be made if the judgement had to be adjusted somehow, with its premises modified or its line of reasoning redirected, in order to achieve coherence with other such judgements. So, though these considered judgements (alias standing pre-theoretical prejudices) often afford a philosopher a fruitful starting-point for his ponderings, and may even be all that in practice his arguments need to rest on, they are not the ultimate premises that may in principle need to be evoked to justify his conclusions. Challenge a considered judgement and you will eventually come up against one or more immediate and unreflective intuitions.

The analytical concept of intuition has to be clarified in another respect also. To call a person's inclination to judge that p 'untutored'

---

[46] Op. cit., p. 20.

is to exclude certain kinds of causal origin for the inclination. It must not arise in the person's mind because it is believed to have been deliberately inculcated by another person or consciously learned from one. Nor may it arise in his mind because *p* is believed to be entailed by some other propositions that have been so taught or learned, or because he is consciously applying to the situation under consideration some general proposition that has been so taught or learned. Perhaps it seems odd that the ultimate premises for a philosopher's categorical reasoning should thus be supposed ineligible to profit consciously from his education (though of course they may well do so unconsciously). But the point is that analytical philosophy is concerned with what *is* a reason for what, not with what is taken by scientists, lawyers, or others to be a reason for what. It has normative implications that the history or sociology of ideas does not have. Hence, even when a philosopher's premiss accords with the official tenets of some non-philosophical doctrine, it must be assumed to have an independent standing and authority. Only thus can it provide, without circularity, a deductive or inductive basis for passing judgement on that doctrine. Only thus can analytical philosophy carry out a radical critique in which nothing is taken for granted. But philosophers need not concern themselves to determine how far the actual origins of such untutored inclinations are cultural and how far they are genetic. In the twentieth century that issue is one to be studied by the empirical methods of anthropology and developmental psychology.

This sense of the term 'intuition', or a sense close to it, began to prevail in the later 1940s. It then became fairly common, at least in North America, for intuitions to be explicitly invoked by philosophers–sometimes even by ex-members of the Vienna Circle–who were deeply committed to empiricist principles. No doubt the shift of meaning was made easier by the fact that no popular metaphysical writer was any longer appealing to intuition as a special cognitive faculty: empiricists could simply move in and take over the term for their own purposes. Thus, in 1948, Hempel and Oppenheim claimed to recognize a point in their analysis of explanation where 'the customary intuitive idea of explanation becomes too vague to provide further guide for rational reconstruction'.[47] But they were quite content to be guided by this intuitive idea up to that point. They were quite content to take the legitimacy of a certain pattern of explanation

[47] C. G. Hempel and P. Oppenheim, 'Studies in the Logic of Explanation', *Philosophy of Science*, 15, 1948, p. 161.

as being vouched for by the fact that it 'surely is intuitively unobjectionable'.[48] Similarly, Carnap wrote in 1963 that 'the reasons to be given for accepting any axiom of inductive logic ... are based upon our intuitive judgements concerning inductive validity, i.e. concerning inductive rationality of practical decisions (e.g. about bets).'[49] More specifically, one of Carnap's proposed conditions of adequacy for a confirmation-function c was that 'c should be as simple as possible without violating any intuitive requirements'. Carnap required that 'if c is simpler than c', but there is no case in which the values of c or the relations between these values appear intuitively less acceptable than those of c', then c is preferable to c'.'[50] And, in 1960, Quine gave his own explicit account of this new usage. He remarked that 'twice I have been startled to find my use of "intuitive" misconstrued as alluding to some special and mysterious avenue of knowledge'. Instead, he pointed out, 'by an intuitive account I mean one in which terms are used in habitual ways, without reflecting on how they might be defined or what presuppositions they might conceal.'[51]

Further examples of such explicit appeals to intuition as a basis for philosophical reasoning may be cited from the writings of Scheffler, Kemeny, Kyburg, Levi, Hintikka,[52] and many others. In regard to the meaningfulness of a notion Kripke has stated that he does not know what could be more conclusive than intuitive evidence, and he has also appealed to intuition to support, for example, the existence of a difference (with far-reaching implications) between what the phrase 'one meter' designates and what the phrase 'the length of S at t_o' designates, where S is actually one metre long at t_o.[53] Again, Putnam's science-fiction story about Twin Earth was designed to evoke agreement with the proposition that, in what he called 'the intuitive pre-

[48] Ibid.

[49] 'Replies and Expositions', p. 978.

[50] Ibid., pp. 977-8.

[51] *Word and Object*, p. 36.

[52] I. Scheffler, 'Prospects of a Modest Empiricism', *Reviews of Metaphysics*, 10, 1957, p. 625; J. G. Kemeny, 'Carnap's Theory of Probability and Induction', in Schilpp, op. cit., p. 713; H. E. Kyburg, 'Probability, Rationality and a Rule of Detachment', in Y. Bar-Hillel (ed.), *Logic, Methodology and Philosophy of Science*, Amsterdam: North-Holland, 1965, p. 303 and id., 'Comments on Salmon's "Inductive Evidence"', *American Philosophical Quarterly*, 2, 1965, p. 276; I. Levi, *Gambling with Truth*, New York: Alfred A. Knopf, 1967, p. 154; J. Hintikka, 'Induction by Enumeration and Induction by Elimination', in I. Lakatos (ed.), *The Problem of Inductive Logic*, Amsterdam: North-Holland, 1968, p. 216.

[53] S. Kripke, 'Naming and Necessity', in D. Davidson and G. Harman (eds.), *Semantics of Natural Language*, Dordrecht: Reidel, 1972, pp. 266 and 274-5.

analytical usage' of the word 'meaning', the meaning of a term is not a function of the psychological state of the speaker by itself.[54] And rather similar appeals to any philosopher's inherent knowledge of ordinary language were cited for analogous purposes by Austin and others even though they did not use the word 'intuition' in this connection. According to Austin we can build up our analysis of the vocabulary of action, for example, 'by examining what we should say when, and so why and what we should mean by it'.[55] Declarations of 'what we should say when' can thus function as intuitive premisses for philosophical reasoning, much as avowals of intuitions about confirmation or explanation can. Both forms of deliverance may reasonably be taken to emerge from tacit acknowledgement of a system of relevant rules—rules of speech or rules of thought—and therefore to constitute evidence about the content of these rules.

Correspondingly Williams, in a discussion of moral luck,[56] declares that 'my procedure in general will be to invite reflection about how to think and feel about some rather less usual situations, in the light of an appeal to how we—many people—tend to think about other more usual situations'. For instance, he invites us to consider in this way what we might think about a man like Gauguin, who repudiated other claims on him in order to realize his gifts as a painter, or about a lorry-driver who, through no fault of his own, runs over a child. Williams himself explicitly eschews use of the word 'intuition'. But he clearly bases his arguments on appeals to premisses that fall under that term as I am using it here. And the same is true of Goodman, although he prefers to speak of 'philosophic conscience' rather than of intuition.[57]

Moreover, just as Austin held that principles implicit in ordinary language might sometimes need to be overridden,[58] so too Carnap remarked that 'from experience with my own intuitive judgements and those of friends whom I often asked for reactions to particular results, I have learned that isolated intuitive judgements are very often unreliable'.[59] Indeed, the genesis of an important paradox has some-

---

[54] H. Putnam, *Mind, Language and Reality, Philosophical Papers*, vol. 2), Cambridge: CUP, 1975, p. 224.

[55] J. L. Austin, 'A Plea for Excuses', *Proceedings of the Aristotelian Society*, 57, 1957, p. 7.

[56] B. A. O. Williams, 'Moral Luck', *Proceedings of the Aristotelian Society*, supp. vol. 50, 1976, p. 117 ff.

[57] N. Goodman, *Fact, Fiction and Forecast*, London: Athlone Press, 1954, p. 38.

[58] Op. cit., p. 11.

[59] 'Replies and Expositions', p. 994.

times been allegedly traced to 'a misleading intuition', as in Hempel's work on confirmation.[60]

In thus admitting fallibility, contemporary philosophers' use of appeals to intuition or linguistic sensitivity has been somewhat more tentative than Thomas Reid's philosophy of common sense, since Reid regarded common sense as an infallible arbiter of self-evident truth. Reid wrote that 'a conclusion drawn by a train of just reasoning from true principles cannot possible contradict any decision of common sense, because truth will always be consistent with itself'.[61] But Carnap and Austin agreed that, even where a person's intuition or linguistic sensitivity is quite appropriately invoked, it may not always be conclusive.

Intuitions play different roles in philosophical reasoning, however, in accordance with whether they concern singular issues or general ones. This point seems to have been more conspicuously acknowledged by those who thought of intuition as a faculty of knowledge than by those who now think of it as an inclination of judgement. Thus in ethical theory Sidgwick distinguished what he called 'three phases of Intuitionism', and he termed these 'Perceptional, Dogmatic and Philosophical', respectively.[62] Perceptional intuitionism appeals to the dictates of a person's conscience in response to particular quandaries on particular occasions. 'We may of course form general propositions by induction from these particular conscientious judgements, and arrange them systematically', said Sidgwick, but he felt that some people might object to doing this because the elaboration of such casuistry might, in practice, interfere with the guidance of conscience. Dogmatic intuitionism, on the other hand, assumes that ordinary people 'can discern certain general rules with really clear and finally valid intuition'. And Sidgwick himself thought of such intuitions about general principles, not particular cases, as the primary subject-matter for philosophical reflection.[63] He was thus mainly concerned with 'intuitions of the rightness or goodness (or the reverse) of particular kinds of external effects of human violation'. But he himself held that such intuitions may be shown to involve error by being shown to contradict each other, though subsequent reflection and comparison may correct the error.

---

[60] C. G. Hempel, 'Studies in the Logic of Confirmation', *Mind*, 54, 1945, p. 9.

[61] T. Reid, 'Essays on the Intellectual Powers of Man', essay 6, ch. II, in Sir William Hamilton (ed.), *The Works of Thomas Reid, D.D.*, vol. 1, Edinburgh: James Thin, 1895, p. 425.

[62] H. Sidgwick, *The Methods of Ethics*, London: Macmillan, 7th edn., 1907, pp. 96-103.

[63] Ibid., pp. 210-16. Cf. Collingwood, op. cit., p. 168.

Ross also came to think of general principles as knowable by intuition. But he insisted that what are self-evident to normal people are prima-facie obligations, not absolute ones.[64] If any conflicts of moral principle are suspected, therefore, they must be apparent rather than real: one or other of the principles at issue cannot really be as extensively applicable as the intuition of its prima-facie content supposed. Moreover, 'what comes first in time is the apprehension of the self-evident *prima-facie* rightness of an individual act of a particular type'. It is from this apprehension, according to Ross, that 'we come by reflection to apprehend the self-evident general principle of *prima-facie* duty'.[65] Accordingly, in Sidgwick's terminology, Ross is to be classified as more of a perceptional intuitionist than a dogmatic one. So too is Prichard.

If we do doubt whether there is really an obligation to originate A in a situation B, the remedy lies not in any process of general thinking, but in getting face to face with a particular instance of the situation B, and then directly appreciating the obligation to originate A in that situation.[66]

Note that the difference between distributive and collective generality is important here. Even if in each case of a certain type a person would intuit that a particular kind of inference may be drawn, that is not the same as his intuiting that in every case of that type this kind of inference may be drawn.

Finally, a philosophical intuitionist, in Sidgwick's terminology, is one who seeks intuitions of fundamental principles that are not evident to ordinary people, in order to explain, justify, or even rectify the morality of common sense. Presumably Plato may be said to afford a good example of this third species of ethical intuitionism, in holding that a philosopher's intellect operates like an eye of the soul when it finally grasps the Forms.[67]

Though Sidgwick drew his three-fold distinction, and I have illustrated it, with reference to the traditional conception of intuition as a faculty of knowledge, it is clear that the distinction applies just as well to contemporary analytical philosophers' conceptions of it as an inclination of judgement or belief without implication of veracity or knowledge. Intuitions about individual cases (where these involve

---

[64] W. D. Ross, *Foundations of Ethics*, Oxford: OUP, 1939, pp. 82-6.
[65] *The Right and the Good*, p. 33. Cf. *The Foundations of Ethics*, p. 84.
[66] H. A. Prichard, 'Does Moral Philosophy Rest on a Mistake?', *Mind*, 71, 1912, p. 37.
[67] *Republic*, 553 D.

moral, conceptual, epistemological, or suchlike issues) set up premisses for philosophical induction, just as judicial decisions in
individual cases set up premisses for jurisprudential induction.
Intuitions about general rules set up premisses or patterns of inference
for philosophical deduction, or may even set up a basis for inductive
theory-construction. Intuitions about fundamental principles determine global issues, such as realism versus anti-realism, or regulative
ideals, such as those of consistency and comprehensiveness, and thus
they set constraints on the operation of both inductive and deductive
reasoning.

Of course, this three-fold classification has to be applied with an
appropriate degree of carefulness. Some linguistic intuitions, for
example, appear to be singular in one respect and general in another.
Such an intuition may seem to count as individual, if it is invoked in
support of a higher-order generalization, as when we generalize about
the use of an individual word in our language in order to support a
generalization about the meanings of all words of that kind. But the
very same intuition clearly counts as general if it is itself the focus of
philosophical attention, as when we are concerned to establish the
meaning of that particular word in the language and may appeal for
support to an intuition about its meaning in a particular utterance.
Strictly speaking, therefore, we should describe this situation as one in
which there is a hierarchy of generalizations–what Bacon called 'a
pyramid of axioms'. Such hierarchies of more and more far-reaching
explanations are characteristic of inductive reasoning in any domain
in which it operates.

§ 9 THE DOMINANCE OF SINGULAR INTUITIONS OVER
GENERAL ONES

Summary. There are good reasons why singular intuitions should be preferred
to general ones as a source of data in philosophical reasoning. The analogy
with experimental reasoning is especially powerful in this connection. But
some recourse to intuitions about fundamental principles, such as to ideals of
consistency and comprehensiveness, is unavoidable.

Analytical philosophers have undoubtedly often invoked intuitions on
general issues, as premisses for their deductions or their theoretical
constructions. They have, in Sidgwick's terminology, often been

'dogmatic intuitionists'. But they have also, on other occasions, often been 'perceptional intuitionists' and argued inductively. And there are at least four reasons why the data obtained by appealing to singular intuitions should normally be thought to constitute more secure premisses for philosophical reasoning, even if the arguments therefrom—being inductive—are less certain.

The first is that, with equally determinate formulations and in relation to the same kind of subject-matter, we are more likely to get agreement to accept a singular proposition than a general one, when each is sponsored by intuition: the commitment is much smaller. Agreement about general rules carries with it a commitment to agree about the results of applying those rules to individual cases also. If you agree that feeding the poor and needy should take precedence over helping those you love to enjoy themselves, then you will, if consistent, also agree that you should give alms to each of the starving beggars who now confronts you rather than pay for your children to ride on the roundabouts. On the other hand it is often possible for two people to agree about the rightness of an individual act, like giving alms on a particular occasion, without agreeing about the reasons for so doing, i.e. about the rules or principles from which this rightness flows. Analogously common law judges who do give the same statement of the law ought to give similar decisions on similar findings of fact in individual cases. But judges who just give similar decisions in similar cases may well back their decisions with different statements of the law. In short, the extent of the commitment is so much less in regard to the acceptance of singular intuitions than of general ones, that it is inherently more probable that people will agree about the former than about the latter.

A second reason for treating singular intuitions as a more acceptable source of data than general ones is that philosophical enquiry is normally concerned to resolve general issues rather than singular ones. Hence a direct appeal to general intuitions runs the risk of begging the question on a central issue. But an appeal to singular intuitions removes discussion to a different type of question. The moral philosopher who asserts that family obligations should always take precedence over obligations to strangers may not have reflected sufficiently on the possibility of a particular situation in which he comes face to face with a stranger who is actually starving. The epistemologist who asserts that major scientific advances can *never* be made by building more and more qualifications into an initial hypothesis may not have reflected sufficiently on the steps by which Mendel's original model of independent assortment was subsequently improved in accuracy.[68]

Thirdly, it is relevant here that at least in ethics most philosophers, like Ross, have seen that every general intuition needs to be protected, implicitly or explicitly, by an 'other things being equal' clause, because the difficulty of foreseeing all future combinations of circumstances makes it necessary to guard against the possibility that a general principle which has been formulated with excessive precision may have too harsh an incidence in some particular situation.[69] So a singular moral intuition or deliverance of conscience, which is typically forced into unconditionality by its nearness to the point of actual decision, is normally free to exploit any 'other things being equal' clause and to override the principle that this clause qualifies. The superior determinateness and immediacy of the singular intuition establish a title to logical priority. It is thus a person's singular intuitions to which any theory about his guiding principles ought ultimately to accommodate itself. An analogous order of precedence is evident when a clinician, administrator, craftsman, chess-master, etc. is teaching his skill to an apprentice, or providing data for computer-simulation of it via an exercise in expert systems analysis. Any hypothesis he is inclined to advance that such-and-such a general rule is an element in his skill would normally be withdrawn or appropriately qualified if, in some instance, it clashes with what he is inclined to say he would do in that particular case. The point of apprenticeship is to have the opportunity to learn by example.

Fourthly, the analogy with scientific reasoning affords a powerful additional argument. Unless there is some special reason, intrinsic to the ethical or philosophical context, why considerations of simplicity and uniformity should not be operative here, the standard patterns of inductive reasoning will be available in regard to intuitions, as in regard to observations. The singular should not only be deducible from the general but also, in appropriate circumstances, give it inductive support. Just as events that are similar in relevant respects are taken to cause similar effects, so too law-suits that are similar in relevant respects are taken to require similar judgements and a person who intuits a particular moral duty for an agent in a given concrete

[68] See R. D. Rosenkrantz, *Inference, Method and Decision*, Dordrecht: Reidel, 1977, pp. 100-3, cf. pp. 125-7.
[69] *The Right and the Good*, pp. 19-20.

situation is thereby committed to accepting that the same moral duty exists for any other agent in any relevantly similar situation. This powerful analogy is wasted if singular intuitions are not treated as being normally a more acceptable basis for philosophical reasoning than general ones. For, just as in suitable circumstances a single experiment (see § 7 above) may support a scientific hypothesis, so too even a single well-chosen example of intuitively valid scientific reasoning about a particular experimental result may give some support to a philosophical theory about the structure of experimental reasoning in that branch of natural science.

Of course, if a scientific theory explains a much wider variety of accepted regularities in a particular field than any other theory does, it is not to be rejected because of a single counter-instance or pattern of counter-instance. Newton's laws of motion were not rejected before a better theory became available, despite their known inability to explain such anomalies as those in the perihelion of Mercury.[70] But the dominance of an outstandingly powerful theory over an observed anomaly in natural science does not give respectability to the dominance of a general *intuition* over a singular one in philosophy. If some piece of inductive reasoning in philosophy does indeed allow a general theory to prevail over a contrary low-level intuition, this does not happen because the theory itself seems intuitively correct, but because it explains many other low-level intuitions (see § 11 below). The analogy with scientific reasoning is a close one, but it has to be accurately traced out.

This analogy also has the advantage of making clear that it is not the having of an intuition, whether singular or general, that counts as a datum for philosophical reasoning, but rather the content of the intuition. For it is not the physicist's observation of the pointer's position on a dial that counts as an evidential datum in the laboratory, but the event observed. Otherwise optics, and perhaps acoustics, would be all the science that there is. The datum that the moralist has to take into account is the rightness or wrongness of a particular action, not the deliverance of conscience that pronounces it right (or wrong); the logician's datum is the validity (or invalidity) of a particular inference, not the intuition that assures us of it; and the philosopher of language's datum is the admissibility (or absurdity) of a certain locution, not the actual practice of using (or avoiding) it. Philosophical

[70] A. Einstein and L. Infeld, *The Evolution of Physics*, Cambridge: CUP, 1938, pp. 252-4.

induction no more aims at a theory about intuitions or linguistic practice than physics or chemistry aims at a theory about observations. Philosophical analysis is not concerned to articulate the various different norms of reasoning that different people actually respect, but rather the universal norms that they should all respect. No room exists therefore for an accusation that philosophers who argue from singular intuitions are regressing into nineteenth-century psychologizing or passing over into the kind of naturalized epistemology that has been rejected earlier in the present book (§ 5).

Similarly, when an analytical philosopher of science cites evidence from the history of science in relation to problems about its epistemology, he is not strictly concerned with the conclusions that famous scientists have held to be well-supported or the fact that they have so held them. To generalize about such conclusions, and the circumstances under which they have arisen, is a job for the historian or sociologist of science. Philosophers are concerned rather to share, and get their readers to share, a scientist's normative judgement that, on the basis of available background knowledge, such-and-such a conclusion is supported to this-or-that extent by such-and-such data. For instance, when Whewell argues the high value of consilience as a criterion of merit for scientific theories, what he cites as evidence are a number of intuitive judgements about this that were made by Newton, Fresnel, etc. in particular cases and are shared by anyone who considers those cases. One such example that Whewell gives is the conviction induced by Newton's discovery that 'the force of Universal Gravitation, which had been inferred from the *Perturbations* of the moon and planets by the sun and by each other, also accounted for the fact, apparently altogether dissimilar and remote, of the *Precession of the Equinoxes*.'[71]

An interesting parallel may also be drawn here with intuitions of grammatical well-formedness. Where the aim is to use the evidence afforded by such intuitions in order to justify a thesis about the grammatical rules respected by a particular speaker, it has sometimes been maintained[72] that the speaker's utterances constitute hard behavioural data, concern with which would maintain the scientific status of linguistics, while avowed intuitions are subjective acts of con-

---

[71] W. Whewell, *The Philosophy of the Inductive Sciences*, London: Frank Cass, 2nd edn., 1847, part 2, p. 66.
[72] e.g. G. Sampson, *The Form of Language*, London: Weidenfeld and Nicolson, 1975, pp. 60-84.

sciousness, concern with which can serve only to drag linguistics back into the dark ages. However, the comparison should not be drawn in these terms. The differences between an utterance of a particular string of phonemes in recorded speech, on the one side, and an avowal of the string's grammaticalness, on the other, as data for grammar, is just that while the former constitutes an actual occurrence of the string in human speech the latter establishes a potential occurrence. Both are signs of an intuition of grammaticalness, in the sense of an inclination to judge, without evidence or inference, that the string is grammatical. But, in the one case this inclination is implicit in the utterance, in the other it is explicitly avowed. Moreover, avowals of grammaticalness or ungrammaticalness may be able to supply data on crucial issues that actually recorded utterances fail to determine, because these avowals may relate to systematically varied contexts or to strings of words that, for accidental reasons, no one ever utters in real life. So it is exclusive reliance on the observation of actual utterances, not reliance on avowals of grammaticalness, that fails to mirror essential features of scientific method.

The point is that the inductive method in natural science normally requires us not to rely on observations of the phenomena that happen to present themselves to our passive consciousness, but actively to manipulate circumstances so that we can deliberately control the experimental situation, as far as we can, in respect of every factor that we think might be causally relevant. An analogue of this occurs in grammatical enquiry whenever we investigate what features of a sentence are dependent on what: at the simplest, for instance, we tell whether the form of a verb depends only on the number of the subject, or also on its gender, by experimenting with a native informant—we check out his intuitions over suitably varied strings of morphemes. Of course, it would be theoretically possible for a grammarian, instead of being content to elicit the intuitions of native informants, to try to elicit an actual utterance of each string in question. But, quite apart from the practical difficulty of contriving this even where the string of morphemes is well-formed, it would remain very difficult to determine in any particular case whether failure to elicit utterance of a particular string was due to the intrinsic ungrammaticalness of the string or to some misjudgement of the circumstances, motivation, beliefs, etc. to which the utterance of the expression would be appropriate. Negative evidence emerges naturally from the investigation of avowed intuitions, not from that of utterances.

The situation in ethics is interestingly analogous. Many accidental contingencies restrict the variety of moral quandaries in which a particular person actually finds himself. So the actual intuitive decisions of conscience that he makes on such issues in his own life are correspondingly limited. But in order to build up inductive support for some kind of ethical theory a philosopher may need to consider several possible combinations of morally relevant circumstances that are not to be found within his own limited range of experience. What is right or wrong in those combinations of circumstances has to be determined by an exercise of conscience in relation to imagined situations, rather like an avowal of grammaticalness in relation to a sentence that is mentioned but not used (i.e. described or spelt out but not asserted). No doubt it is better to rely on real-life decisions of conscience if one can, just as a grammarian may prefer to rely on real-life utterances if he can: there is less risk that the intuitions may be biased, or otherwise influenced, by the preferred theory. But some recourse to intuitions about imaginary situations or utterances may be unavoidable. Similarly a philosopher of science needs to take his examples from the actual history of science wherever this is possible. But he may not be able to dispense altogether with appeals to avowed intuitions about imaginary cases or his own thought-experiments.

Someone may object that there is nevertheless an important disanalogy between standard inductive paradigms of reasoning about factual issues and supposedly inductive patterns of reasoning about normative issues. Harman has argued, for example, that scientific theories have an explanatory role in relation to particular observings that ethical theories do not have in relation to particular exercises of our moral sense.[73] He has pointed out that neither the relevant moral principles nor the wrongness of the act contribute anything towards explaining why you have the moral feelings that you do when you see some children setting fire to a cat: they can serve only to justify those feelings. 'It seems to be completely irrelevant to our explanation whether your intuitive immediate judgement is true or false.'[74]

This objection is easily answered. If the explanation in question is of some matter of fact–i.e. if it is an explanation that a causal or statistical hypothesis or a scientific theory might provide–then of course one should not expect any normative judgement to provide that type of explanation. Indeed, if a philosopher claims that norms can

[73] G. Harman, *The Nature of Morality: An Introduction to Ethics*, New York: OUP, 1977, pp. 1-9.   [74] Ibid., p. 6.

constitute a topic for inductive generalization as well as facts can, then an intrinsic part of what he claims is that inductive generalization need not be tied up exclusively with factual explanation in terms of causes, probabilities, etc. However, if the explanation sought is not of why you have the moral feelings that you do but rather of why the moral feelings that you have are the right ones to have—i.e. if the explanation sought is not an explanation of your attitude's *de facto* psychological properties but of its *de jure* normative status—then the relevant moral principle or the wrongness of the act may provide a perfectly good explanation. You are right to be outraged by what the children are doing to the cat, we might say, because it is an act of sadistic cruelty. So, to the task of explaining the rightness of your outrage it is by no means irrelevant whether your intuitive judgement is true or false.

Good reasons exist, therefore, for taking singular intuitions to be more acceptable than general ones as sources of data in ethics and other branches of analytical philosophy. Wherever possible, intuitions on general issues should not be treated as a source of premises. Admittedly, if a person of outstanding ability and experience in a particular field of empirical or mathematical research declares his strong belief in the operation of some specified general principle within that field, then, even though he has little or no evidence to support this belief, we are entitled to give him some special credit. If he has often been right before, he may be right here too, just as a well-reputed clinician's diagnoses are trusted even when he cannot produce much argument for them. After all, such hunches are normally checkable. So in these circumstances a hunch about a general principle seems to have considerably greater value than in run-of-the-mill philosophical situations, where a philosopher of science, say, declares that he finds some particular measure of simplicity or some particular axiom of induction to be 'intuitive', but has no relevant record of successful hunches to establish his credibility or the outstanding efficiency of his mental 'black box'. One can almost see a grain of justification here in the doctrines of Plato and Spinoza—in the view that exceptionally able and deeply enquiring minds may be privileged, after much intellectual effort, to have a few intuitive insights into general truths. But there is really a substantial difference between crediting what someone says because of his tested ability and experience, and crediting it because of some untestable metaphysical supposition about the affinity of Reason and Reality. It is only the former, not the latter, that is occasionally appropriate in the case of general hunches, as is apparent from our readiness to consider treating them as unsuccessful, if they conflict with singular data of the appropriately accredited type.

Perhaps someone may also object that in one important respect general intuitions are superior to single ones as a source of philosophical premises. In an intuition about an issue of general principles, it might be claimed, we stand at a distance from the pressures of an immediate, concrete context. So we are much less likely to confound, say, what is epistemologically correct with what it is in practice reasonable to believe. But this point has a bearing only on heuristic philosophical reasoning. General intuitions may well guide us towards conclusions that are likely in the end to be defensible. But, in constructing an argument to defend or justify such conclusions, we need to let singular intuitions dominate over general ones for the reasons already stated, even though as a preliminary to the argument certain singular intuitions may have to be discounted in one of the ways discussed in § 9 below.

Sidgwick, however, distinguishes three categories of intuitions, and what I have been arguing so far is just that the first of these are more acceptable than the second as sources of premises for philosophical reasoning. So what about Sidgwick's suggestion of a third category, which he called 'philosophical intuitions'? If these operate over the same issues as intuitions of the second category, though at an even more general level, they are obviously even more unacceptable as sources of premises. But if, as has been suggested, there are lines of philosophical induction that run from singular intuitions to a system of general principles, then we have to envisage certain regulative ideals as controlling these lines of reasoning. Some such ideals have an incontrovertible claim to logical priority, in the sense that unless we are willing to accept them the reasoning is unwarranted; and, so far as we are inclined just to assume them without further reflection, that inclination could well be counted as an intuition. For example, ideals of consistency and comprehensiveness, in one form or another, seem to be indispensable intuitions of this kind for those engaged in the construction of philosophical theories, since any attempt to construct arguments for those ideals, or to generalize them out of singular intuitions, seems to be governed in its turn by analogous ideals.

The relatively a priori status of such ideals is perhaps most easily seen in connection with constructing theories about issues of fact.

Every time we change our accepted system of factual propositions in the face of adverse sensory evidence we have two other options that are also open: we could instead sacrifice the ideal of consistency and just incorporate the adverse evidence alongside the unmodified system that it refutes, or we could sacrifice the ideal of comprehensiveness and just take no notice of the new evidence. The unattractiveness of either of these two options is the measure of our intuitive conviction about the value of consistency and comprehensiveness as regulative ideals, since it is both those ideals that we have to invoke in order to justify our preference for adjusting our accepted system of factual propositions in the light of the new evidence. And the same point can be made about our accepted system of fundamental principles of inference and deliberation–the system that analytical philosophy is concerned to shape.

§ 10 PHILOSOPHY AS A FORM OF TRANSITION FROM BELIEF TO ACCEPTANCE

Summary. A philosopher who tests his hypothesis against his own intuition is not thereby just deciding in favour of his own cause but testing against brute fact, because in the relevant sense intuition is a form of belief, not of acceptance. Acceptance is voluntary, belief not. Acceptance of a set of propositions commits one to its consequences, belief in it does not. Philosophy, by building on intuitions, can replace muddled and inconsistent beliefs by a coherent and acceptable system of principles.

A possible objection to what has been said about the role of intuition in philosophical reasoning runs as follows. 'Intuitions', it may be said, 'are essentially subjective attitudes of mind that are of no value as sources of premises for philosophical reasoning, whether inductive or deductive. All reasoning in philosophy, whether inductive or deductive, has to be hypothetical. It is always from assumed premises. It tells us what we are committed to *if* we hold certain views, and presents us with one or more ways of introducing a kind of reflective equilibrium into our naturally disordered tangle of principles, prejudices, and individual judgements. It cannot tell us what views we *should* hold. Neither singular intuitions nor general ones provide the kind of brute facts against which hypotheses or theories need to be tested in order to gain respectability. A philosopher who tests his hypotheses successfully against his own intuitions is merely deciding in favour of his own cause. Once you agree that intuitions cannot provide knowledge–as Spinoza, Sidgwick, etc., thought they could–you ought also to agree that they cannot provide premisses for any kind of philosophical reasoning.'

The nub of this objection is that a philosopher who tests his hypotheses or assumptions successfully against his own intuitions is thereby just deciding in favour of his own cause. But a closer examination of the relevant concept of intuition will show that this is not so. Specifically, we need to explore the difference between believing a proposition's truth and accepting it, because intuition, as a certain kind of inclination to judge, is a form of belief, not acceptance. Only if intuition were a form of acceptance would a philosopher who invoked it be deciding his own case. And what is at issue here is not just a difference of meaning, in relevant contexts, between the words 'believe' and 'accept'. It is not just a feature of linguistic idiom or of so-called 'ordinary language'. Such features may well vary somewhat from speaker to speaker. Instead, we are concerned with certain differences in reality that deserve recognition irrespective of the variety of linguistic oppositions by which they are marked within particular languages or idiolects–and irrespective also of whatever problems face the empirical psychology of human judgement. But these differences have undoubtedly been obscured by the tendency of certain writers (Levi, Kyburg, etc.[75]) to use the terms 'believe' and 'accept' interchangeably.

Very often we accept what we believe and believe what we accept. But a person who does not fully believe that p can nevertheless accept that p. That is to say, without being in a subjective state of conviction that p he can decide to go along with that proposition in practice as an unquestioned premiss for his own or others' proofs, arguments, inferences, and deliberations. For example, this might happen if he has a hunch that not-p, though the balance of presently available evidence makes p the only socially acceptable opinion. Equally, a person can fully believe that p without fully accepting it. That is to say, he could be convinced that p while nevertheless rejecting the use of that proposition as a premiss for certain proofs, etc. For example, a juror might be in that situation if, because of his personal acquain-

---

[75] e.g. I. Levi, *Decisions and Revisions, Philosophical Essays on Knowledge and Value*, Cambridge: CUP, 1984, p. 15; H. E. Kyburg, 'Rational Belief', *The Behavioural and Brain Sciences*, 6, 1983, p. 236.

tance with a witness, he believes the witness untrustworthy but feels that he ought to put his belief out of his mind in judging the case before the court.

Again, accepting that p is no reason at all for believing that p. But having a belief that p is normally some reason for accepting that p, even though it may well not be the only, or the best, reason or even a sufficient one. There is just a presumption that a belief would not have arisen at all without there having been some data in its favour.

Both acceptance and belief can be either fickle or fixed, about what is or about what ought to be. But acceptance is standardly thought of as being voluntary, while belief is not. You may decide to believe *in* God, or to believe–i.e. trust–a friend. But you cannot decide to believe *that* it will rain to-morrow, or to believe *that* it will not. You can decide only to accept that it will, or to accept that it will not: the belief may ensue, but it may not. So people are held responsible and accountable for what they accept, not for what they believe. A juror is culpable for adopting beliefs that he had about the defendant before the trial as premises on which to base conclusions about the defendant's guilt. But he is not culpable for having those beliefs: he could not help having them. People are often at fault for not acquainting themselves with relevant facts. But they are hardly to be blamed (though they may be subjects for pity, contempt, admiration, or wonder) if they remain incredulous even after acquainting themselves with evidence that is normally adequate to sustain the relevant belief. When Descartes held that in human judgement 'the will is much wider in its range and compass than the understanding',[76] he is most favourably construed as asserting the voluntariness of acceptance. And when Hume wrote that 'belief is more properly an act of the sensitive, than of the cogitative part of our nature', and that 'Nature, by an absolute and uncontroulable necessity has determin'd us to judge as well as to breathe and feel',[77] he is most favourably construed as asserting the passivity and involuntariness of belief. Analogously, to practise Cartesian doubt on a proposition is deliberately to call in question the acceptability of that proposition, whereas to have an ordinary, natural doubt about its truth is to have an involuntary reluctance to believe it. No doubt there are many degrees and forms both of acceptance and belief. Also, it is often

---

[76] R. Descartes, *The Philosophical Works* (trans. E. S. Haldane and G. R. T. Ross), vol. 1, Cambridge: CUP, 1931, p. 175.
[77] D. Hume, *A Treatise of Human Nature* (ed. L. A. Selby-Bigge), Oxford: OUP, 1983, p. 183.

difficult to know whether to classify a person's state of mind at a particular time as one of belief, of acceptance, or of both. But the difference between the two concepts is clear enough.

Only in these terms can the possibility of self-deception be made clearly conceivable (although the expression 'self-deception' is sometimes used rather loosely to cover quite a variety of different states of mind). A person cannot intelligibly be said to persuade himself into believing that p while at precisely the same time still believing that not-p. But the explorer's father, who is said to deceive himself into thinking that his son is still alive, may well be supposed both to believe truly, albeit dispositionally, that he is dead and also to have somehow persuaded himself–most of the time–into ignoring this belief and suppressing its manifestations, and even into accepting that the son is still alive. He is thus both agent and victim of his own wishful thinking. Such behaviour may legitimately be termed a self-deceit, since for anyone wilfully to persuade someone else to accept a proposition that is contrary to what the persuader himself correctly believes to be true is certainly a deceit if the persuader achieves his result by purposely concealing his own belief, or by purposely misrepresenting the evidence or its implications. Similarly, we need the possibility of a difference between believing that an act ought to be done and accepting that it ought in order to account for the possibility of the difference–familiar to moral philosophers[78]–between what an agent's conscience tells him to do and what his inclinations tempt him to decide to do. The dictates of a person's conscience are not under his immediate control but he is normally free not to accept them.

Since acceptance involves a voluntary choice of premises, a person is committed to accepting all the deductive consequences of any set of propositions that he accepts, whether or not he is able or disposed to work out those consequences himself. That is, he is obliged to accept any or all of these consequences if the question arises. If he announces his acceptance to other people, he has a commitment to those people specifically insofar as he has created a presumption about how he will think and act. And, even if he has not *announced* his decision to accept that p, this decision is nothing if not a self-imposed undertaking to think and act as if it is true that p. But you are not intellectually committed by a belief, however strong, to any implication of that

---

[78] e.g. Aristotle, *Nicomachean Ethics*, 1145^a 15-1152^a 36, and J. Butler, *The Works of Joseph Butler, DCL* (ed. W. E. Gladstone), Oxford: OUP, 1896, vol. 2, sermons II and III, esp. p. 59.

belief. That is because states of mind that arise in you, or grow on you, or come to dominate you, no more impose any intellectual obligations on you than do the electoral campaign posters that people stick on your walls without your consent. Of course, if you do not believe the immediate and obvious consequences of the proposition that p, it may seem doubtful whether you really believe p at all. But, when you are thought to believe that p, you are not thereby expected to believe any of the remoter or less obvious consequences of the proposition that p.

This particular difference between belief and acceptance is easy to miss because anyone's stating that he believes that p certainly does normally commit him to accepting any logical consequences of the proposition that p. But that commitment stems just from the fact that asserting 'I believe that p' to someone else is normally a way of stating one's acceptance of its being true that p: by making the first-person confession one normally expresses acquiescence in one's own belief. Third-person assertions may be contrasted here. 'John believes that p' does not impute John's commitment to accepting p's logical consequences, since John may have made no relevant statements or decisions. So commitment is not implicit in the concept of belief, as it is in that of acceptance.

Accordingly, if in a particular context you unconditionally accept each of the set of propositions $p, q, r \ldots$ you thereby accept, or are committed to accepting, the conjunction p & q & r & ... as one of the consequences of that set. It is often only because of this that others, by exposing an inconsistency within such a conjunction, may persuade you to change your mind about a particular proposition. But there is nothing odd about the description of someone both as believing each of $p, q, r \ldots$ and also as not believing (or accepting) the conjunction p & q & r & ..., since he may well believe (or accept) that somewhere or other among his beliefs–he doesn't know where–at least one error is present. Indeed, so far from its being irrational for a person to think that he has at least one mistaken belief, it may well be irrational for him to think that he has not got at least one mistaken belief, in view of the widespread evidence in favour of the generalization that everyone is, at least occasionally, led into errors of belief by his own misunderstandings, muddled associations, wishful thinking, carelessness, or mental or physical laziness, or by the mistakes or deceits of others. So, circumstances may occur in which you both believe and accept that p, and that q, and that r, and that ..., and in which you would, therefore, be irrational not to *accept* also that p & q & r & . . ., but quite rational not to *believe* that p & q & r & . . ..

Correspondingly, there can be no such thing as a primitive *theory* of matter or mind–for example, a so-called 'folk psychology'–embedded involuntarily and unreflectively in a community's language or culture. Theories are open to acceptance or rejection. But it may be that some systems of beliefs are fostered by our natural language, cultural heritage, etc. and subverted by our natural science.

It is clear, therefore, that a philosopher who tests his hypotheses or assumptions against his own intuitions is not thereby just deciding in favour of his own cause. Analytical philosophy has something to analyse. Intuitive beliefs, like beliefs of any other kind, are brute facts that are not subject to voluntary control. Whether deliverances of moral conscience or of inferential practice, they cannot be created at will by anyone, and *a fortiori* they cannot be created by a philosopher in order to confirm his own hypotheses or assumptions (though various influences, including the study of philosophy, may help to transform them). Rather, the process of philosophical reflection, so far as it proceeds by deduction or induction from intuitions, can be seen as a way of bringing beliefs before the tribunal of acceptance. That is how it enables us to avoid the 'unexamined life', as (according to Plato) Socrates saw.[79] If intuitive beliefs about the rightness of such-and-such particular acts, for example, are captured successfully within an ethical system, over wide variations in the kind of situation involved, then whoever accepts the system on the basis of those intuitions also accepts thereby the propositions sponsored by the cuitions. In this sense philosophers may be said to find reasons for accepting what they intuitively believe. But, if some intuitively held principles need to be modified or rejected in order that the system may be both consistent and comprehensive, then whoever accepts the system on these terms thereby accepts whatever consequences it generates in place of the original ones. When philosophical analysis proceeds from intuitively sanctioned premises to a reasoned con-clusion, it may be described as moving from analysandum to analysans. It seeks to ensure that any muddles or inconsistencies in our unreasoned inclinations and passive prejudices are replaced by an explicitly formulated, consciously co-ordinated, adequately reasoned, and freely adopted system of acceptable principles. If, on a particular issue, a philosopher still accepts some propositions that are incon-

[79] Plato, *Apology* 38 A.

sistent with others that he has come consciously to accept, he has not yet completed the coherent analytical reconstruction or idealization of his own patterns of reasoning. A good philosopher seeks, like Socrates or Spinoza, to be as well-integrated a person as he can.

§ 11 WHEN CAN AN INTUITION BE DISREGARDED?

Summary. The three ways in which awkward or unwelcome intuitions may be disregarded in the inductive reasonings of analytical philosophers are analogous to those in which observations may sometimes be disregarded in experimental science or judicial decisions in jurisprudence. An intuition may just be written off as unauthoritative, in the face of some allegedly canonical counter-intuition. Or it may be put down to an inadequate awareness of the range of issues affecting relevant intuitions. Or it may be disregarded because the relevant generalization is treated as an idealization. Otherwise, if no intuition is to be discarded, the generalization at issue may need revision or qualification, or the problem may have to be thought of as not yet fully resolved.

Both Carnap and Austin held–in their very different ways (§ 8)–that an intuition might sometimes need to be disregarded. A similar point was made by Goodman when he remarked that an inference is rejected if it violates a rule we are unwilling to amend, even though rules of inference are themselves justified only by reference to judgements rejecting or accepting particular deductive inferences.[80] But how is this compatible with the thesis that intuition provides the premisses for a mode of inductive reasoning in philosophy which is, *mutatis mutandis*, the same as the kind of induction that operates in evaluating experimental evidence for scientific hypotheses or in the jurisprudence of common law? A scientist is not allowed to pick out the experimental data that fit his hypothesis and throw away the data that do not. In a court of common law a judge is not allowed to pick out just the precedents that fit his preferred version of the law and to disregard those that do not. So, would not a moral philosopher, for instance, who argues inductively for a system of principles which he knows to run counter to the dictates of his own conscience in a particular case, be dishonest? Surely a philosopher is no more entitled to disregard the data supplied by his intuitions than a scientist is entitled to disregard the data supplied by observation of his own

[80] Op. cit., p. 67.

experimental results, or a judge to disregard the data supplied by his own researches in the law reports?

These questions have to be answered, and the answer, as it emerges, will help us to see some structure in an important range of different types of reasoning that are available in analytical philosophy. The situation is rather more complex than the remarks of Carnap, Austin, or Goodman suggest.

Let us grant, at the outset, that an analytical philosopher cannot just ignore an adverse intuition that persists in his mind. If it still lingers there after he has formed the conclusion that it belies, he has not yet resolved his problem adequately. It is like a replicable anomaly in natural science, or like a novel line of decisions in the courts, which has yet to be accommodated within an acceptable system of principles. The philosopher may even have quite a good theory, but he ought not to think it the best possible one.

However, there are also ways in which prima-facie counter-evidence to a particular hypothesis turns out not to operate as replicable counter-evidence after all. In natural science this may happen in one or other of three main ways. Sometimes an observation or measurement in the experiment turns out to have been faulty, and so the report of what occurred was incorrect. Sometimes a hidden variable was interfering with the action of the controlled variables in the experiment, so that factors other than those reported were influencing the result. In either of these two types of case the replicability of the experiment would be unreliable. And in a third type of case the experiment is satisfactorily replicable, but the hypothesis is treated as an idealization to which the real world only conforms under an unrealizable *ceteris paribus* condition. Similarly a supposed legal precedent may be discounted in one or other of three analogous ways. Sometimes the previous case may be shown to have been wrongly decided, or to have been heard by a judge whose decisions are not binding in the instant case, so that the alleged precedent lacks authority. Sometimes the previous case had features that were significantly different from those of the instant case, so that the alleged precedent is irrelevant. And sometimes the conclusion is that the principles underlying the law would be best codified by our establishing a new nexus of legal roles and relations which would not quite accord at every point with relevant precedents. Accordingly, we need to investigate how analogous possibilities may affect philosophical inductions. We need to investigate the circumstances under which an analytical philosopher may suppose himself entitled to disregard the data of his own intuition.

The most obvious philosophical analogues of faulty experimental observation are where some recognizably adventitious element of wishful thinking, self-interest, pupillage, or emotional prejudice has entered into the intuition. But there are also more interesting kinds of analogue, where the unacceptable intuition is attributed to some intellectual rather than motivational preoccupation.

Consider, for example, the classical pattern of argument for epistemological scepticism that relies on some such intuition as 'I don't know that I am not dreaming' or 'I don't know that a demon, or a demonic scientist, is not deceiving my sensory faculties'. From such a premiss the sceptic infers inductively the general conclusion that he can have no *knowledge* of external objects at any time. One way of trying to counter this pattern of sceptical argument is to write off the intuition, just as an experimenter might claim that a certain supposed phenomenon was in fact a perceptual illusion. Thus Moore claimed that he *knew* the truth of what he expressed by the combination of certain gestures with saying the words 'There is one hand and here is another', and that he therefore possessed a premiss of known truth from which he could prove the existence of objects external to his mind. It would follow, Moore claimed, that any intuitions to the contrary have to be rejected, since the claim to knowledge on which he based his argument is more certain than any premiss on which an argument to the contrary might be based.[81] So this type of reasoning in analytical philosophy seeks to shut off the possibility of criticizing our normal cognitive practices from the outside, as it were. Whenever the sceptic invokes intuitions that cast doubt on the whole assumption that knowledge is obtainable, his Moorean opponent insists on confining discussion within the framework of that assumption by citing some intuitively recognizable exemplar of knowledge. The intuitions invoked by the sceptic are thus to be written off, in the face of supposedly more acceptable premisses, as due to a misdirectedness of intellectual attention.

Another example of this type of manœuvre is to be found in Quine's treatment of the sceptical issue. Quine likens 'the archaic and unconscious hypothesis of ordinary physical objects' to a physicist's hypothesis about the existence of molecules: 'the positing of those

---

[81] G. E. Moore, 'Proof of an External World', in G. E. Moore, *Philosophical Papers*, London: Allen and Unwin, 1959, pp. 127-50.

extraordinary things is just a vivid analogue of the positing or acknowledging of ordinary things'.[82] Hence any discussion or criticism of the one hypothesis is, in principle, on all fours with discussion or criticism of the other. Both must come to judgement before the tribunal of sensory experience in accordance with accepted principles of scientific method. What is being resisted is again the sceptic's attempt to establish a source of epistemological criticism that is external to the enterprise of ordinary knowledge-seeking. Instead, if there are any doubts about the reliability of this or that hypothesis, or any problems about the nature of empirical knowledge, it is for science itself to resolve them. So, here too, the sceptic's intuitions are being swept aside as misdirected. Specifically, they are being swept aside in favour of the intuitions about evidence, simplicity, conservation, sufficient reason, etc.[83] on which Quine's theory of scientific method is built, because that theory provides the manual on which he proposes to rely in conducting the critical examination of sceptical worries before the tribunal of experience.

My object here is not to pass judgement on the adequacy or inadequacy of these anti-sceptical arguments. They are cited rather as instances of a certain type of manœuvre in philosophical reasoning that is analogous to the rejection of a particular observation or measurement in experimental science, or to the denial of authority to an alleged precedent in jurisprudence. Similarly, examples can also be deployed that illustrate the alternative type of intuition-rejecting manœuvre, whereby fault is found, not so much with the direction of interest shown by the intuition, but rather with its ability to reveal all that is relevant in the situation. The supposed trouble now is not that the intuition exhibits a clear concern with the wrong issue but rather that it arises from a confused concern with the right one.

Take Carnap's treatment of the concept of existence, for example. Carnap did not believe that sceptical worries about the existence of an objective world could be dissolved–as Moore and Quine argued–by appeals to intuitions about perceivable fact. Instead, whenever someone introduces a rule-governed, linguistic framework for talking about a certain kind of entity, we have to distinguish, said Carnap, between two different ways in which questions about existence may be asked. Some questions arise within the framework, such as the question 'Are unicorns real?' within the ordinary framework for the system

[82] *Word and Object*, p. 22.
[83] Ibid., pp. 17-21.

of spatio-temporally ordered things, or 'Is there a prime number greater than a hundred?' within the framework for the system of natural numbers. Other questions may be raised about the existence or reality of such a system as a whole, as in 'Does an objective world exist?' or 'Are numbers real?' If these latter questions were asked within the appropriate framework they would be trivial and their answers would have to be affirmative. So, according to Carnap, philosophers who suppose them to be non-trivial must be asking them outside any definite framework. But then, argued Carnap, they must be pseudo-questions because no rules have been specified in accordance with which they may be answered. Questions can indeed arise about a framework as a whole. But such questions are practical ones, not cognitive ones. We have certainly to make the choice whether or not to accept and use the forms of expression in a particular framework. But we do this, according to Carnap, on the basis of practical considerations. For example, the 'thing' language may be thought to have greater simplicity, efficiency, and fruitfulness than the language of 'sense-data'.[84]

Thus Carnap is to be seen as insisting that in discussing an epistemological issue philosophers should not seek their premises only from a viewpoint that is internal to some appropriate linguistic framework, but should also bear in mind what can or cannot be thought about the acceptability of the framework itself. It is only when this distinction has been properly clarified that we can understand the confusion that gives rise to the sceptic's doubts. In other words, we can then disregard the intuition on which the sceptic relies because we have brought out into the open its underlying conflation of two very different kinds of issue, where intuitions underwritten by the rules of the framework are relevant to one kind of issue and intuitions about the value of the framework are relevant to the other. The situation is analogous to the discovery that a hidden, uncontrolled variable has been interfering with the outcome of scientific experiment and, consequently, that observations of the outcome are unreliable evidence in relation to the hypothesis that the experiment was designed to test.

Something like this is also argued when philosophers distinguish, as (adapting an earlier distinction of Frege's) Austin taught many to do,[85]

---

[84] R. Carnap, *Meaning and Necessity, A Study in Semantics and Modal Logic*, Chicago: Chicago UP, enlarged edn., 1956, pp. 205-21.

[85] J. L. Austin, *How to Do Things with Words*, Oxford: OUP, 1962, pp. 94-163. See also H. P. Grice, 'The Causal Theory of Perception', *Proceedings of the Aristotelian Society*,

between the meaning of a word or sentence and the force, or forces, of its utterance. Here too, our intuition may have been misled hitherto by our failure to draw a relevant distinction. Thus Hare cited a number of sentences in which the word 'good' occurs in order to build an intuitive foundation for his argument that this word's meaning is to make a commendation,[86] and Toulmin argued analogously that the characteristic use of the word 'probably' is to qualify a commitment.[87] But, by directing attention to cases in which these words occur in the antecedents of conditional sentences, in indirect discourse, etc. Searle sought to show that they often occur without being able to make any commendation or qualify any commitment.[88] Searle argued therefore– in accordance with Austin's seminal idea–that we ought to distinguish the standard meaning that such a word has in any context from the commendatory, or commitment-qualifying, force that this meaning generates in simple, present-tense, categorical utterances like 'He is a good man' or 'Probably it will rain'. And in general, if Austin is right, we do well to disregard those intuitions about meaning that conflate the meaning of a word or sentence with the force or forces of its utterance. Indeed, those intuitions should then fade away as the power of Austin's examples is exercised on us and our intuitions become more sharply focused, either on the semantics of sentences, or on the pragmatics of speech-acts.

Moreover, just as the discovery of a hidden variable that is affecting experimental outcomes is often fruitful of further progress in natural science, so too Austin's work on speech-acts opened up yet further avenues for others to explore. We may note, for example, that Austin's enquiry into the forces of human utterances led him to discuss various kinds of felicity that an utterance might have in its context by virtue of its force.[89] As a result the assertibility of a statement may plausibly be distinguished from its truth-value, so that, as Stroud has claimed, 'someone might be fully justified in saying he knows some particular theory about the world around him without its being true that he does know that thing'.[90] A certain proposition might be reasonable for him

---

supp. vol. 35, 1961, pp. 126-32, and D. K. Lewis, 'Scorekeeping in a Language Game', *The Journal of Philosophical Logic*, 8, 1979, pp. 339-59.

[86] R. M. Hare, *The Language of Morals*, Oxford: OUP, 1952, pp. 79-136.

[87] S. Toulmin, 'Probability', *Proceedings of the Aristotelian Society*, supp. vol. 24, 1950, pp. 27-62.

[88] J. R. Searle, *Speech Acts: An Essay in the Philosophy of Language*, Cambridge: CUP, 1969, pp. 136-41.   [89] Op. cit., pp. 132-46.

[90] B. Stroud, *The Significance of Philosophical Scepticism*, Oxford: OUP, 1984, p. 63.

to believe, or satisfactory to accept, even though it is not actually true. In this way at least some kinds of anti-sceptical intuition, such as Moore's, may come to be legitimately discounted and disregarded, when the question that they purport to answer is appropriately subdivided into one question about the assertibility of a particular statement and another about its truth.

Nor is this pattern of inductive reasoning confined to cases in which one genre of confused intuition collapses into two sharper and more specialized genres. An intuition is also legitimately disregarded, and may even be replaceable by a contrary one, when it has been evoked by the description of an imaginary state of affairs, as an example of the presence of some characteristic or relation that is at issue, but the description is incomplete, or otherwise faulty, in some relevant respect. For example, Radford once supported the thesis that knowledge does not imply belief by describing an imaginary conversation in which one of the participants, Jean, gives a series of very hesitant, yet mostly correct, answers to questions about the dates of Tudor and Stuart monarchs.[91] Radford's story tends to evoke the intuition that Jean *knew* most of those dates (presumably because he, Jean, could not have got almost all of them right accidentally), together with the intuition that Jean did not *believe* that Elizabeth died in 1603, etc. (presumably because he was so hesitant about saying this). But the cogency of Radford's example is greatly reduced when we consider what might have happened if Jean had been asked the same questions one week later. If Jean tended to give the same answers on such a later occasion also, we might then be much more inclined to judge that he *believed* that Elizabeth died in 1603, etc. (since, whatever a person's hesitancy of manner, persistent assertion of the same proposition creates a presumption that he believes it). And if, on the later occasion, Jean tended to give different answers, we might then be inclined to think that he had no real *knowledge* of most of the dates (but got them right the first time by a lucky fluke). So, what has happened here is that a relevant issue–the issue about what would happen if Jean were asked the same question again–was left quite unexplored by the original experiment on our intuitions. Radford's story contained insufficient information to test out the robustness of our intuitions in relation to this variable. But, whatever way the story is suitably expanded, it can no longer elicit so readily the particular combination of intuitions that

[91] C. Radford, 'Knowledge by Examples', *Analysis*, 27, 1966, pp. 1-11.

is needed in order to support the thesis that knowledge does not imply belief.

Moreover, there is a third, and quite different, way in which awkward intuitions are sometimes discounted. When Carnap remarked that 'isolated intuitive judgements are often unreliable',[92] he had in mind the difficulty of constructing any systematic analysis of, say, confirmation without having to ignore some discordant intuitions while so doing. Analogously, Galileo disregarded the effects of atmospheric friction, etc. when he hypothesized a rate of acceleration for falling bodies. This is the method of idealization–of which Euclidean geometry was perhaps the first important example, with its theorems about points that have position without magnitude, or about lines that have length without breadth. It is the frequent use of this method in natural science that lies behind the claims of philosophers like Cartwright that the fundamental laws of physics are false to the facts.[93] And the more precise and systematic a philosophical recon-struction is, the more likely it is to have made–intentionally or unintentionally–some analogous abstractions and idealizations. For example, David Lewis's account of how linguistic meaning can derive from social conventions[94] pays no attention to the operation of emotive meanings, as when the use of certain expressions tends to evoke feelings of contempt or disgust for what they designate–by virtue of the associations that have built up around those expres-sions.[95] To accept Lewis's theory one needs to disregard the intuition that possession of such a causally emotive power is often a reason for the use of one particular expression rather than another. But Lewis's theory does at least supply a plausible account of how meaningful language is possible in an emotionless speech-community. Similarly both Leibniz[96] and several modern philosophers, like Russell,[97] have put forward various analyses in the form of theories about the syntax or semantics of a (logically or scientifically) ideal language. But in doing so they have necessarily had to override many intuitions about

[92] 'Replies and Expositions', p. 994.
[93] N. Cartwright, *How the Laws of Physics Lie*, Oxford: OUP, 1983, pp. 54-73.
[94] D. K. Lewis, *Convention: A Philosophical Study*, Cambridge, Mass: Harvard UP, 1969.
[95] Cf. C. K. Ogden and I. A. Richards, *The Meaning of Meaning*, London: Routledge and Kegan Paul, 10th edn., 1949, pp. 231-42.
[96] See R. M. Yost, *Leibniz and Philosophical Analysis*, Berkeley: California UP, 1954.
[97] See B. Russell, 'The Philosophy of Logical Atomism', *The Monist*, 28, 1918, p. 520.

how words actually function in our practically-oriented natural languages.

Nevertheless, despite the existence of these three ways of discounting intuitions, we may sometimes face an apparent conflict of intuitions that is best resolved, not so much by our disregarding some or all of the conflicting intuitions, but rather by reformulating or reinterpreting some of the generalizations that may claim their support. For example, suppose you accept the rule (of so-called 'strict implication') that if p-and-not-q is self-contradictory, then q is deducible from p, and suppose you accept this rule because you find such a judgement intuitively convincing in a variety of individual cases. Your rule then implies that for any q whatever, if p is self-contradictory, q is deducible from p (since p-and-not-q will also be self-contradictory whenever p is). So are you just to disregard the conflicting intuition that, say, 'It will rain to-morrow' is surely not deducible from 'Sheep are not sheep'?

Such intuitions seem altogether too robust to be easily schooled into silence. One possible move, therefore, might be to qualify your criterion of deducibility by a requirement that p must be suitably relevant to q, along some such lines as those followed by Anderson and Belnap.[98] Or you might instead insist on distinguishing between a rule of deducibility and its conditions of application. Then perhaps, you can claim, like Pap,[99] that it is part of the conditions of application for any rule of the form 'When the relation between p and q is R, then q is deducible from p' that it should be possible to conceive the truth of p, since in applying the rule we need to be able to think 'If p is true, then q is also.' It follows that a particular q may be said to be 'deducible' from a particular p in the relatively weak sense in which this means that there is a rule that licenses the deduction, but at the same time 'not deducible' from that p in the rather stronger sense in which this means that the conditions for applying the relevant rule can never be satisfied. Once the latent ambiguity is brought out into the open you can claim that, when properly understood, your intuitions here are not in conflict with one another at all. In the weaker sense of 'deducible' anything whatever is indeed deducible from a self-contradictory premiss: in the stronger sense it is not. But, if for this

---

[98] See, for example, A. R. Anderson and N. D. Belnap, Jr., *Entailment: The Logic of Relevance and Necessity*, Princeton, NJ: Princeton UP, 1975.

[99] A. Pap, 'Strict Implication, Entailment and Modal Iteration', *The Philosophical Review*, 64, 1955, pp. 604-13.

reason you prefer to theorize about deducibility only in the stronger, reinterpreted sense, you must be prepared to pay the price. No deductions by *reductio ad absurdum* will be possible.

Thus any philosophical generalization that a philosopher supports by inductive reasoning needs to be thought capable of eventual revision, in order to fit into a statable system of principles that are consistent both with one another and with all his replicable singular intuitions. If at any one time the principles of reason are not delineated in too dogmatic and conclusive a manner, the prospect of eliminating any conflict of intuitions is left open. In other words, so far as we reason inductively we should be fallibilists in our philosophy as well as in our science. For example, if we are to reason inductively, what is sometimes called the 'rationalist' position in ethics[100]–the thesis that equally important moral rules never conflict in particular cases–is tenable only if it is thought of as stating a regulative ideal that guides the indefinite improvement of our ethical system, rather than as describing a kind of theory that we may at some stage be confident of having reached. At the same time, however, we have to remember that, as in natural science, when some proviso or qualification is forced on us by the data, the theory thus modified will carry much greater conviction if the modification can also be shown to have an independent rationale. Inductive reasoners sometimes build into their theory a sequence of *ad hoc*, uncorroborated responses to counter-examples which are warranted by no other virtue than that of being a means to ward off falsification. When this happens in science Lakatos stigmatized it as a 'degenerating problem-shift',[101] and Schlesinger has rightly deprecated it in analytical philosophy.[102]

Finally, we must also admit that an awkwardly unexplained or discordant intuition may sometimes remain with us just because we have, so far, found no adequate grounds for rejecting it. Such an intuition is analogous to the continued observation of some puzzling and anomalous phenomenon in natural science, for which we still seek a satisfactory explanation. For example, that is how Stroud treats his

---

[100] e.g. A. Donagan, 'Consistency in Rational Moral Systems', *The Journal of Philosophy*, 81, 1984, pp. 291-309.

[101] I. Lakatos, 'Falsificationism and the Methodology of Scientific Research Programmes', in I. Lakatos and A. E. Musgrave (eds.), *Criticism and the Growth of Knowledge*, Cambridge: CUP, 1970, p. 118.

[102] G. Schlesinger, 'The Method of Counterexample', in J. H. Fetzer (ed.), *Principles of Philosophical Reasoning*, Totowa, NJ: Rowman and Allanheld, 1984, pp. 151-71.

intuition of the possibility that he is dreaming:[103] he feels that he has to leave the case for scepticism as yet unrefuted. And that was how Newtonians had to treat the motion of the apsides of the moon until Clairaut showed its derivability from Newton's laws,[104] and how they had to go on treating certain features of the perihelion of Mercury. But the known existence of a counter-instance need not be taken as forcing the inductive validity of a generalization down to zero. A zero value is unavoidable under those conditions, if inductive validity is measured in terms of mathematical probability.[105] But if inductive reasoning is conceived on Baconian lines a theory may, in appropriate circumstances, be attributed a non-zero level of support from available evidence, even when that evidence is known to include anomalies.[106] This was certainly how Newtonian mechanics was treated for a couple of centuries, because the enormously wide range of phenomena to which it did apply greatly outweighed the few anomalies that stood against it. And in a moral dilemma such as Williams describes you may quite consistently have felt a predominance of inclination towards your chosen principle of conduct even though you still retain a lingering regret that you rejected a course of action which was not without merit.[107] Analogously, even if an intuition like Stroud's remains to count against your own particular, anti-sceptical position, that position could still be a fairly strong one if it enjoys a wide range of support from other kinds of intuition.

§ 12 WHY DO ANALYTICAL PHILOSOPHERS DISAGREE?

Summary. The divergences of theory that are a characteristic feature of analytical philosophy are quite compatible with rationality of dialogue. They are attributable partly to differences of basic intuition and partly to the inevitable under-determination of general philosophical theories by particular intuitive data. So progress here is not measured by consensus.

Even though the premisses sanctioned by a philosopher's intuitions are not at his beck and call (see § 10), and are implicitly claimed, when he cites them, to be shared by all right-thinking people, they may not

---

[103] Op. cit., pp. 272-3.
[104] See the appendix by Florian Cajori in I. Newton, *Mathematical Principles of Natural Philosophy* (trans. A. Motte), Berkeley: California UP, 1962, p. 650.
[105] Cohen, *The Probable and the Provable*, pp. 188-90.
[106] Ibid., pp. 162-6.   [107] Cf. 'Moral Luck', p. 127.

in fact be shared by anyone else at all. And certainly they do not describe publicly observable events or regularities, like the data of scientific enquiry. Nor are they even embodied in publicly available pronouncements, as are the premises of jurisprudential induction. But this absence of indisputable objectivity does not matter. It would, indeed, matter if analytical philosophers should be expected to converge towards consensus in respect of *any* problems they investigate. But in fact, as pointed out in § 3, it is divergence, not convergence, that has marked the development of analytical philosophy in the past thirty years, where many fundamental philosophical issues are concerned. As the movement has expanded to take in wider circles of cultural influence, more and more of the traditional controversies have reappeared within an analytical framework. Holism has again raised its standard against atomism, essentialism against conventionalism, realism against phenomenalism, religionism against positivism. So a theory about the nature of analytical philosophy should be able to explain such divergence.

One source of divergence obviously lies in interpersonal differences of intuition, whether these be about general or particular issues, whether the reasonings that they ground are inductive or deductive, and whether the differences be differences of intuition about the same issues or differences in the issues about which different people have intuitions. For example, I for one do not share several of Carnap's intuitions about the measurement of confirmation in experimental science. So I can at best accept Carnap's conclusions only hypothetically not categorically. But from a third party's point of view that does not serve to falsify Carnap's theory of confirmation, let alone show it to be worthless. The theory may still be categorically acceptable to those who share Carnap's intuitions and believe that they can discern a field to which these intuitions apply.

Indeed, an analytical philosopher normally tries to choose just those examples and illustrations that will get his readers to share his own intuitions. Russell recognized this when he wrote 'Philosophical argument, strictly speaking, consists mainly of an endeavour to cause the reader to perceive what has been perceived by the author.'[108] In the process, as we saw in § 11, the reader's old intuitions may be replaced by new ones. But was Russell right to suggest that the connection between a philosopher's citation of some relevantly authoritative

[108] B. Russell, *The Principles of Mathematics*, London: Allen and Unwin, 2nd edn., 1937, p. 130.

scientific paradigm and the assertion of his own analytical thesis is largely a non-rational one? Does a description of Newton's work on colour refraction, for example, or of von Frisch's work on bees function only to help cause assent to a thesis about the structure of experimental reasoning, without giving it any logical support? On the other hand, if we allow such a citation to provide logical support for the thesis, are we not treating this thesis as a historical or sociological account of what certain kinds of people have taken as a reason for what, rather than as a philosophical account of what *is* a reason for what?

The answer to these questions is that, as we saw in § 9, an analytical philosopher of science must come intuitively to share an influential scientist's judgement before he is entitled to cite it categorically as a premiss for his inductive reasoning in support of an analytical generalization. Moreover, even where influential scientists differ, he cannot afford to ignore all of their judgements altogether without running the risk of replacing the quest for valid and fruitful principles of existing scientific thought by the quest for a new and idiosyncratic system of his own. So, first, a few well-chosen exemplars of authoritative, scientific reasoning serve to identify the target of the analytical enquiry. And, secondly, for each such exemplary judgement that is cited a presumption of correctness operates–at least if a categorical philosophical analysis is being attempted rather than a hypothetical one. In other words a citation of the selected exemplars is not just causally and non-rationally connected with acceptance of the analysis, nor, on the other hand, does it in itself state inductive evidence in relation to this acceptance. Instead, there is an unavoidable presumption of correctness in each case, to be checked against the philosopher's intuition, and where a philosopher's analytical generalization fails to conform with this presumption he owes an explanation to his readers.

It is, therefore, a serious criticism of Carnap's 1950 theory about the confirmation of scientific hypotheses, for example, that he nowhere seeks to compare his own intuitions with exemplars from the history of science, or to apply his analysis to such concrete instances of scientific achievement. The only concrete application of his theory that he actually explores is with regard to the evidential confirmation of hypotheses about the winners of imaginary chess tournaments,[109] which is scarcely a central or typical subject of scientific enquiry. Indeed, if he

---

[109] *Logical Foundations of Probability*, pp. 382-6 and 394-6.

had attended to the structure of any major exemplar of experimental reasoning, like Newton's work on refraction or von Frisch's on bees, he would have had to make fundamental alterations to his own system.[110]

In regard to the meaning of a word in ordinary speech, of course, as in regard to the grammaticality of a sentence, there are no authoritative speakers within the relevant speech-community. Modern linguistics does not assign a normative status to the speech of kings or courtiers, or to the writings of classical authors. The intuitions of any one native speaker of a particular natural language deserve as much respect as those of any other. These speakers may not both be equally good at contriving explicit formulations of their intuitions, but in any case the evidence of their practice is available. So, where such native speakers' intuitions differ, linguists have to hypothesize dialectal or even idiolectal peculiarities. This reconciles the differences of intuitions.

But philosophical analysis is a normative activity. So, where people differ in their intuitions about a concept–e.g. in their intuitions about what is implicit in some identified word-meaning, like the meaning of 'the' in definite descriptions–their intuitions may support opposing analytical theories. And an analogous point can be made about ethical intuitions, at any rate by those who do not attach especial value to the intuitions of people whom they suppose to be endowed with some religious authority. Nevertheless, philosophers need to bear in mind that to publish philosophical arguments based on one's own intuitions is a worthwhile activity only if it is reasonable to expect that a substantial part of one's reading public will share most of those intuitions. The eccentricity of a person's intuitions does not invalidate them as a basis for philosophical argument.[111] The system based on them is still *his* philosophy. But a pragmatic constraint operates. Construction of the system may be judged a waste of effort if its key intuitions are not widely shared and it does not have sufficient common ground or subject-matter to attract other philosophers into dialogue. The more marginal it is to the continuing dialogue, the less historical importance it will have.

Two considerations normally help, however, to ensure that, if a philosopher constructs novel and coherent arguments on the basis of

---

[110] Cf. Cohen, *The Probable and the Provable*, pp. 129-32, 147 and 149.

[111] *Pace*, in the case of semantic intuitions, Arne Naess, *Interpretation and Preciseness*, Oslo: J. Dyburad, 1953, pp. vii-xiv.

his own robust intuitions, the publication of his arguments will make an effective contribution to the pertinent dialogue.

The first consideration is that whatever genetic or cultural factors explain the author's own intuitions will usually bear also on the judgements of many other people. Indeed, if it were possible to count comparable units of judgement in any major area of human thought, one would normally expect only a few of a person's intuitions, if any, to be echoed by those of no other people, quite a lot to be echoed by those of many others, and the great majority to be echoed by those of almost everyone else in the same culture, especially where elementary logical or arithmetical issues are involved. How else could we live together? Admittedly some psychologists have claimed that very many people are systematically prone to fallacious judgements on certain elementary logical or mathematical issues. These psychologists have thus implied the existence of widespread disagreement on such issues–disagreement between correct and incorrect reasoners. But we shall see later (§§ 15-19) that there is no substance in these claims or their implications. If there is any kind of issue about which replicable disagreements of intuition are relatively likely, it concerns rather the application of this or that familiar concept to imaginary cases with novel or unfamiliar characteristics–such as when questions are asked about brains in vats or about look-alike Earths.

The other relevant consideration is that, even where different participants in a philosophical dialogue do not share the same intuitions in regard to the premisses of categorical argument, the hypothetical formulation of the argument may still be acceptable to all of them. If they have enough logic in common, they may appreciate the strength or validity of the argument, even though they do not share all its premisses. For example, whether or not they have intuitions that sustain a utilitarian ethic, they might accept some of Lyons's arguments about the relationships between different forms of act-utilitarianism and rule-utilitarianism.[112] The hypothetical mode of procedure is thus especially well adapted to dialogue on topics where there is a shortage of agreed data. And it can make a substantial contribution to philosophical awareness by clarifying the interconnections between different elements in the analytical options at issue. Indeed, this is probably one of the most important ways in which philosophers can learn from one another and improve the overall quality of their dialogue. It is also a way in which widespread

---

[112] D. Lyons, *Forms and Limits of Utilitarianism*, Oxford: OUP, 1965.

agreement may be reached that such-and-such a combination of theses is untenable or that such-and-such a thesis needs qualification or that such-and-such an argument needs supplementation. One good example of this was the reaction to Prior's brilliantly ironical treatment of the concept of analytically valid inference,[113] where he demonstrated that, *if* an inference needs no more than analytic validity, *then* we can infer anything from anything.

Nor are conflicts of intuition the only, let alone the most interesting, source of legitimate divergence in philosophical conclusions. Sometimes, in otherwise well-constructed deductive arguments, this divergence stems from variations in the kinds of premises selected, as when one moral philosopher starts from intuitions about meanings and another from intuitions about conduct. Sometimes divergence stems from an underlying difference in the degree of importance attached to simplicity of systematization. Supporters of ordinary language analysis, for example, may think that Strawson's account of definite descriptions is not disadvantaged by needing a three-valued logic for its formalization.[114]

Moreover, we have to remember also, once we accept the possibility of inductive reasoning within analytical philosophy, that inductive extrapolations are always underdetermined by their data. In such induction about matters of fact Goodman's 'grue' paradox,[115] like the problem of selecting a curve-function to fit a finite set of points, illustrates how there are always indefinitely many general hypotheses that we can take to be supported by the same set of particular data within their domain. An analogous problem arises in jurisprudence about how to extract the *ratio decidendi*–the relevant legal rule–from particular common law judgements. In any kind of extrapolating induction the problem is always how to pick out, from among the features that run through all the evidential items, those features that are to be held relevant to the task of analogizing or generalization. The only way to narrow down and justify this choice is by deduction from some prior constraint, resting on previously determined knowledge or policy, such as a restriction on the terminology or content of acceptable hypotheses, or a commitment to sufficiently specific criteria of comparative simplicity, or a regard for certain practical, evaluative, or

---

[113] A. N. Prior, 'The Runabout Inference Ticket', *Analysis*, 21, 1960, pp. 38-9.
[114] See E. J. Lemmon, 'Quantifying and Modal Operators', *Proceedings of the Aristotelian Society*, 58, 1958, pp. 245-68.
[115] *Fact, Fiction and Forecast*, pp. 74-5.

ontological considerations. And in induction about philosophical issues any such relatively a priori constraint–like a requirement for theories of substance and personal identity to be consistent with some particular religious beliefs about transubstantiation and immortality– is bound to be much more controversial than this kind of restraint would be in natural science or jurisprudence, because it would itself be sanctioned only by intuition, faith, or assumption and not by previous experience or agreed public policy.

So, even if everyone so far had similar deliverances of conscience in similar moral quandaries, similar intuitions about how to assess the evidential value of a particular experimental test on a particular hypo- thesis, similar perceptions of sense or nonsense in particular utter- ances, similar discountings of intuitions (as in § 11), and so on–even then there would still be indefinitely much room for variation in inductively supported resolutions of the same philosophical problem. We can certainly understand here why, as already argued in § 3, the objectivity of facts about linguistic practice could never suffice to guarantee eventual philosophical consensus. And, in general, rea- soned co-operation in the details of everyday life is quite compatible with deep philosophical disagreement. Indeed, the possibility of agreement as the eventual outcome of a rational dialogue between two analytical philosophers rests on the existence of a quite extensive range of prior agreement between them about the general and par- ticular issues concerned. And even a very small number of funda- mental disagreements may generate widely divergent treatments of the same issues. Kuipers, for example, has discussed the question: how should philosophers of science explicate the intuition that we get diminishing returns from repeated tests and the intuition that new kinds of test have superior value to old kinds? He has argued that these intuitions can be justified by reference to the theory of probability, just as well as by invoking the expectations of future events that are en- gendered by past experience. But Kuipers' argument will not satisfy his Popperian opponents, who have principled objections to both forms of justification in the epistemology of science.[116]

Nevertheless, its inevitable lack of interpersonal objectivity does not render philosophy incapable of rational argument. Rather, the

[116] T. A. K. Kuipers, 'Non-Inductive Explication of Two Inductive Intuitions', *The British Journal for the Philosophy of Science*, 34, 1983, pp. 209-23, and D. Miller, 'Can Science do without Induction?' in L. J. Cohen and M. Hesse (eds.), *Applications of Inductive Logic*, Oxford: OUP, 1980, pp. 109-29.

need for premises on which cogent arguments may be built, or for acceptable principles of inference, forces philosophy into the framework of dialogue. Since such philosophical premises or principles cannot be rooted in independent facts, like the experimental data that are used to check scientific hypotheses, they must instead be rooted in anticipated concessions by those who are parties to the dispute. So a categorical philosophical argument, whether deductive or inductive, is inevitably addressed to actual or potential participants in the same dialogue, in the hope or expectation that at crucial points it will encounter intuitions matching those of its author, whereas a scientific argument need have no such addresses because it does not rest on intuitions. Cogent philosophical argument is always *ad hominem* at certain points, in a way that cogent scientific argument need not be. That is why the history of analytical philosophy is peculiarly the history of a dialogue, not of a succession of monologues. And that is also why it is wrong to claim that, because in practice justificatory arguments always give out at some stage, it is pointless to offer any of them. A person who asks for a reason for something ought to be willing to state what kinds of propositions he does accept, in order to allow at least the possibility of there being some pragmatically adequate (e.g. locally acceptable) premises for the justification that he requests. Otherwise his request does not have to be taken seriously.

Indeed, at bottom, it is because of this *ad hominem* quality that analytical philosophy is sometimes said to be an activity rather than a system of propositions. Other schools—Thomist, Kantian, Hegelian, Marxist, phenomenologist, existentialist, and so on—come out each with its own core of shared doctrine and self-satisfied consensus. But the school of analytical philosophy issues instead, on topic after topic, in a motley jumble of opposed reasonings, where each philosopher's line of argument runs *from* what many others think a rather selective subset of the very wide variety of actual or possible intuitions *to* what many others think a rather idiosyncratic set of clarifications and explanations. It is tempting, therefore, to suppose that the point of the enterprise lies in the process rather than the product. But, despite the absence of consensus about premises or conclusions, each exercise in analytical philosophy is nevertheless intended as a piece of reasoning. So, even if philosophical achievement were to be equated with the activity of producing such an exercise instead of with the finished product, its content would still have to admit of reconstruction as a rationally coherent system of propositions in appropriate deductive or inductive relationships to one another. Characterization of an analytical achievement would still be parasitical on the articulation of such a system.

Schlick seems to have thought otherwise. At least he argued that the analysis of a meaning should not be regarded as consisting in a system of propositions, because the meaning of any analytical proposition is itself a matter for analysis.[117] But, because philosophy proceeds within the framework of a dialogue, it can normally build on anticipated concessions of intelligibility. So in practice Schlick's argument has no force.

Perhaps someone will object instead that I am wrong to treat divergence as normal, and convergence as abnormal, in my account of analytical philosophy. 'You are too pessimistic', it may be said. 'Why should not the practice of philosophy lead in the end to a broad unanimity in intuitions about what is a reason for what and also to a broad agreement about the best way to systematize those intuitions? And would not this be the final attainment of fundamental truth?

There are three points that need to be made in reply to such an objection.

The first concerns the facts. Claims about what may happen 'in the end' have no definite reference. So, if we are to take the objection seriously, we must assign its reference to some actual date. Suppose instead, therefore, that analytical philosophers reverted after a century (or two centuries, or three) to some fairly high level of consensus, and began to disagree, like most scientists, only about minor issues or new problems. The fact is that on the evidence of what has happened in the present century we should not expect this period of consensus to last for long, if social conditions for free intellectual discussion still exist.

Secondly, suppose that the evidence of what has happened in the past century (and in twenty-three previous ones, and in all attempts hitherto to set philosophy 'on the sure path of a science'[118]) is somehow unrepresentative, so that in fact this eventual consensus persists for centuries even under conditions of free discussion. Well, that would still be consistent with the present account of the structure and subject-matter of analytical philosophy. Analytical philosophy would still involve deductive and inductive reasoning about what is a

---

[117] M. Schlick, 'The Future of Philosophy (1931)' in id., *Philosophical Papers*, vol. 2, p. 220.

[118] I. Kant, *Critique of Pure Reason*, Riga: Hartknoch, 1787, preface to 2nd edn. (trans. N. K. Smith, London: Macmillan, 1950).

reason for what. And continuance of consensus could still not be taken as a sign that 'fundamental truth' had been attained. Even in mathematics and natural science long-lasting consensus is notoriously not a sign that fundamental truth has been attained.

Thirdly, it is by no means self-evident that the view to be called 'pessimistic' here is the one that expects no lasting consensus. One might instead regard this as the optimistic view, if one thinks that continued discussion of a rich diversity of inductively and deductively well-reasoned theories is as much a sign of progress and vitality in philosophical dialogue as continued variation in creative styles is a sign of progress and vitality in art, music, or literature. Think of analytical philosophy here as being rather like mathematics or natural science, and you cannot regard eventual consensus as inherently undesirable. Think of it instead (whatever its analogies elsewhere with the sciences) as being, on the matter of consensus, rather like art, music, or literature, and you may well regard eventual consensus as inherently undesirable. Admittedly, any careful exponent of a properly grounded categorical argument must assume that another philosopher's failure to agree with his conclusion is some kind of a defect and that failure to treat his argument as at least hypothetically valid is an even worse one. But to assume thus that consensus about certain philosophical arguments is desirable is quite different from supposing that consensus about every philosophical argument is desirable. One can hold firmly to this or that side of the debate on one or more substantive philosophical issues while still remaining a pluralist in one's metaphilosophy at large (as is further argued in § 19 below). For example, one might feel committed to the categorical validity of certain fundamental logical principles, while attaching a high value to the co-existence of conflicting philosophical doctrines about political society.

In the end, then, popular parlance is right in assuming that everyone is logically entitled to his own philosophy–his own self consciously accepted system of principles and priorities–even where, as in the philosophy of science, part of this system ought also to echo certain others' intuitions. If, for reasons already given, it is in the very nature of analytical philosophy to admit of divergent conclusions about fundamental issues, we should not regard the occasional outbreaks of consensus that occur in this or that circle of acquaintance as signs of progress. The school of fawning disciples that sometimes collects around a powerful philosophical mind does little to advance the subject. Rather (as suggested already in § 1) we should measure progress in a particular problem-area by the quality of the dialogue: i.e. by the diversity of well-reasoned solutions that have been proposed, and by the thoroughness, accuracy, imaginativeness, and sophistication with which the implications and presuppositions of particular solutions have been explored (and often even agreed) so that the choice of solution has been opened up to the possibility of rational decision. In philosophy, as in art, it is the originality and professionalism of a contribution that count, not the number of its imitators. And when virtual unanimity about most fundamental principles appears inevitable within an interconnected group of problems we should salute this event as heralding the birth of a new science rather than as constituting a new sign of maturity in the already long-established discipline of philosophy. To complain, as Kekes does, that in 2,500 years 'it is impossible to find a single instance of philosophical knowledge'[119] reflects a profound misperception of the nature of philosophy, or at least of analytical philosophy. If there is still no agreed knowledge about 'whether there is a spiritual element in reality, what things are good or bad, how to live well, whether anything exists that we cannot observe, whether human beings are determined or free, what sort of society is the best, and so on',[120] then that is at least one reason for supposing the hope for such so-called 'knowledge' to be a will-o'-the-wisp.

But to speak thus in favour of overall philosophical pluralism we have to evaluate for the moment from an external point of view. We have to speak *about* the self-conscious choice of a system of principles and priorities that each philosopher has to make, rather than *from within* the particular system that is actually or potentially our own and is in conflict with the systems of many others. We have to consult our intuitions about the methods and purposes of analytical philosophy, and to feed those intuitions with an adequate list of examples and illustrations from recent philosophical history (compare the relation between history and philosophy of science described on pp. 86 and 109), while ignoring as far as possible our intuitions on controversial issues of substance. We cannot ignore altogether any issues of substance that bear directly on metaphilosophical problems, such as questions about intuition or tacit reasoning. But we can certainly avoid commitment to the familiar causes, like positivism, nominalism, or conventionalism, with which analytical philosophy has often been wrongly identified.

[119] *The Nature of Philosophy*, p. 4.   [120] Ibid., p. 5.

§ 13 IS PHILOSOPHY OF SCIENCE AN EMPIRICAL ENQUIRY?

Summary. It may be objected that appeals to empirical, scientific tests can and should replace philosophical appeals to intuition. This objection is valid against the claims of certain logical positivist philosophers to be able to develop a priori global criteria of demarcation, explanation, and confirmation. But the historicist reaction to those claims ignored the possibility of shifting the focus of philosophical generalization.

'Human knowledge' it may be said, 'has progressed enormously since the seventeenth century as a result of the systematic submission of new theories to empirical tests. Appeals to conscience may still be in order in ethics. But it is too late to put the clock back by supposing that there is a potential body of knowledge about reasoning, called "analytical philosophy of science", which can emerge from tests against intuition rather than observation. No room exists here for competition with empirical enquiry, though the relevant empirical enquiry may be part either of science itself or of the history or sociology of science.'

This objection does have force against the curious tendency that existed for a while in modern analytical philosophy to treat certain kinds of scientific problem as philosophical rather than scientific issues. That tendency owed its origin to the apparent paradigm afforded, in the earlier part of the present century, by the recent achievements of Frege and Russell in the logical analysis of mathematical concepts and their purported derivation of all classical mathematics from purely logical principles. To many in the generation of the Vienna Circle the epistemology of mathematics appeared as a relatively well-advanced and well-understood subject which the epistemology of science would do well to emulate. So, since Frege and Russell claimed to have formulated the fundamental laws of numerical reasoning in logical terminology as an unchallengeable set of a priori truths, it was natural that Schlick, Carnap, Hempel, and others should seek to achieve as similar a result as they could for scientific reasoning.

First, there was the problem of how to demarcate the frontiers of cognitive respectability. The aim here was to distinguish genuinely scientific hypotheses from metaphysical and transcendental ones, and the solution of the problem was sought in an a priori criterion of empirical verifiability. Thus Ayer wanted to formulate his criterion in the jejune vocabulary of formal logic, augmented solely by the

epistemological concept of an 'observation-statement'.[121] The project
ran into a morass of probably insuperable technical difficulties and
was abandoned because of them.[122] But what was also wrong was not
only that the project was inherently prejudiced against analogically
based meanings and realist analyses of scientific theory (as already
noted in § 4 above), but also that it was largely misdirected as a
contribution to the philosophy of scientific reasoning. The problems
about cognitive significance or respectability that mostly engage
modern scientists' attention are not ones that are capable of armchair
solution by philosophers. New laboratory instruments, new chemical
tests, more powerful computers or rocketry–these are the means that
scientists use to solve their problems of cognitive significance by
converting untestable hypotheses into testable ones. Just to emphasize
the epistemological centrality of observation was perhaps a valuable
and progressive move in the age of Locke and Hume, when modern
science was still not yet fully established and appeals to observation
needed to be favourably contrasted with appeals to authority or
revelation. But in the twentieth century, when the intellectual
credentials of science are no longer a crucial issue, we need a more
sophisticated conception of the problem of cognitive respectability.
The important problems of demarcation need to be thought of as
being *within* science, not *about* it. In this perspective it is not so much
empiricism that sets limits to respectable scientific enquiry, as the
logical positivists supposed. Rather, it is science that progressively
pushes back the horizons of empiricism by developing new techniques
for testing hypotheses. So, in order to demarcate the frontiers of
cognitive respectability, we need, in practice, to assume a plurality of
changing criteria that differ according to the field of enquiry and the
current state of progress in experimental gadgetry and other relevant
technology, rather than a single eternal principle. We assume a
plurality of specific constraints on the formation of hypotheses and
cannot derive those detailed assumptions from any general requirement about testability.

An analogous point can be made in regard to the problem of how to
gauge the value of a scientific explanation. Here again the problem
was viewed as calling for an a priori, once-and-for-all solution by

---

[121] *Language, Truth and Logic*, 2nd edn., 1946, p. 11.
[122] M. L. Pokriefka, 'Ayer's Definition of Empirical Significance Revisited', *Analysis*,
43, 1983, pp. 166-70, and 'More on Empirical Significance', *Analysis*, 44, 1983, pp. 92-3.

philosophers. So Hempel and Oppenheim,[123] on the basis of their relevant intuitions, proposed to define a numerical measure for the explanatory or predictive power of a scientific theory, and this measure, defined in purely logical and mathematical terms, was to be of quite general application. Yet the history of science is replete with examples of scientists' finding, as a result of new discoveries, that some existing theory has more, or less, explanatory power than it was previously supposed to have. Every attempt to use a theory to explain something is also a test of the theory's validity or range of application. Experimental investigations into the properties of subatomic particles, for example, have long since shown that classical mechanics is less comprehensive in its explanatory scope than would otherwse have been apparent. Scientifically important problems about explanatory power thus have an irreducibly local and empirical element in them: they do not admit of a priori solution by philosophers in terms of a global measure for logical content.

A third form of the same tendency is to be found in discussions of how to evaluate the support given by empirical evidence to scientific hypotheses. In 1950 Carnap's highly influential treatise on the subject[124] assumed that the problem was soluble by an inductive logic that would generate theorems with the same a priori status as those of the classical deductive logic constructed by Frege and Russell. An assignment of a value to a confirmation-function for given arguments, i.e. an assessment of the degree to which one specified proposition confirms another, was to be treated as an analytic proposition. It was to be derivable from intuitively valid axioms, that *inter alia* selected a preferred measure for the range of possible worlds in which a proposition is true, and it would not be open to correction in the light of new scientific knowledge. Nor was this measure expected to vary in any way with the subject-matter of enquiry.

Yet here too the judgements that scientists actually make require a different epistemology (as already remarked in § 2). For example, the results of the original tests on thalidomide seemed to support the hypothesis that it was safe to use. We now know, as a result of many tragic events, that this was a mistake, in that the pregnancy or non-pregnancy of the subjects on whom the drug was tested was not put at issue and there was therefore no controlled experiment to test whether the drug had teratogenic properties. It was thus an empirical discovery

---

[123] Op. cit.
[124] *Logical Foundations of Probability*.

that revealed the incorrectness of earlier judgements about the strength of support that the original evidence provided. And, in general, criteria for assessing the experimentally attested reliability of a scientific hypothesis in pharmacology or elsewhere can be expected to improve *pari passu* with the advancement of knowledge in that particular field. The validity of these criteria is relative to their field of application and the state of background knowledge at the time. Such criteria are not to be thought of as globally valid–as timeless and unchanging truths of logic that can be excogitated by the mathematical ingenuity of philosophers. Carnap thought of his confirmation-measures in relation to a given scientific vocabulary which determined the variety of possible worlds to be taken into account. He seems not to have recognized that the validity of such measures depended, at least in part, on whether or not the contents of this vocabulary were in fact relevant, and their weighting appropriate, to the various aspects of nature with which the measures were concerned. And that fault, typifying Carnap's a priori approach to the problem, has been inherited by Hintikka[125] and his school. For example, Niiniluoto and Tuomela[126] have written about differences between confirmation-assessments in richer and poorer sub-languages, but in doing so they have said nothing about how we may, or should, decide which sub-language is safe to use for a particular task, or about when we need to modify or enrich the sub-language already in use.

Against this mistakenly a priorist tendency in analytical philosophy of science an excessive reaction became apparent among some thinkers in North America in the 1950s and 1960s. Historical or socio-logical knowledge, not intuition, was now supposed to play the crucial role. The formal and schematic logical analyses of scientific reasoning that had emulated Frege-Russell paradigms were replaced by an insistence on the value of concrete factual studies of actual incidents in the development of modern science. Emphasis was placed on differences rather than similarities, whether these were between different sciences, between different schools, or between different phases of development. It was now claimed to be a vice, not a virtue, to seek a single system of abstract principles for the appraisal and evaluation of all scientific theories. All was now seen to be flux, where previously the unchanging laws of logic and mathematics were supposed to

[125] 'A Two-Dimensional Continuum of Inductive Methods', loc. cit.
[126] I. Niiniluoto and R. Tuomela, *Theoretical Concepts and Hypothetico-Inductive Inference*, Dordrecht: Reidel, 1973, pp. 165-96.

operate. At the same time stress was often laid on the fact that scientific enquiry is not just an activity of the intellect but also of the imagination, and not just a mental but also an institutional activity, depending for its very existence on an appropriate framework of universities, research establishments, fund administrations, learned societies, academic journals, international conferences, and so on.

Thus Hanson asserted that 'profitable philosophical discussion of any science depends on a thorough familiarity with its history and its present state'.[127] The proper way to discuss methodology was to consider the methodological issues that arose in the stage-by-stage development of, say, modern particle-physics. It was the process of scientific discovery that interested Hanson, not the propositional articulation of what is discovered, nor the analysis of the logical relationship between experimental premises and theoretical conclusions. But the trouble with this kind of treatment is that it drifts on descriptively from one anecdote to another, like a botanist collecting specimens: it does not help us to a deeper understanding of what is common to different scientific discoveries. Just as botanical collecting needs to be complemented by plant-physiology, so too, in the epistemology of science, historical descriptions need to be complemented by philosophical elucidations.

Indeed, from Hanson's position it was not a big jump to the view that each epoch or school of scientific enquiry may be judged by its own standards. So the proper role of historians of science was characterized by Kuhn in these words: 'Rather than seeking the paramount contributions of an older science to our present vintage, they attempt to display the historic integrity of that science in its own time as the creation of a revolutionary new paradigm.'[128] Correspondingly the replacement of one major theory by another cannot be adequately accounted for in terms of some single, self-conscious methodology. 'Because scientists are reasonable men', wrote Kuhn, 'one or another argument will ultimately persuade many of them. But there is no single argument that can or should persuade them all.'[129]

Kuhn's philosophy of science does not press very far into the subject-matter of its enquiry. Even if it were true that no single argument could or should persuade each scientist, it would still

[127] N. R. Hanson, *Patterns of Discovery: An Enquiry into the Conceptual Foundations of Science*, Cambridge: CUP, 1958.
[128] T. S. Kuhn, *The Structure of Scientific Revolutions*, Chicago: Chicago UP, 1962, p. 3.
[129] Ibid., p. 157.

remain a deep and important problem to discover what structural or other features are common to the relevant arguments, irrespective of their detailed content. Deeper theoretical understanding comes from the discovery of underlying unity amid superficial diversity. No one would deny the truth of this for scientific progress. But (as already suggested in § 1) it is equally true for philosophical progress. All scientific theorizing proceeds by abstraction. It concerns itself with spatial relations, with number, with motion, with the evolution of biological species, and so on. If a theory attempted to concern itself instead with, say, the concrete aggregate of actual animals, which not only have shapes and numbers and the ability to move and breed but also an indefinite variety of other characteristics, the theoretical enterprise would inevitably choke on a superfluity of detail. But this is just as true for theories about science as for theories within science. A theory of scientific progress must be expected to abstract and elucidate one or more pervasive aspects of this progress, not just to recapitulate the totality of things and events that constitute the actual course of scientific development from period to period. Otherwise it has failed, as judged by the kind of standard that it should respect.

In a similar vein Feyerabend has argued not only for the impossibility of drawing rational comparisons between certain competing scientific theories, like classical and relativistic mechanics, but also for the thesis that those who take different sides in such a dispute 'think differently, speak a different language, live in a different world'.[130] The languages in which the theories are expressed must be incommensurable, according to Feyerabend, so that no common data can be described to which the two competing theories may both be related.

But, though the issue cannot be fully discussed here, Feyerabend's scepticism can easily be seen to rest on an assumption that invalidates it. He has to assume that it is possible to identify when two or more theories are competing with one another for acceptance. Only if that kind of situation is identifiable does it become possible for the sceptic to enter into the dialogue in which philosophers like Carnap and Hempel have been taking part and to claim, as against them, that any choice between competing scientific theories is irrational. To deny that there is any competition at all would involve a degree of paradox that even the sceptic's thesis has to avoid if it seeks a hearing at all. But

---

[130] K. Feyerabend, 'Explanation, Reduction and Empiricism' in F. Feigl and G. Maxwell (eds.), *Minnesota Studies in the Philosophy of Science*, vol. 3, Minneapolis: Minnesota UP, 1962, pp. 51-2.

competition between theories is conceivable only in relation to at least some shared framework of problems and objectives, even if there is disagreement about the relative importance of different elements in this framework. Once such a framework is given, the grounds for Feyerabend's scepticism disappear, because one cannot understand a problem without also understanding what would count as a solution of it and one cannot understand an objective without also understanding what would count as an achievement of it.

Again, Toulmin conceives the development of science in terms of the evolution of various intellectual disciplines rather than as a mere succession of accepted theories. Each discipline may be seen not only as a body of concepts, methods and aims, but also as a profession, comprising the organized set of institutions, roles, and men whose business it is to apply those concepts and methods in order to achieve those aims. Toulmin then seeks to give a Darwinian account both of the coherence and continuity by which we identify disciplines as distinct and also of the long-term changes by which disciplines are transformed. Intellectual novelties are constantly competing for survival within particular disciplines, and the demands of their intellectual environment engender a process of selection that determines which of these novelties can survive. Moreover, says Toulmin, the rationality of natural science has nothing intrinsically to do with formal entailments and contradictions, with inductive logic or with the probability calculus. Fundamentally, he argues, this is because 'the establishment of new or modified concepts involves–in the nature of the case–non-stereotyped procedures, which can be expressed only in non-formal arguments, framed in terms of "meta-statements" about those novel or modified concepts'.[131]

One serious objection to Toulmin's evolutionary model of scientific progress, as to most other evolutionary models (such as Popper's theory of objective knowledge[132]), is that speciation, which was the central topic of Darwin's great book, has no important analogue in the progress of science. Specifically in Toulmin's case the analogy between disciplines and species is a poor one, and the relation of a concept to the intellectual discipline to which it belongs is more like that of a unique component to the system embracing it than like that of a non-unique member to its species or population. And if you try to shift the analogy by treating scientific concepts as species of which the

---

[131] S. Toulmin, *Human Understanding*, vol. 1, Oxford: OUP, 1972, p. 487.
[132] *Objective Knowledge: An Evolutionary Approach*.

members are thoughts in the minds of individual scientists you lose any plausible analogue for the evolving discipline.

The most important flaw in Toulmin's sociology of science, however, is its inability to give an adequate account of rationality. Nor should this be surprising. Darwin's theory was originally put forward as an alternative to those accounts that sought to explain adaptedness by reference to some kind of rational design. Instead of appealing, like orthodox theology, to God's rational plan, it contrived a pattern of explanation, via natural selection among random mutations, which had no need to assume the occurrence of any rational act. And not only was Divine rationality–i.e. the application of Divine knowledge for the fulfilment of Divine purpose–irrelevant to Darwinian explanation: no other kind of rationality was allowed to have a part in it either. In particular no heritable innovations were to be traced back in Lamarckian style to learned adaptations. Hence no evolutionary change of any kind came about through the application of intelligence and knowledge to the solution of a problem. That was at the heart of Darwin's idea. That is what still surprises some people almost as much as it shocked nineteenth-century theologians. And that is why Darwinian evolution is so deeply inappropriate a model (*pace* Toulmin, Popper, and others) for the understanding of scientific progress–as if scientific progress could occur without the application of intelligence and existing knowledge to the solution of new problems.

Nor is there anything analogous to random mutation that plays a regular part in the task of generating new scientific hypotheses. A rational scientist approaches this task by at least reading through a lot of the existing literature–not by throwing dice or spinning a roulette wheel. The factors influencing his construction of new hypotheses to test are thus not decoupled from factors influencing the results of such tests, as the Darwinian analogy requires them to be.

Moreover, even if we were to think of new scientific ideas has having to meet an evolutionary challenge we should still need to investigate the precise mechanisms by which an idea's degree of success in meeting this challenge is determined. It may well be the case that each discipline has its own, changing criteria of assessment–its own changing patterns of controlled experimentation. If so, that merely accentuates the need to identify some rational structure that is common to all such assessments. Just as Mendelian genetics is needed to fill out our understanding of Darwinian evolution, so too some kind of inductive logic is needed in order to articulate the rational principles which constrain the selection of hypotheses on the basis of controlled experiment.

The overall position, then, is something like this. No doubt Carnap, Hempel, and others at one time invoked intuitions in relation to certain problems about confirmation, explanation, etc. that are really part of the domain of scientific enquiry. They based logico-mathematical arguments on those intuitions in order to achieve an a priori global resolution for issues that in fact require empirical determination in local contexts. But it does not follow from this that philosophical accounts of scientific rationality must instead take a historical or sociological form and that no general questions arise about confirmation or explanation which can properly be answered by philosophical analyses and arguments based on intuitively given premisses.

What is necessary instead is to discern the appropriate domain for philosophical generalization about scientific reasoning—i.e. to discern the level of abstraction or generality at which the analysis of this reasoning is possible. The historicists (Hanson, Kuhn, etc.) were right to think that no measure of explanatory power or evidential support has a priori status or global applicability. But they were wrong to infer from this that rationality in science can therefore be a subject only for anecdotal narrative or sociological description. Just because the actual criteria of demarcation, of explanatory power, or of evidential support are tied in some way to the particular field of enquiry and vary with the state of relevant scientific knowledge, there may well be general normative conditions which all such ties and variations ought ideally to satisfy.

First, philosophers are entitled to look for invariant principles governing the way in which background knowledge determines the actual criteria of demarcation, explanation, or support. For example, if experience with testing other drugs should affect the choice of which variables are to be controlled in experiments designed to test evidential support for the non-toxicity of a new drug, the question how such experience is best applied in thus selecting variables seems to pose a relatively general problem for the epistemology of science.

Secondly, if the structure of properly controlled experiment has certain cardinal features that are invariant across all disciplinary frontiers, then these features may impose universally operative constraints on the logical relations that different assessments of evidential support bear to one another within any local context. The philosophical analysis of scientific reasoning should then aim at constructing a logical syntax of evidential support which will provide universally applicable answers to questions like 'Does every variation of experimental conditions have equal value?', 'Does the replication of an experiment increase its evidential value?', 'Can a hypothesis enjoy more support than any of its logical consequences?', 'Must the conjunction of the two hypotheses enjoy less support than either conjunct?', and so on.

Moreover, in both the above enquiries[133] the issue will not be 'What is scientific reasoning actually like?' but rather 'What should scientific reasoning ideally be like?' So statements of empirical fact, whether about actual experimental results or about the behaviour of scientists, cannot serve as the crucial premises. At some point it will be necessary to appeal to intuitions.

Of course, there are many philosophical issues to which certain kinds of empirical facts or scientific findings are relevant. One can hardly discuss the ethics of euthanasia, for example, without paying some attention to the current state of medical practice and life-support technology. But these facts or findings are relevant as potential reasons for performing such-and-such an act for adopting such-and-such an attitude. Analytical philosophy, within its general concern for the appraisal of reasons, may seek to evaluate that potentiality. But it can do so only by reference to normative principles that require to be tested against our intuitions. No amount of empirical knowledge is an adequate substitute for the normative premises that this kind of test can supply.

An objection is foreseeable from those who, like Barnes and Bloor,[134] take the social causation of this or that feature of scientific enquiry to be the primary subject-matter of study for anyone interested in the nature of science. 'Every culture', we shall be told, 'has its beliefs, its reasons for preferring one belief to another, and its standards for regarding one reason as more cogent than another. So everyone's evaluations are context-bound, and no one should formu-

---

[133] Cf. Cohen, *The Implications of Induction*, esp. pp. 35-95 and 207-37, and id., *The Probable and the Provable*, pp. 121-244.

[134] B. Barnes and D. Bloor, 'Relativism, Rationalism and the Sociology of Knowledge', in M. Hollis and S. Lukes, *Rationality and Relativism*, Oxford: Blackwell, 1982, pp. 21-47. Cf. the papers in J. R. Brown (ed.), *Scientific Rationality: The Sociological Turn*, Dordrecht: Reidel, 1984.

late the justification of his preferences in absolute or context-independent terms. It follows that rationally and irrationally held beliefs do not fall into different natural kinds, but are subject to similar patterns of explanation in sociological terms. And it is only through such explanations that we can get to grips with the fundamental problems about the nature of science.'

The trouble with this argument is not that it is self-refuting, as some may be tempted to complain, but rather that it is a *non sequitur*. If each culture in fact has its own supposed standards of rationality, then so does the culture of those who, like Barnes and Bloor, are currently interested in the history and sociology of science. What follows from the relativist's premiss is not that no one should formulate the justification of his preferences in absolute or context-independent terms, but that everyone must inevitably do this, because it is integral to any formulation that invokes supposed standards of rationality. To invoke such standards is to claim their independence of cultural differences. The normative analysis of rationality is thus not a problem that just disappears if the relativist's premiss is true. Rather, we should expect it to arise independently in each culture and to provoke different resolutions. And perhaps the wide-ranging conflicts of doctrine that are so common in analytical philosophy (see § 3 and § 11 above) are partly due to deep-seated cultural differences that are reflected in differences of intuition on relevant issues. As a historian or sociologist one should certainly study the causation equally of those scientific developments that one thinks rational and of those that one thinks irrational. But pursuit of this important historical or sociological study is not an adequate substitute for a philosophical analysis of the standards—whether customary or innovative—by reference to which one should assess such a development's rationality. So in metaphilosophy we can afford to leave unresolved the grand and glorious issue about which relativists and anti-relativists conceive themselves to be doing battle. Whichever side is right, and even if the issue is a pseudo-problem, there is still room for any philosopher of science to pursue the normative analysis of scientific rationality, and to pursue it, as he must, within the structure of his own intellectual perspective.

§ 14 DEDUCTIVISM AND INDUCTIVISM AS ALTERNATIVE STRATEGIES IN ANALYTICAL PHILOSOPHY

Summary. Argument in favour of a sceptical conclusion tends to be deductive in pattern, not inductive. But non-sceptical conclusions are also often supported deductively. Deductive philosophical arguments are common among empiricist philosophers as well as among rationalist ones, and inductive arguments are common among rationalist philosophers as well as among empiricist ones. A deductivist inclination tends to foster interest in traditional problems and promotion of global theses. An inductivist inclination tends to foster interest in problems arising out of contemporary non-philosophical concerns and to encourage a more localized focus.

It is clear that the difference (described in § 7 above) between categorical and hypothetical modes of procedure in philosophical reasoning has some impact on the choice between deductive and inductive patterns of argumentation. A deductive pattern associates more persuasively with the hypothetical mode than with the categorical one, because premises for the deduction of philosophical conclusions are likely to be general propositions rather than singular ones and are therefore less convincingly sustained by intuition. Perhaps it was partly because he started with the help of a singular intuition–'I think, therefore I am'–that Descartes felt able to promote a categorical epistemology by deductive argument. Again, Carnap's theory of confirmation attempted to combine deductive argumentation with the categorical mode of procedure. But several of the intuitions on which it is based are too weak to be persuasive. At the same time an inductive pattern of philosophical argumentation tends to favour the categorical mode, because it is not difficult in the course of philosophical dialogue to find premises for inductive generalization that are relatively unassailable and uncontroversial. The description of some imaginary moral quandary can be fleshed out in such a way that almost everyone would agree intuitively with its proposed solution whether or not they agree to the system of generalizations that the solution is supposed to support. Similarly, if an example of a relevant judgement is drawn from some authoritative contribution to the development of science, it will normally elicit matching intuitions from a philosopher's readers (§ 9). To argue hypothetically from such a premiss, rather than categorically, tends to appear rather as a stylistic affectation of scruple than as a serious admission of uncertainty.

However, one should not forget that, though the premisses of inductive reasoning in philosophy may often enjoy a superior certainty (when compared with those of deductive reasoning), its conclusions (unlike deductive ones) also suffer from a characteristic type of fallibility. To criticize a deductive argument in philosophy one normally assumes its validity and searches it for express or tacit premisses that are of disputable acceptability. It is a rather superficial criticism to charge the argument with being a *non sequitur* merely because a requisite premiss has not been stated, so long as an appropriate additional premiss is readily acceptable in the context. But to criticize an inductive argument one normally tries instead to call its supposed level of validity into question by exploiting its exposure to the possibility of counter-examples. The existing conclusion may fit existing premisses (if none of these are to be discarded for the kind of reason discussed in § 11), but it may not also fit new premisses: at any particular time an inductive hypothesis is always underdetermined by the data then available. And philosophers sometimes tend to underestimate the extent of inductive support that needs to be assembled for a philosophical thesis before they are entitled to a significant degree of confidence that no such counter-example to it is available.

So the distinctions between categorical and hypothetical modes of procedure, and between deductive and inductive patterns of argumentation, are just as important in understanding the nature of analytical philosophy as is the distinction between semantic ascent and semantic descent which was discussed in §§ 2 above. Without exploiting some such taxonomy it is not possible to explain the differences that arise within modern analytical philosophy and its classical antecedents not only on points of detail (for which differences of intuition or of inductive systematization are often responsible) but also in regard to the whole tone of discussion. Admittedly very many different steps of reasoning may be identifiable within the concrete complexity of an actual philosophical monograph, and neither the mode of procedure nor the pattern of argumentation needs to be homogenous throughout, any more than the strategy of semantic orientation needs to be uniform. For example, a categorical argument may be given to support the principle of inference upon which a hypothetical argument relies, or the premisses of a deductive argument may be given an inductive foundation. Also the literary style of a monograph and its distribution of emphasis may have a considerable effect on its readers. But a pervasive tone may nevertheless be given to a particular discussion by the relative importance of the part played within it by one mode of procedure, or by one pattern of argumentation, rather than another.

Thus Schlick introduces his theory of meaning by invoking singular intuitions in support of it.[135] In support of the fundamental principle that 'the meaning of a proposition can be given only by giving the rule of its verification in experience', he cites the obvious nonsense of someone's saying 'Take me to a country where the sky is three times as blue as in England': the request is meaningless because its satisfaction is unverifiable. And he also appeals to the fact that Einstein answered the question 'What do we mean when we speak of two events at distant places happening simultaneously?' by describing an experimental method for ascertaining the simultaneity of such events. Thus far the movement of thought is inductive. Yet the pervasive tone of verificationist philosophy is deductive, since the anti-metaphysical conclusions drawn from its fundamental principle are allowed to override any intuitions that many people may be known to share about the meanings or meaningfulness of such sentences as 'God exists', 'God is good', etc. This deductivist approach is especially evident in Ayer's version of verificationism, where the fundamental principle is 'demonstrated'[136] from other general propositions and it is deduced from this principle that ethical sentences lack literal significance just as much as metaphysical ones do and that distinctively moral problems are not more susceptible of rational resolution than are distinctively metaphysical ones.

An alternative possibility for the theory of meaning would be to pursue a uniformly inductive approach. We could look at each of various specimens of discourse that seem prima-facie meaningful in order to test whether a proposed criterion of meaningfulness is sufficiently ecumenical to embrace them all. But such an approach would be unlikely to lead to positivist conclusions. Indeed this kind of approach was certainly implicit in the moves that were made by religionists like I. Ramsey[137] to rebut the positivist argument.

An inevitable variation is to be noted here in the type of argument that is best suited to support a particular type of philosophical

---

[135] M. Schlick, 'Meaning and Verification', *The Philosophical Review*, 45, 1936, pp. 339-69, in id., *Philosophical Papers*, vol. 2, pp. 456-81.

[136] *Language, Truth and Logic*, 2nd edn., p. 41.

[137] I. Ramsey, 'On the Possibility and Purpose of a Metaphysical Theology', in I. Ramsey (ed.), *Prospect for Metaphysics: Essays of Metaphysical Exploration*, London: Allen and Unwin, 1961, pp. 153-77.

enterprise. Those who wish to cast doubt on the legitimacy of certain everyday claims to knowledge, on the reality of certain familiarly accepted entities, on the merit of certain popular values, or on the meaningfulness of certain familiar kinds of assertion, can hardly hope to construct a cogent argument on a uniformly inductive basis. They are trying to refute general views that are widely held; and their natural course is to argue deductively from carefully selected premisses, since the general current of singular intuitions is bound to be running against them. So they might try to build on assumptions to which a respectable sector of orthodox opinion is already implicitly committed. For example, Hobbes, who notoriously came to be fascinated by the Euclidean model of reasoning, purported to deduce his theory of political sovereignty mainly from premisses about the nature of motion in human beings, and he claimed eventually to be able to derive the–surely paradoxical–proposition that in no state can any act of the sovereign be unjust.[138] Analogously Spinoza's heterodox equation of God with Nature was expounded in the explicitly Euclidean form of his *Ethics* as an allegedly demonstrable consequence of familiar metaphysical principles. And another common pattern of deductive argument for paradoxical conclusions is by *modus tollendo tollens*. For example, Unger has put forward two such arguments.[139] In outline, one is that everyone who knows that rocks exist must also know that he is not being deceived into believing this by a malign scientist, and that since he cannot know the latter he cannot know the former. The other is that, if one knows, it is all right to be certain, and that, since it is never all right to be absolutely certain, one never has knowledge.

The best that sceptics can do in inductive terms is either to aim at discounting (in one or other of the ways discussed in § 11) any familiar intuitions that are inconsistent with their sceptical thesis, or (like Schlick) just to argue from one or two kinds of intuition and ignore the rest. Thus Hume, in his *Treatise*, first challenges his reader to produce a single simple idea that is not a copy of a corresponding impression. And he then abandons the inductive pattern of argumentation so as to be free to use his inductively supported principle–the principle that every simple idea is a copy of a previous impression–as the foundation of his deductive arguments that we have no rational title to believe in

---

[138] T. Hobbes, *Leviathan*, 1651, pts. 1 and 2; J. Locke, *Two Treatises of Government*, 1690, bk. 2, para. 102.

[139] P. Unger, *Ignorance: A Case for Scepticism*, Oxford: OUP, 1975, pp. 8 and 98-105.

the existence of causal connexions, objective moral values, continuing selves, or physical processes independent of our experiences.

But, if Hume had been more of an inductivist, some of his conclusions might have been very different. For example, if he had persevered with his inductive approach sufficiently to respect people's intuitions about the logical derivability of counterfactual conditionals from causal generalizations, he might have found it difficult to analyse causal generalizations as statements of *de facto* uniformities in the way that he did. Most people think that 'Friction causes heat' entails 'If I were to rub two twigs together they would get hot' even if in fact they themselves never actually rub two twigs together. But a statement of a *de facto* uniformity tells us nothing about what would happen under other conditions than actually occur. Similarly, anyone who is normally ready to argue inductively from particular ethical intuitions, can hardly accept the logical-positivist doctrine that moral judgements cannot legitimately constitute premises or conclusions of rational argument.

So, within analytical philosophy, both deductivism and inductivism may run into characteristic perils if allowed to dominate excessively. Deductivism may degenerate into excessive paradox, because it tends to encourage starting from too selective a set of intuitions (while those that lead in a different direction are ignored). But inductivism may degenerate into excessive conservatism, because it tends to encourage too indiscriminate a respect for prima-facie intuitions. Philosophical analyses attract little credit if they imply that nothing is as it is commonly supposed to be, and little interest if they imply that everything is.

Perhaps the starkest contrast, in this regard, between stated metaphilosophies is that between Russell's deductivist view of philosophy in 1918 and Wittgenstein's inductivist view a quarter of a century later. According to Russell his aim was to argue from 'perfectly plain truisms', and he held that 'the point of philosophy is to start with something so simple as not to seem worth stating, and to end with something so paradoxical that no one will believe it'.[140] According to Wittgenstein in his later years, however, 'the work of the philosopher consists in assembling reminders for a particular purpose', and 'if one tried to advance *theses* in philosophy, it would never be possible to

[140] 'The Philosophy of Logical Atomism', in B. Russell, *Logic and Knowledge, Essays 1901–1950* (ed. R. C. Marsh), London: Allen and Unwin, 1956, p. 193.

question them, because everyone would agree to them'.[141] Such are the extremes of difference for which a choice between deductive and inductive strategies may be largely responsible.

Of course, though sceptical or revolutionary conclusions can be promoted only by predominately deductive arguments, a deductive type of argument need not necessarily lead in a sceptical or revolutionary direction. Thus, most notably, Descartes' attempt to refute epistemological scepticism and lay new foundations for familiar beliefs purported to proceed through a sequence of deductive stages: first, a turning of the sceptic's doubt against himself in the inference from 'I doubt' to 'I exist'; then proof of the existence of God; then proof of the existence of an external world; and finally proof of the laws of nature.[142] Similarly Kant's attempted demonstration of his categorical imperative, as a rock-firm foundation for moral judgement, was as determinedly deductivist in character as was to be expected from his explicit assertion 'Nor could anything be more fatal to morality than that we should wish to derive it from examples'.[143] The citation of examples is necessary in order to express or evoke singular intuitions, so, if we agree with Kant that examples are not to be exploited in this way, philosophical induction is impossible. (Actually Kant's argument here for his rejection of induction is a *non sequitur*. His premiss is that everything which a person takes as an example of morality must first have been tested against principles of morality in that person's mind. But the most that would follow from this, if it were true, would be that the principles must be consciously *or* unconsciously present in a person's mind before any particular application of them, not that they must be *consciously* present there before then. Hence citation of the example may still function to bring the principle into consciousness, and, if so, it may legitimately be seen, without circularity, as expressing intuitive support for the principle.)

Again, inductivist arguments need not lead to conservative conclusions. For example, Quine's system of regimentation for human discourse is hardly to be thought conservative in view of its hostile attitude to logical modalities, intentional objects, and subjunctive conditionals.[144] But Quine's arguments are based mainly on appeals to

---

[141] L. Wittgenstein, *Philosophical Investigations*, Oxford: Blackwell, 1953, para. 128.

[142] R. Descartes, *Discourse on Method*, London: J. M. Dent, 1912, pp. 33-5.

[143] I. Kant, *Fundamental Principles of the Metaphysic of Morals* (trans. T. K. Abbott), London: Longmans, Green, 3rd edn., 1907, p. 30.

[144] *Word and Object*, pp. 157-61.

the intuitions that utterance of this or that particular sentence may provoke. What ensures that Quine's intuitions do not appear to have a conservative force is that they are concerned with underlying logical properties and relations as determinants of how our use of linguistic forms would ideally be regimented. All sentences, in Quine's scheme, would carry their logic on their face, which few do now. Our language is to be changed, though our logic, presumably, is not.

Indeed, since choice of theory is always underdetermined by the data for inductive reasoning, a philosophical policy of always saving the phenomena is quite compatible with wide variations in the chosen theory's degree of imaginativeness and innovation. Frege's approach to indirect discourse was substantially more conservative than Quine's own in regard to the intersubstitutability of identically referring terms in unformalized natural language.[145] He allowed this intersubstitutability to operate even in indirect discourse, while Quine did not.

It is interesting also to notice that the choice between deductive and inductive patterns of argument can be quite independent of any preference for rationalist or empiricist epistemology. Admittedly Descartes claimed to have continued his chain of deductive reasoning in such a way as to resolve all doubt about the precise content of the laws of nature. So the deductivism of his philosophical method was continuous with his epistemological rationalism. Hume and Ayer, on the other hand, enlisted philosophical deduction, as we have seen, in the service of their empiricist epistemologies. And inductivism distributes its favours with a comparable impartiality. For example, Whewell's approach to the philosophy of science was predominantly inductive. He found it necessary to write a history of science before he could begin work on its philosophy. But this inductivism was directed towards the defence of a quasi-Kantian epistemology. In seeking to show how physics owes its ideas of space, force, etc. to the active contribution of the mind rather than to passive experience, and how scientific laws owe their universality and necessity to the same source, Whewell sought his evidence largely from the history of science. Quine, on the other hand, has no room for necessity in a scientific theory as he conceives it and he regards such a theory's universality of application as subject to judgement by the tribunal of experience. But he supports this thoroughly empiricist epistemology by a charac-

---

[145] Compare G. Frege, 'On Sense and Reference', in P. Geach and M. Black (eds.), *Translations from the Philosophical Writings of Gottlob Frege*, Oxford: Blackwell, 1952, pp. 56-78, with Quine, *Word and Object*, pp. 141-6.

teristically inductive pattern of reasoning, though unlike Whewell his attention is fixed on contemporary science rather than on the whole history of science. Specifically, he argues about the logical and terminological resources that we require in order to be able to reconstruct contemporary scientific theory, along with the judgements made about it by contemporary scientists, in an explicitly regimented notation. And, since a comprehensive and complete survey of modern science would be an absurdly ponderous basis for his argument, Quine's reasoning inevitably adopts an inductivist structure. The uniformities of procedure and statement that exist in modern science allow a few examples to claim representative status.

In ethics, however, the connection between method of reasoning and substantive theory may be a little closer than in epistemology. If induction is your preferred method of argument for use in philosophical reasoning about particular principles of right and wrong, then neither a Kantian nor a utilitarian ethic is easily sustainable since either may generate principles that your inductive reasoning rejects. But deductivism is not complementarily restrictive in regard to an intuitionist ethic. With appropriate premises (for example, theistic ones like Butler's[146]) we could certainly construct a deductive argument in favour of a person's attaching overriding authority in a moral quandary to the dictates of his own conscience.

It is also worth nothing that the philosophy of mathematics and the philosophy of natural science are different from one another in regard to how their subject-matter tends to affect their methods of reasoning. The philosophy of mathematics has to accommodate a substantial body of deductive reasoning if only because its conclusions must conform to the constraints imposed by important metamathematical results, such as Gödel's proof of the incompleteness of elementary number theory. But the philosophy of natural science has to proceed very largely on inductivist lines because it cannot afford to ignore the powerful intuitions that are evoked by references to familiar paradigms of scientific discovery like Newtonian mechanics or the decipherment of DNA.

Aristotle long ago pointed out[147] that Socrates' definitions were reached by inductive argument. But perhaps Plato, despite the metaphysical claims advanced by his theory of Forms, was the archetypal

---

[146] Op. cit., vol. 2, sermon II, pp. 50-66.
[147] *Metaphysics* M 4, 1078^b 29-32.

inductivist in philosophy, as Bacon[148] acknowledged. Not only was he particularly fond of argument by analogy, which is a standard inductivist method (see § 7 above). He also recommended that students should work their way into the subject by first studying the special sciences and then examining the assumptions on which these rest. And that recommendation can be seen as an attempt to ensure that no one should come to metaphysics without an adequate awareness of the range of inferential intuitions–i.e. of particular inferences made in accordance with unexamined assumptions–that occur within the special sciences.

Thus an inductivist inclination leads a philosopher to pluck his problems alive from out of the myriad local perplexities that are generated among his contemporaries about particular features of science, politics, art, religion, language, or other cultural activities. This is because the singular intuitions that his theories seek to accommodate are normally at home only in such localized contexts. A deductivist approach, however, so far as it takes its origin from some general principle or principles, is freer to occupy itself with issues of a more global nature and to find its problems more clearly delineated in the reflections of other philosophers than in the departmentalized reasonings of non-philosophical specialists. Hence a deductivist inclination will encourage interest in the philosophical tradition and promote ever deeper and more sophisticated treatments of traditionally familiar issues in pure philosophy, irrespective of their relevance to non-philosophical concerns in contemporary culture. Indeed this feature of deductivism tends to foster the belief that there have been no new issues in philosophy since Plato wrote his dialogues. An inductivist inclination, on the other and, may sometimes help to bring new issues into the philosophical tradition or new aspects of old ones. But to the extent that these problems have not profited from so long an exposure to the dialectical subtleties of philosophical investigation the questions thus brought to light may at least at first be, or appear, substantially less profound. They may sometimes also exhibit a kind of hybrid quality, because of being closely interconnected as yet with issues in other disciplines. And the internal coherence of proposed answers to these questions may not be as finely honed as that of philosophical theories which satisfy a more deductivist inclination. It is deductive development that searches out any deep-rooted inconsistencies.

[148] Op. cit., bk. 1, aphorism 105.

Indeed, that is why for critical purposes philosophical dialogue tends to profit more decisively from deductive than from inductive reasoning. As shown in § 11 there are various ways of buttressing a philosophical position against inductive counter-examples. But a deep-rooted inconsistency is more difficult to eradicate. For example, in a recent book Benenson argues in favour of what he claims to be an anti-realist analysis for any ordinary judgement that a specified outcome has this or that degree of mathematical probability. Such a judgement, he says, is elliptical for a statement of the considerations by reference to which we determine its truth, namely the evidence for the probability and the underlying partial entailment between the evidence and the outcome.[149] Now it may be tempting to raise the inductivist criticism that this account does not cover certain describable varieties of probability judgement. But there is a deeper trouble, which becomes evident when we trace out deductive implications. Benenson fails to discuss how an anti-realist rejection of bivalence could be reconciled with the complementational law of negation in mathematical probability. If we don't have 'If E entails the falsity of not-H, then E entails H', why should we still have 'If p (not-H/E) = 0, then p(H/E) = 1'? In the philosophy of meaning an anti-realism that does not reject bivalence is only superficial. But an anti-realism that does reject bivalence is not easily combined with Benenson's interpretation of the classical calculus of chance as a theory of partial entailment.

Unfortunately, however, the growing professionalization of philosophy has made it particularly easy for deductivist analytical philosophy to detach itself from the central issues of contemporary culture. The denser the milieu of journals, graduate schools, research institutes, etc. within which contemporary philosophical dialogue takes place, the easier it is for a philosopher who takes his problems exclusively from other philosophers to believe that these problems merit discussion just because they are also discussed by other philosophers. The Vienna Circle contained more non-philosophers than philosophers, and was deeply interested in the theoretical problems of non-philosophical disciplines. But the effect of the post-1945 expansion of university life throughout the world has been that an immense forum of purely philosophical discussion has now been created, within which philosophers can much more easily cease to be con-

[149] F. C. Benenson, *Probability, Objectivity and Evidence*, London: Routledge and Kegan Paul, 1984.

cerned about the relevance of their work to other intellectual issues. Their self-esteem is sufficiently maintained by the approval of other participants in the professional dialogue or even by the approval of just their own immediate colleagues, if the latter are sufficiently numerous. This effect has been enhanced by the vastly greater opportunities now available for philosophers to publish at article-length rather than at book-length: indeed some influential writers (for example, H. P. Grice, D. Davidson, and H. Putnam) have published almost exclusively in this way. What happens is that within the narrow span of a minutely argued article in a professional journal it is an obvious waste of space to rehearse whatever non-philosophical considerations may have given rise to, or be at stake in the general issue under discussion, and so newcomers to the profession are sometimes no longer made aware that these considerations still exist.

Deductive arguments are nevertheless capable of influencing the patterns of non-philosophical activity in various ways. Philosophical ideas filter out into literature, art, science, politics, etc. through many different channels. And, when deductivist conclusions do eventually come to exercise some influence, they may have very great scope and power. Consider, for example, the debt of the Romantic movement to deductions from Spinoza's identification of God with Nature, or the reformatory impact of Bentham's utilitarianism.

It is not that an inductivist inclination prevents philosophers from arriving eventually at global conclusions. Indeed, while the deductivist has no inherent motive for increasing the level of generality at which his theory operates, the inductivist moves naturally, where he can, towards greater and greater generality. Only inductivism incorporates an ideal of synoptic comprehensiveness. A well-tested, yet unrefuted principle that subsumes and explains subordinate principles and also generates new knowledge, has a superior inductive claim to acceptance, as Bacon long ago recognized. But according to the inductivist such conclusions are not to be 'anticipated', as Bacon called it, in a premature straining after comprehensiveness.[150] They are to be reached instead by appropriately argued stages. Consider, for example, the classical problem of universals. The deductivist may seek to set up a general argument for realism, say, or for conceptualism, or for nominalism, or perhaps he will argue that the problem itself is a bogus one, issuing from a futile metaphysical urge

[150] Op. cit., bk. 1, aphorism 26.

to transcend language.[151] The inductivist will look instead at the strength of the case for asserting the truth of a realist (or a conceptualist, or a nominalist) analysis of certain specified categories of predicates in their appropriate contexts of discourse. This was the approach adopted by Quine[152] in regard to mathematical theories, and I have shown elsewhere how it may also, and quite separately, be applied to botanical taxonomy and to legal terminology.[153] An inductivist philosopher who found a strong local case for realism, say, in each of a wide variety of different subject-matters would thereby acquire some title to assert the global merit of realism. That is, in the end he might come to the same conclusion as a deductivist though by a different route. But he might find instead that the strength of the case for realism tended to vary from subject-matter to subject-matter, and that would be the kind of conclusion which the deductivist is much less likely to reach.

The globalist tendency of some deductivist philosophy is also to be seen in epistemology. For example, Chisholm[154] has proposed definitions and axioms for such notions as '*e* inductively confers evidence upon *h*' without attempting to establish that these principles apply to actual patterns of reasoning in specific areas of human activity such as experimental science or judicial procedure. He is content to make completely general claims about what any human being would think in epistemically problematic situations; and, because these global claims are thus not immediately exposed to any of the local intuitive tests that specificity would lay them open to, they may easily give an impression of greater plausibility than they deserve to do and may thereby lend themselves to a particularly inconclusive style of controversy where solid ground is hard to find.

This difference between the typically global preoccupations of deductivist philosophy and the–at least initially–local concerns of inductivist philosophy is illustrated in yet another context by discussions of determinism. Consider the impact of determinism on

[151] e.g. D. M. Armstrong, *A Theory of Universals*, Cambridge: CUP, 1978, and D. F. Pears, 'Universals', *The Philosophical Quarterly*, 1, 1951, pp. 218-27, respectively.

[152] W. V. O. Quine, *From a Logical Point of View*, Cambridge, Mass: Harvard UP, 1953, pp. 14-15; see also id., 'What Price Bivalence?', *The Journal of Philosophy*, 78, 1981, pp. 90-5.

[153] Cohen, *The Diversity of Meaning*, pp. 135-8; and id., 'Theory and Definition in Jurisprudence', *Proceedings of the Aristotelian Society*, supp. vol. 29, 1955, pp. 213-38.

[154] R. M. Chisholm, 'On the Nature of Empirical Evidence', in L. Foster and J. W. Swanson (eds.), *Experience and Theory*, London: Duckworth, 1970, pp. 103-34.

interpersonal attitudes. Strawson,[155] for example, has stressed, with characteristic insight and eloquence, how much it matters to us whether the actions of other people–and particularly of *some* other people–reflect attitudes towards us of goodwill, affection, or esteem on the one hand or of contempt, indifference, or malevolence on the other. Resentment, anger, gratitude, forgiveness, love, etc. are then typical reactions with which we respond to their attitudes. But two main sorts of considerations, says Strawson, can make us modify or mollify our reactions. Perhaps the other person was in some temporarily abnormal condition, such as strain or hypnosis. Or perhaps he is altogether psychologically abnormal or morally undeveloped. In the latter case our attitudes may be so profoundly modified that we can come to think of the other person rather as an object for social policy than as someone with whom to share a human relationship. So Strawson then poses the question: could, or should, acceptance of the determinist thesis lead us always to look on everyone as objects in this way? And his–deductively structured–answer to this question is a negative one. Our human commitment to participation in ordinary interpersonal relationships, he thinks, is too thoroughgoing and deeply rooted for us to take seriously the thought that some general theoretical conviction about determinism might make us abandon that commitment. A sustained objectivity of interpersonal attitude, and the human isolation which that would entail, does not seem to be something of which human beings would be capable. Nor, he hints, would it be rational for us to choose such an impoverishment of human life on the ground that, as we thought, determinism was true.

Moreover, in addition to the reactive attitudes so far considered, which are essentially those of the beneficiaries or offended parties themselves, there are kindred attitudes of moral indignation and moral disapprobation about what is done to others. These vicarious analogues of the personal reactive attitudes rest on, and reflect, exactly the same expectation or demand in a generalized form. That is, they rest on or reflect the demand for the manifestation of a reasonable degree of goodwill or regard, on the part of others, not simply towards oneself but towards all those on whose behalf moral indignation may be felt. Correspondingly, if we did believe the truth of determinism we would be no more inclined to reject, let alone be justified in rejecting, these vicarious forms of reaction than the basic interpersonal ones.

[155] P. F. Strawson, *Freedom and Resentment, and Other Essays*, London: Methuen, 1974, pp. 1-25.

And it is to be noted that this global, deductivist argument, for the compatibility of determinism and responsibility, is independent of any precise formulation for the notoriously polymorphous notion of determinism.

Strawson's conclusion is certainly relevant to a conception of the free-will problem that is still often found in philosophical writings. That conception stems from a formulation of the problem that occupied the minds of many seventeenth- and eighteenth-century philosophers when they reflected on the new dominance of mechanics in physical theory: are human actions as cause-bound and predictable as the movements of the planets?

But the sheer generality of this formulation deprives it of relevance to some of the more pressing intellectual problems of contemporary culture. As a global thesis determinism is not only difficult to formulate with satisfactory precision. It is even more difficult, if not impossible, to prove true—especially since classical mechanics lost its old dominance. The strongest contemporary threat to traditional views about moral obligation and moral responsibility comes not from the total, metaphysical type of determinism with which Strawson deals, but from the creeping onset of partial determinisms which are from time to time propounded by psychologists, criminologists, etc. If a certain type of human action, under certain describable conditions, could be explained and perhaps even predicted by a well-substantiated theory, ought we then, and for that reason, to give up talking about that type of action, under those conditions, in terms of moral obligation and moral responsibility? If we knew some fairly precise combination of family experience and social pressure that universally and inevitably, or even very probably, results in criminality, should we cease to criticize such a criminal? This is one of the local problems that is still in the forefront of debate between moralists, social reformers, and so on. Apparently relevant intuitions—oriented towards individual cases—are not easily reconciled here. But Strawson's globally oriented argument gives no indication of how the problem should be resolved. He accepts that it is proper to treat people as objects of social policy, rather than of moral indignation, in some circumstances. But he does not tell us whether the truth of a deterministic theory in relation to a particular kind of action establishes that kind of action as calling for such treatment.

Yet another example of the global preoccupations of deductivist philosophy may be worth mentioning. In exploring the implications of Davidson's truth-conditional semantics some philosophers, like Dummett,[156] have found difficulty in accommodating certain areas of discourse to a principle of bivalence. They claim that some categories of meaningful statement–e.g. certain counterfactual conditionals–may be neither true nor false. Consequently an adequate account of what a person grasps when he understands the meaning of the statement cannot be a specification of the conditions under which such a statement is true. So these philosophers contemplate the possibility of there being deductive support for everywhere replacing what they take to be a realist construal of sentence-meaning by an anti-realist one. According to such an anti-realism understanding the meaning of a declarative sentence cannot be a way to obtain information about how the world actually is. Such understanding consists not in a grasp of the sentence's truth-conditions but in a capacity to recognize whatever is counted as verifying it–i.e. as conclusively establishing it as true, or at least as warranting its assertion.

The issue is a deep and complex one. But it is sufficient here to remark that the deductivist philosopher of meaning characteristically finds his problem arising out of the philosophical literature, because he seeks generalizations for his starting-point and the philosophical literature abounds with implicit or explicit generalizations that have been accepted as premisses by other philosophers: he then proposes his own global solution on the basis of a preferred subset of those premisses. By contrast the inductivist takes as his starting-point some intuitions about particular meanings, such as those echoing a micro-biologist's inclination to judge that the expression 'virus' has a referential function that is analogous to the referential function of expressions denoting macroscopic objects. He may then seek to maintain a realist, or an anti-realist, analysis of a certain group of expressions in scientific theory. But, though his use of the terms 'realism' and 'anti-realism' suggests that his problem is–at its roots–the same as that of the deductivist, this may well be a misidentification. The deductivist's preoccupation with global issues directs him towards an analysis of the concept of meaning, while the inductivist's interest in the evidence afforded by individual cases directs him rather towards analysing the meanings of particular categories of expressions. The deductivist here concerns himself more with the sense,

[156] M. Dummett, 'What is a Theory of Meaning? (II)' in G. Evans and I. McDowell (eds.), *Truth and Meaning: Essays in Semantics*, Oxford: OUP, 1976, pp. 67-137.

intension, or connotation of the word 'meaning', the inductivist with some of its referents–i.e. with certain elements in its extension or denotation. Thus in tackling the problem of meaning the deductivist is led towards a strategy of semantic ascent, while the inductivist is led towards a strategy of semantic descent. So the questions they seek to answer are different though interconnected.

In practice, of course, inductivism and deductivism often complement one another in a single text, just as do the hypothetical and categorical modes of procedure. Such is the tangled web of actual philosophical reasoning. But for the purpose of metaphilosophical analysis it is useful to consider the two patterns of possible reasoning in abstraction from one another and to note the characteristic strengths and characteristic weaknesses of each.

Note too that in giving examples of this difference between inductivism and deductivism–or indeed in illustrating any other metaphilosophical thesis–one can hardly avoid describing philosophical arguments in a rather abstract and simplified fashion that tends to deprive them of any philosophical interest in their own right. Much of their specific content is omitted, and very many subtleties or complexities of formulation are overlooked. Also signpost statements, stipulative definitions, reports or interpretations of other philosophers' views, etc. are all disregarded. But this kind of preoccupation with relevant structural features is a familiar characteristic of philosophical analysis. In reasoning about reasoning metaphilosophy has to concentrate attention on its own task. Analogously a philosopher of science, for instance, would cite only the features of, say, Newton's optics that illustrate the philosophical point being made, in order not to drown that point in a sea of irrelevant scientific detail. Only thus can he ensure that the necessary supporting intuition is evoked in a sufficiently clearcut form.

Of course, this citing of appropriately abstracted features, rather than of a mass of concrete detail, is characteristic of expository rather than heuristic reasoning. When you are searching for an answer to a problem you can't risk ignoring details that may be relevant. But when you think that you have already found the answer you need to streamline the presentation of your argument in order to display its validity effectively. Indeed, the account of philosophical reasoning that has been given in §§ 7-13 sketches the implicit structure of a certain kind of achievement: it does not aim to describe the task that issues in such achievements. It is all oriented towards analysis, or idealized reconstruction, of the publishable end-products of philosophical enquiry, not towards a description or evaluation of the often much lengthier procedures and processes by which these are produced in the mind of a philosopher. I have not intended to say anything, for example, about the question whether analytical philosophers should first formulate a theory, and then test it out, or first assemble and consider the data and then form a theory, or rather use whichever policy seems most fruitful at the time. But it should go without saying that, unless some adequate degree of insight supplies the analytical conclusions that are to be attested by deductive or inductive reasoning, those conclusions may be banal, uninteresting, and unimportant. Rigour of argument, or multiplicity of examples, can rarely compensate adequately for shortage of insight, while an outstandingly perceptive insight may carry such conviction that it makes any argument in its favour seem superfluous.

Moreover, it has to be emphasized that at the level at which deductive and inductive arguments are distinguished from one another there is no third pattern of reasoning available for analytical philosophy. Hegel claimed that deductive reasoning was inadequate for philosophical purposes, because in a deductive proof, such as a mathematical one, the conclusion does not preserve the argument by which it has been established. In his view a dialectical movement of thought is required, whereby the argument is somehow rolled up into the conclusion.[157] But, first, in some ways of individuating the conclusion of a deductive proof–ways once explored by Wittgenstein–the conclusion cannot be understood properly unless one has grasped the proof: the proof, it may be said, creates a new concept.[158] Secondly, even where an analytical philosopher prefers, as most do, to individuate conclusions independently of the arguments for them, he nevertheless generally attaches at least as much importance to philosophical arguments as to philosophical conclusions. Indeed, it is that which gives interest and respectability to analytical exercises in the hypothetical mode of procedure. So most analytical philosophers certainly take a good philosophical argument to be worth preserving beyond the point at which its conclusion has been accepted. And, by preferring to distinguish clearly between an argument and its conclusion, they make it

[157] G. W. F. Hegel, *Phenomenology of Spirit* (trans. A. V. Miller), Oxford: OUP, 1977, pp. 24-8.
[158] L. Wittgenstein, *Remarks on the Foundations of Mathematics* (trans. G. E. M. Anscombe), Oxford: Blackwell, 1956, pp. 78-9 *et passim*.

possible to compare the merits of different arguments for the same conclusion. Thirdly, it is no use objecting that analytical philosophers often seem to clarify the sense in which some traditional thesis–determinism, say, or moral objectivism–is tenable, rather than to assess the strength of support for a supposedly already definitive thesis. The objection is invalid because this clarificatory mode of reasoning, as was pointed out in § 7, does in fact have an inductive structure that is evident also in many legal arguments from judicial precedent.

Nor can analytical philosophy proceed satisfactorily without the backing of either deductive or inductive reasoning–however much this is possible for the philosophy of those who assert, with Samuel Alexander, that they 'dislike argument',[159] or with Derrida that they detest discussion, subtleties, and ratiocinations.[160] Even Schlick, who preferred to think of his philosophy as an activity rather than as a system of propositions,[161] was nevertheless aware, in practice, of the need to construct such arguments. For example, he was ready both to support his verificationist account of meaning by reference to particular instances of its applicability, and also to deduce certain consequences of accepting that account.[162] More recently Nozick has protested, with apparent seriousness, that 'philosophical argument, trying to get someone to believe something, whether he wants to believe it or not, is not . . . a nice way to behave towards someone'.[163] Nozick claims that the proper goal of philosophy is explanation, not argument–for example the explanation of how knowledge of an external world is possible. But this contrast between supposedly alternative goals is illusory, since every explanation needs to be supported by arguments, whether deductive or inductive: it has to be established that the explanation is satisfactory. Indeed, even Nozick's own philosophical writing, with its purported explanations, is not consistent with his professed opposition to philosophical argument. Like Schlick's philosophical writing, it is full of arguments, counter-arguments, and occurrences of words like 'therefore'.[164] Nor is there any merit in Nozick's thesis that philosophical argument is objec-

---

[159] S. Alexander, 'Some Explanations', *Mind*, 30, 1931, p. 423.

[160] J. Derrida, 'Limited Inc abc. . .', *Glyph*, 2, 1977, supplement p. 56.

[161] 'The Future of Philosophy (1930)' in *Philosophical Papers*, vol. 2, pp. 171-5, and 'The Future of Philosophy (1931)', ibid., pp. 210-24.

[162] 'Meaning and Verification', ibid., pp. 456-81, esp. pp. 457 and 468.

[163] *Philosophical Explanations*, p. 13.

[164] Ibid., pp. 75, 277, etc.

tionable because it tries to make people do something whether or not they want to do it. This thesis treats persuasion by argument as a form of coercion—which is scarcely less absurd than treating peace as a form of war or white as a shade of black. Philosophical arguments seek the voluntary acceptance of their conclusions (as remarked in § 10 above). Involuntary beliefs are what such arguments start from, not what they aim at establishing.

Indeed, in the end, what guarantees the distinctive meaningfulness of philosophical statements is the possibility of arguing for or against them in appropriate ways. Where philosophy does not admit of such a possibility, it relapses into a form of poetic monologue or obscurantist mystery-mongering which is outside the mainstream of analytical enquiry. And what is true in this respect of substantive philosophy is true also of metaphilosophy. For in metaphilosophical discussion also we employ either hypothetical or categorical reasoning, and reason either deductively or inductively. For example, what has been said in the present section about the opposition between scepticism and inductivism in epistemology may be classified as a hypothetical and deductive treatment of the issue, in that it elicits implications while deliberately avoiding any commitment either to scepticism or to inductivism; whereas the thesis that both inductive and deductive reasoning are admissible in any branch of analytical philosophy is a categorical and inductive one, in that intuitively recognizable examples of both kinds of reasoning are cited in support of the thesis.

III

Analysis and Rationality

§ 15 ARE PEOPLE PROGRAMMED TO COMMIT DEDUCTIVE FALLACIES?

Summary. Some recent experimental results in psychology are claimed to demonstrate an inherent human tendency to commit certain fallacies in deductive reasoning. But these results are open to alternative and more plausible interpretations, because we can tell the meaning that a person attaches to a logical term only when we know the structure of the inferences that he is inclined to make in contexts in which it occurs. So the results of experimental tests on deductive performance should not be taken to cast any discredit on appeals to intuition in philosophical reasoning.

EVERY replicable intuition, we have seen (§§ 8-14), is a piece of prima-facie evidence about the norms of valid inference. But it is not always easy to reconcile all our intuitions within a comprehensive system of norms and some have to be discounted–by one or other of various characteristically inductive procedures that were described in § 11. Is this the way in which logically and statistically uneducated people should treat any mistakes they make in deductive or probabilistic reasoning–a species of mistake to which some contemporary psychologists claim them to be especially prone? If it were, then the credentials of intuition, as a source of premises for philosophical reasoning, would not be seriously tainted. After being filtered through whatever procedures of discounting were appropriate, people's surviving intuitions would support principles of reasoning that are both normatively acceptable and, under ideal conditions, psychologically effective.

But that is not how these psychologists see the situation. They claim that many of the mistakes that an ordinary person makes are not due to adventitious motivational or intellectual preoccupations, but are systematically generated by his possession of normatively incorrect principles or by his non-possession of correct ones. So, if such a person used his own intuitions as a basis for analytical philosophy, he would arrive by impeccable inductive reasoning at seriously erroneous conclusions. Hence, if the psychologists were right, what they say would seriously discredit the claims of intuition to provide–other things being equal–dependable foundations for inductive reasoning in analytical philosophy. Philosophers would not even be able to rely then (as it was suggested in § 12 that they could) on a hard core of shared logical and mathematical intuitions on the basis of which they can build divergent but mutually intelligible arguments within a common dialogue.

The psychologists do not, of course, claim to have demonstrated *universal* proneness to fallacy. Indeed, that would have been a self-refuting claim. Rather, they themselves, along with at least some of their subjects and a roughly corresponding proportion of the world at large, are alleged not to commit the various errors in question. So their theory is compatible with the correctness of at least some analytical philosophers' claims. But, if they are right that most people are prone to have systematically fallacious intuitions, then most people are inherently unfit to practise analytical philosophy in the form in which I have analysed it in §§ 6-14. Moreover, if some widespread proneness to fallacies has already been discovered, the prevalence of yet other fallacies may still remain to be discovered. So no one at all can be fully confident that any of his own intuitions afford him reliable premises for philosophical argument.

Admittedly, during the first couple of decades after the Second World War experimental psychologists, in keeping with the prevailing optimism of the age, generally took normative theories of deductive and probabilistic reasoning and decision-making to be descriptive of actual human competence. But after the mid-1960s, alongside growing popular pessimism about economic, political, and environmental outcomes, the trend has veered. Very many papers have appeared which claim to have established that logically or statistically untutored adults are inclined to employ one or another of a variety of fallacious procedures in their reasonings or not to employ the correct procedures. The normal person's intuitions on these issues, it is claimed, tend to be persistently irrational. And the faults committed are not attributed just to adventitious factors, like conceit, carelessness, wishful thinking, or preoccupation with salient features. The normal person's competence is said to be flawed, not just his performance. He is said to have some wrong principles, or not to have some right ones. So, since at many points analytical philosophy has to premiss its accounts of reasoning on the data of human intuitions, its meta-philosophy can hardly afford to ignore this extensive literature.

Sometimes it is quite easy to refute the psychologists' arguments. For example, in an experiment contrived by Rips[1] a substantial body of subjects tend not to recognize the validity of arguments involving inferences from premisses of the form '*p*' to conclusions of the form '*p* or *q*'. Rips diagnoses the source of this as a defect in the availability of the rule that logicians call 'disjunction-introduction', which is the rule that Rips's computer-simulation model requires to assess such arguments. But Rips is assuming that the layman always uses and understands the elementary connectives of natural language in a purely truth-functional sense, so that a proposition of the form '*p* or *q*' is true if and only if *p* and *q* are not both false. And, if we are not prepared to take this notoriously controversial assumption for granted, we can just as well construe Rips's results as revealing individual differences in how people use and understand such connectives. In particular those results can be taken to confirm the already well-supported hypothesis that many people do not use 'if', 'and', 'or', etc. in a purely truth-functional role.[2] In order to get closer to evidence that a subject is not operating with the rule of disjunction-introduction, it would be necessary to demonstrate that he does not recognize the validity of an inference from a premiss of the form '*p* is true' to a conclusion of the form '*p* and *q* are not both false'. But no one supposes that any substantial tendency towards this kind of error would be demonstrable.

Another example of the way in which apparent evidence of widespread irrationality turns out, on closer scrutiny, to be ambivalent is in regard to the fallacy of illicit conversion of conditionals–i.e. of arguing from 'If *p* then *q*' to 'If *q* then *p*'. This is an example of supposed proneness to make an invalid inference rather than of supposed proneness not to make a valid one. Indeed, intellectuals have remarked for over two millennia[3] on the tendency of their inferiors to commit this fallacy, and in recent years it has become a topic for experimental study. Wason and Johnson-Laird explain the data on the

---

[1] L. Rips, 'Reasoning as a Central Intellective Ability', in R. J. Sternberg (ed.), *Advances in the Study of Human Intelligence*, vol. 2, Hillsdale, NJ: Erlbaum, 1984, pp. 105-47, esp. pp. 134-7.

[2] L. Jonathan Cohen, 'Some Remarks on Grice's Views about the Logical Particles of Natural Language', in Y. Bar-Hillel (ed.), *Pragmatics of Natural Language*, Dordrecht: Reidel, 1971, pp. 50-68, and 'Can the Conversationalist Hypothesis be Defended?', *Philosophical Studies*, 31, 1977, pp. 81-90.

[3] e.g. Aristotle, *De Sophisticis Elenchis*, 167^b 1-4. Cf. C. L. Hamblin, *Fallacies*, London: Methuen, 1970, pp. 35-7.

grounds that, in situations in which subjects are apparently prone to illicit conversion of conditionals, 'this is not because the subjects possess faulty rules of inference but because they sometimes make unwarranted interpretations of conditional statements'.[4] The subjects are claimed to treat these conditionals as if they were statements of causal connection which allow one to infer from effect to cause as well as from cause to effect.

But it is not clear that such subjects must in fact be supposed even to be making an unwarranted interpretation. We have to bear in mind here that the normative logical theory which systematizes criteria for deducibility treats symbolic formulas as stand-ins for the actual premisses possible in human reasoning. So what are the actual, concrete premisses that are represented by the initial formulas in a primitive or derived rule for natural deduction, when such rules are taken to be the norms relevant to some publicly propounded sequence of reasoning? The mere sentences uttered do not normally constitute all of the premisses conveyed by the total act of communication, since we are entitled to presume that the latter include also any judgements that are implied by the act of uttering those sentences in the contextual circumstances. More specifically, as far as human conversation is governed by rules of relevance, brevity, informativeness, and so on, as required by the purpose in hand,[5] the information provided by the utterance of a solitary conditional sentence, 'If p then q', may be presumed, unless there are contextual indications to the contrary, to be all that is required in the circumstances to satisfy the interest either of someone who wants or needs to know what is also true if p, the antecedent of the conditional, is true, or of someone who wants or needs to know the conditions under which q, the consequent, is true. In the former case (e.g. perhaps, 'If you interrupt him now, he'll be cross') the conditional is convertible because its utterance would normally be pointless unless 'If not-p, then not-q', were also true, and 'If not-p, then not-q' is formally equivalent, by the rule of contraposition, to 'If q, then p', which is itself the converse of 'If p, then q'. In the other case (e.g. perhaps, 'If you give him a tip, he'll let you in') the conditional is convertible because its solitary utterance may be presumed to state the only condition under which the consequent is true.

    [4] P. C. Wason and P. N. Johnson-Laird, *Psychology of Reasoning: Structure and Content*, London: Batsford, 1972, p. 65.
    [5] Cf. H. P. Grice, 'Logic and Conversation', in D. Davidson and G. Harman (eds.), *The Logic of Grammar*, Encino, Calif.: Dickinson, 1975, pp. 64-75.

Hence, if we consider the total content of the message communicated, rather than just the conditional sentence that is uttered, it would not be fallacious or unwarranted for subjects to presume, unless there are specific indications to the contrary, that the converse of the conditional is implicit in the message. A psychological experimenter who wishes to exclude the legitimacy of presuming the converse in such a case must contrive suitable instructions to his subjects. He must either try to teach them how to distinguish between the implications of a sentence uttered and the implications of its utterance, in which case the extent to which they still commit the supposed fallacy may just measure the failure of his attempt to teach the relevant distinction. Or, alternatively, he must spell out a problem to his subjects which contains specific indications that the normal implications of uttering conditional sentences do not apply in regard to it, in which case the extent to which subjects still commit the supposed fallacy may just measure the inadequacy of those indications. In sum, just as in the case of Rips' investigation of supposed fallacies about disjunction-introduction, it looks as though the data are inevitably inconclusive. To be sure that the subjects understood the exact question that the investigators wished to ask them, it would be necessary to impose on them such an apparatus of clarifications and instructions that they could no longer be regarded as untutored laymen and the experiment would then become just a test of their educational progress in the field of philosophical logic.

Very similar considerations apply to cross-cultural tests of logical ability. Apparent errors in answering questions tend to be interpretable as due to misunderstanding of the questions intended. It has been demonstrated for example, that, although performance with formal syllogisms is at chance level among uneducated people in several cultures, inferential reasoning is not necessarily defective.[6] The concept of a deductive problem in which only the information given should be considered is something inculcated by education and is not readily understood by the uneducated. For example, an illiterate Mexican may be told 'To carry corn from his farm José needs a horse and cart; he has the horse; but he does not have the cart.' The question is then put 'Can José carry corn from his farm?' The illiterate Mexican replies 'Yes' on the grounds–quite reasonable in his culture–that José

[6] S. Scribner, 'Modes of Thinking and Ways of Speaking: Culture and Logic Reconsidered', in P. N. Johnson-Laird and P. C. Wason (eds.), *Thinking: Readings in Cognitive Science*, Cambridge: CUP, 1977, pp. 483-500.

will borrow a cart. He may not have grasped the precise question intended. But he has certainly shown his ability to reason about particular cases.

It is thus extremely difficult to establish that any deductive fallacy is regularly committed by untutored laymen. The fact is that the role which a person assigns to a particular logical particle, such as 'or', 'if', etc., in his interpretation or understanding of his own and other people's utterances is indistinguishable from the patterns of logical contradiction, necessary truth, and logically valid inference to which he supposes that the use of these particles gives rise. So, in order to find out what he means, you normally have to assume that he is not committing any logical errors. On the further assumption that he intends his usage to be uniform, you may be able to convict him occasionally of committing a logical fallacy, because occasionally he may deviate from the norms implicit in his usual practice. And no doubt the causes of those deviations–inattention, forgetfulness, wishful thinking, complexity of argument, preoccupation with the salient or familiar, etc.–are well worth investigating. But what is impossible, in regard to logical deducibility, is to achieve some firm determination of how a person *understands* occurrences of logical particles that is quite independent of determining what his singular *intuitions* are about logical contradiction and deducibility. So it is not that logical intuition has to be regarded as a mysteriously transcendent faculty for acquiring knowledge of inferences that are safe not just in the actual world but also in all possible worlds. Rather, understanding and intuition here are just different sides of the same coin. It is different with experimental tasks that hinge on the use of non-logical words. In an appropriate context one can easily determine the species of plant, say, that a person supposes a given word to name, without at the same time determining what he believes about the properties, behaviour, life-cycle, etc. of that plant. He may be able to identify lupins when he sees them but knows nothing about their food-value, mode of reproduction, optimal soil conditions, or susceptibility to frost. But logical words do not admit of any analogous differentiation between verbal skills and factual knowledge. In their case nominal and real essence, as it were, are intrinsically indistinguishable.

Perhaps it will be objected that if the meaning of a logical particle is linked to its role in reasoning, then being prone to a certain kind of logical fallacy must merely be linked with assigning some correspondingly undesirable meaning to one or more logical particles. So, if some such assignment were common, the corresponding fallacy would also be common.

But what would it be like to have in one's language a connective that generated invalid inferences? We can take as an imaginary example the logical properties that Prior[7] attributed to the word 'tonk'. These properties combine to ensure that in a language containing 'tonk' any conclusion whatever can apparently be obtained from any premiss whatever. So, if we detected the presence of a connective 'tonk' with this meaning in a person's language because of the nature of his inferential behaviour when the sound 'tonk' occurs in utterances, we would know that his system of norms for deductive inference was unsound, in the sense that it would not guarantee that the conclusion of an inference would always be true if its premisses were. But there is no evidence that any natural language has ever contained such a connective. Indeed the situation is at worst self-correcting. If a language embodied a logic that was unsound in the above sense, its speakers could hardly be expected to survive the hazards of nature in sufficient numbers to be able to pass on the language to later generations. Nor, therefore, would it be surprising if, as Belnap suggests,[8] our concept of deducibility, by requiring soundness, rules out a priori the use of any such language. Our very idea of a 'tonk' language would then be incoherent.

Perhaps someone will now object that the proneness of untutored laymen to *certain* kinds of deductive fallacy is not only experimentally demonstrable but also rather difficult to eradicate. In these cases, the objection will run, invalid intuitions seem particularly liable to recur, much as we find it difficult to prevent perceptual illusions–the mirage on the hot road, the Müller-Lyer, etc.–from recurring even after we have established that they are illusions. Consider, for example, Wason's four-card trick.[9] The subjects are presented with four laboratory cards showing, respectively, 'A', 'D', '4' and '7', and they know from previous experience that every card, of which these are a subset, has a letter on one side and a number on the other. They are then given the rule 'If a card has a vowel on one side, then it has an even number on the other side' and are asked to say which cards need to be turned over in order to determine whether the rule is true or false

---

[7] A. N. Prior, 'The Runabout Inference Ticket', *Analysis*, 21:2, 1960, pp. 38-9.
[8] N. D. Belnap, Jr., 'Tonk, Plonk and Plink', *Analysis*, 22:6, 1962, pp. 130-4.
[9] P. C. Wason, 'Reasoning', in B. Foss (ed.), *New Horizons in Psychology*, vol. 1, Harmondsworth: Penguin, 1966, pp. 135-51.

in relation to the four cards presented. The most frequent answers are 'A and 4' and 'Only A', which are both wrong, while the right answer, 'A and 7', is given spontaneously by very few subjects. And even after various remedial procedures have been employed many subjects continue to give the wrong answer.[10]

It is undeniably important to explain why this intellectual conjuring trick so often and so persistently succeeds. But the experiment presents no evidence of a defect in logical competence. Many subjects are obviously unable to contrapose their application of the rule appropriately. They fail to consider how the rule should be checked in the form 'If a card has an odd number on one side, it has a consonant on the other'. But this failure does not establish any general inability to contrapose, as other experiments make clear. Results are quite different with a familiar, real-life rule like 'Every time I go to Manchester, I go by train'.[11] Nor is contraposition always appropriate. We do not test the hypothesis 'All crows are black' by examining non-black things in order to check whether or not they are crows.[12] So the psychological problem is just to determine which features of the experiment distract subjects from applying appropriate principles of reasoning that they are quite capable of applying in other cases. If subjects are adequately trained to allow for *those* features, they will not persist in giving incorrect answers, any more than an audience will continue to be taken in by an ordinary conjuror when they have been adequately trained about what to keep their eyes on. Of course, some subjects may be very much more difficult to train successfully here than others are. But educationalists will hardly be surprised if this is so.

Indeed, if the computational hypothesis (discussed in §§ 20-4 below) is taken to provide a correct framework for cognitive psychology, so that the human brain is assumed to be equipped to process information and acquire new programs in much the same way as a

[10] P. N. Johnson-Laird and P. C. Wason, 'A Theoretical Analysis of Insight into a Reasoning Task', *Cognitive Psychology*, 1, 1970, pp. 134-48.

[11] P. C. Wason and D. Shapiro, 'Natural and Contrived Experience in a Reasoning Problem', *Quarterly Journal of Experimental Psychology*, 23, 1971, pp. 63-71. Cf. also P. N. Johnson-Laird, P. Legrenzi and M. S. Legrenzi, 'Reasoning and a Sense of Reality', *British Journal of Psychology*, 63, 1972, pp. 395-400; P. C. Van Duyne, 'Realism and Linguistic Complexity', *British Journal of Psychology*, 65, 1974, pp. 59-67; K. J. Manktelow and J. St. B. T. Evans, 'Facilitation of Reasoning by Realism: Effect or Non-Effect', *British Journal of Psychology*, 70, 1979, pp. 477-88.

[12] Cf. C. G. Hempel, 'Studies in the Logic of Confirmation', *Mind*, 54, 1945, pp. 1-26 and 97-121.

digital computer, it is in any case difficult to see how any kind of inclination towards deductive irrationality can be supposed to exist in a human mind except through an accidental weakness in performance. Digital computers, with their binary logic-gates, are mechanizations of Boolean algebra. So the mind must at least have a competence for processing complexes of Boolean operations, even if the exercise of this competence is always liable to be impaired, interrupted, or inhibited in a variety of ways. If a mental procedure is describable by a cognitive psychologist in terms of a program that is implementable on a digital computer, how can such a procedure be contrary to what Boole[13] called 'the fundamental laws of those operations of the mind by which reasoning is performed'?

§ 16 ARE PEOPLE PROGRAMMED TO COMMIT FALLACIES IN PROBABILISTIC REASONING?

Summary. If people were intuitively inclined to use fallacious procedures for estimating probabilities, serious doubt would arise about the assumption of rationality on which analytical philosophy depends. For example, in experiments where subjects are asked to solve the taxicab problem, investigators claim that most subjects' answers wrongly ignore base-rates when testimonial evidence is available, and the existence of a base-rate fallacy is said to be confirmed by other experiments. However, two considerations suggest that the investigators' interpretation of the data in such experiments requires radical revision.

The situation in regard to intuitive judgements of probability is somewhat different from that which holds in regard to intuitive judgements of deducibility. This is because probabilistic reasoning requires the assignment of cardinal, ordinal, or comparative values to a probability-function and the method of estimating such values is often not fully determined by the definition of the function. Nor is the definition of the function determined always by its method of estimation. For example, suppose that, for any finite and sufficiently large number of As, the (conditional) probability of an A's being also a B is defined as the relative frequency of Bs among the As. This definition is applicable over a wide range of issues, since in any case, so far as we know, the number of terrestrial organisms (human beings,

[13] G. Boole, *An Investigation of the Laws of Thought*, London: Walton and Maberly, 1854, p. 1. I speak here only of what is called 'simulated understanding' in §21 below.

rats, roses, etc.) in the history of the universe is finite. And clearly the definition of the function and its mode of estimation are often independent of one another. This is because the size of a probability in an indeterminately large natural population has to be estimated from samples, and samples may differ from one another in size or structure. So it is, in principle, possible to discover that a subject conceives of some probability in a large population as a relative frequency and yet makes the mistake of judging that a small sample always provides as good a basis for this estimate as a large one. Such an attribution of error could well be incontrovertible, because the subject's judgement would not be open to reinterpretation on the ground of there being some ambivalence in the experimental data like that in the case of supposed fallacies in deductive reasoning (§ 15).

Nevertheless, though some psychologists have in fact claimed that lay subjects are prone to quite a wide variety of systematic errors in the estimation of probabilities, the experimental data that have so far been produced in this connection all turn out to be open to a more plausible interpretation. The investigator's beliefs that fallacies have to be imputed to their subjects turn out to be due in each case to unjustified assumptions about the nature of the probability-function in terms of which the subjects conceive their task. Nor does this view stem from an arbitrary charitableness. It would beg the question in the present context just to adopt a policy of always, or nearly always, imposing *ad hoc* an interpretation of subjects' responses in which those responses appear correct. Instead we can begin to see how the conception of probability in terms of which a subject comes to construe his task is cued uniformly for him in each case by the wording and content of his instructions and the situation in which these instructions are given (against the background of his own experience and education and any other individual differences that are relevant to his cognitive performance). And, even when our interpretations of subjects' responses are thus based not on charity but on an appropriate hypothesis about cueing, we still find no evidence of systematic fallacy.

The matter requires some rather detailed investigation, though it is neither possible nor necessary to survey here all the literature on the subject. The challenge that this extensive literature presents must certainly be faced.[14] But examination of a few central issues will suffice to show how weak the challenge really is.

[14] Cf. L. Jonathan Cohen, 'On the Psychology of Prediction: Whose is the Fallacy?', *Cognition*, 7, 1979, pp. 385-407 and ibid., 8, 1980, pp. 89-92; id., 'Can Human Irrationality

Consider first the paradox of the taxi-cabs, where most people's pre-theoretical intuitions seem grossly at odds with elementary statistical theory. Let it be accepted that the vehicle involved in a certain road accident in Smithville was a taxi-cab and that 85% of Smithville cabs are blue and 15% green. Let it be accepted too that a witness has identified the cab in the accident as green and that, when he is tested over equal numbers of blue and green cabs in conditions similar to those of the accident, he gives the correct colour in 80% of cases and the other colour in only 20%. Then what is the probability, expressed as a percentage, that the cab in the accident was blue? There is robust experimental evidence[15] to the effect that most statistically untutored people tend to estimate this probability as 20%. They thus seem to rely solely on the witness's testimony and to ignore altogether the specified base-rate—namely the distribution of cab-colours. But if, when the probability in question is calculated by means of Bayes's theorem, the specified base-rate is treated as the relevant prior probability, the required posterior probability amounts instead to approximately 60%.[16] So most people's intuitive judgements *seem* to be in error here. If they are really so—and that is what is claimed by the psychologists, Tversky and Kahneman, who originally propounded the problem—then we have at least one piece of evidence

be Experimentally Demonstrated?', *The Behavioural and Brain Sciences*, 4, 1981, pp. 317-70; id., 'Are People Programmed to Commit Fallacies? Further Thoughts about the Interpretation of Experimental Data on Probability Judgement', *Journal for the Theory of Social Behaviour*, 12, 1982, pp. 251-74; id., 'The Controversy about Rationality', *The Behavioural and Brain Sciences*, 6, 1983, pp. 510-17; id., 'Can Irrationality be Discussed Accurately?', ibid., 7, 1984, pp. 736-8.

[15] D. Kahneman and A. Tversky, 'On the Psychology of Prediction', *Oregon Research Institute Research Bulletin*, 12, 1972, whole of vol. 4; D. Lyon and P. Slovic, 'Dominance of Accuracy Information and Neglect of Base-rates in Probability Estimation', *Acta Psychologica*, 40, 1976, pp. 287-98; M. Bar-Hillel, 'The Base-rate Fallacy in Probability Judgements', *Acta Psychologica*, 44, 1980, pp. 2311-33, and id., 'The Base-rate Fallacy Controversy', in R. W. Scholz (ed.), *Decision Making Under Uncertainty*, Amsterdam: Elsevier Science Publishers, 1983, pp. 39-61.

[16] If H is the hypothesis that the cab in question is green and E states that the witness says that H is true, then by Bayes's theorem, where $p(E) > 0$,

$$p(H/E) = \frac{p(E/H) \times p(H)}{p(E)}$$

Now the likelihood ratio $p(E/H)$ is given as 0.8 and $p(H)$ is taken to be 0.15. So $p(E/H) \times p(H) = 0.12$. At the same time, with the other likelihood ratio $p(E/\text{not-}H) = 0.2$, we have $p(E) = (pE \And H) + p(E \And \text{not-}H) = (p(H) \times p(E/H)) + (p(\text{not-}H) \times p(E/\text{not-}H)) = 0.29$. Therefore $p(H/E) = 12/29$, and, since all the cabs are either green or blue, the probability that the cab is blue, given E, is 17/29.

against the assumption of human rationality on which analytical philosophy depends.

Perhaps someone will be tempted, at first, to suggest that in the experiments which establish how most people respond to the problem the judgements which articulate this response are not to be counted as 'intuitive' in the sense defined in § 8 above. Intuitions, in the relevant sense, are supposed not to be checkable by sensory perception. For, if they involved a form of empirical judgement, any theories based on them would belong to natural science, not philosophy. But a judgement that the probability of the Smithville cab's being blue is, say, 20% is indeed a kind of empirical judgement because it is taken to be checkable against the circumstances of the case. The judgement's correctness or incorrectness is assessable in the light of empirical facts about the base-rate, the witness's reliability, etc. Perhaps, therefore, someone will be tempted to conclude that, whatever the correct solution of the problem, experimental data about how people respond to it are irrelevant to metaphilosophical issues about the rationality of intuitions.

However, these experimental data are not so easily disposed of. The estimate of a 20%, or 60%, probability is indeed in part an empirical judgement in that one of the things you need to do in order to see whether it is correct is to look at the facts. But that is not all you need to do. Even when you know all the facts that might be relevant you still have to select the ones that are actually relevant, and then apply the pertinent algorithm for inferring the requisite probability from the relevant facts. And it is this selective procedure, coupled with the ensuing inference, that intrudes an element of intuition into the judgement at issue. So the question arises, not only whether subjects in the experiments use a correct inferential algorithm, but also whether it is correct for them to ignore the specified base-rate in applying this algorithm.

That question is raised in the present context because of its metaphilosophical implications. But it is important in many other contexts also and illustrates very clearly how the use of inductive argument from singular intuitions, as remarked in § 14 above, tends to link philosophy quite closely to perplexities that arise in other areas of contemporary culture. Thus the impact of base-rates on diagnostic evidence is sometimes a crucial issue in medical decisions. Suppose that certain symptoms are shared by a rare (15%) and a common (85%) disease, that the only relevant test establishes which of the two diseases is present with no better than 80% accuracy, and that performance of the test in the case in hand indicates the presence of the less common disease. Is the test worth doing at all if the relatively low base-rate of the disease has to be taken into account? But, if you yourself had those symptoms and the right choice of therapy was a matter of life or death, would you agree to being automatically diagnosed, without any test, as having the commoner disease? Correspondingly the impact of base-rates on testimonial evidence is of great forensic importance, and many analogous issues arise in business, administration, and military intelligence.[17]

A prima-facie attractive move is to claim that the specified base-rate distribution is largely irrelevant to any question about the probability that the cab in a particular accident was blue. The specified base-rate, it might be said, gives us a probability for the blueness of any cab that is picked out at random in the town, but a probability for the blueness of any cab that is involved in an accident in the town is a very different matter. The psychologists, on this view, have chosen the wrong prior probability as a premiss for their Bayesian calculation. The correct prior should rather be 50% than 80%, reflecting the lack of relevant information. And this defence of the common answer to the taxicab problem seems to be supported by the fact that people's inclination to use base-rate statistics as premisses for their calculations is known to increase as those statistics become more immediately relevant to the specific outcome at issue—especially if the relevance is causal.[18]

Such a defence, however, does not account for all the relevant experimental data. The trouble is that, when told only the distribution of cab-colours in the town and then asked to estimate the probability, on that evidence, that the cab involved in the accident is blue, most people do reply with a figure of 85%.[19] That is to say, there is robust experimental evidence that, when they are not told anything about the witness's testimony, most people's intuitions are quite content to equate the probability at issue with the specified base-rate. One can therefore hardly defend the common response to the original problem by claiming that this base-rate is an intrinsically inappropriate

[17] It is sometimes said that an analogous issue lies at the heart of the controversy (about the evidence for miracles) between D. Hume, *An Enquiry Concerning Human Understanding*, Oxford: OUP, 1902, pp. 109-31, and R. Price, *Four Dissertations*, London: Millar and Cadell, 2nd edn., 1768, pp. 384-464. But in that issue the two likelihood ratios are not complementary.

[18] See Bar-Hillel, 'The Base-rate Fallacy in Probability Judgements', loc. cit.

[19] Lyon and Slovic, op. cit., p. 294.

premiss for Bayesian calculations. Rather, it might plausibly be claimed, those who do not treat this base-rate as the prior probability in their tacit Bayesian calculations are just being inconsistent.

Moreover, some quite differently structured experiments also seem to provide evidence of this base-rate fallacy.[20] Subjects are shown brief personality descriptions of several individuals, allegedly sampled at random from a group of 100 professionals each of whom is an engineer or a lawyer. In one experimental condition they are told that the group from which the descriptions had been drawn consisted of 70 engineers and 30 lawyers, in another that it consisted of 30 engineers and 70 lawyers. All subjects are then asked to assess, for each description, the probability that it belonged to an engineer rather than to a lawyer. If the mathematical probability that any particular description belongs to an engineer rather than to a lawyer is calculated in accordance with Bayes's theorem, it should apparently be higher under the first condition than under the second. But in fact people tend to estimate the probability at approximately the same figure in both cases. They are said to violate Bayes's rule and to be dominated here, as in the taxicab experiment, by a 'heuristic' of representativeness. This is a principle–which is said to work successfully in some cases but not in others–for judging the probability of an outcome just by the extent to which it 'represents' the evidence. And, though subjects thus fail to equate the relevant prior probability with the specified base-rate when they are given the additional descriptive information about particular individuals, they nevertheless judge the probability that a particular individual is an engineer to be 70% or 30% respectively, when they are not given these descriptions. That is to say, when there is no additional information they equate the probability at issue with the specified base-rate, as in the taxi-cab problem. And the results of this experiment also count against the hypothesis that in the taxi-cab case subjects are just inclined to confuse the probability in question with its converse–i.e. to confuse the required probability that the cab is blue given that the witness says it is, with the stated probability that the witness says it's blue given that it is blue.

Nevertheless, at least two important considerations count against the psychologists' view that most subjects in these experiments are ignoring prior probabilities and are therefore applying an incorrect procedure for estimating mathematical probabilities.

[20] A. Tversky and D. Kahneman, 'Judgement under Uncertainty: Heuristics and Biases', *Science*, 125, 1974, pp. 1124-31.

First, there is a certain oddity about the claim that some people make incorrect judgements of probability by systematically ignoring Bayes's theorem. That theorem is so elementary a principle in the classical mathematics of probability—so near to its heart—that anyone who systematically ignores it could well be interpreted as operating with some non-classical probability-function rather than as supplying incorrect values for the classical one. If Bayes's theorem required, as Bernoulli's 'law of large numbers' theorem does, a proof of several non-obvious stages, it is at least conceivable that people might possess some defining set of mathematical principles for classical probability without possessing Bayes's theorem. As already remarked in § 10 above, a person who is known to believe that p is not necessarily expected to believe any of the remoter or less obvious consequences of p. But Bayes's theorem is not like that. If you accept the multiplicational law for the probability of a conjunction, plus the commutativity of conjunction, you already have Bayes's theorem in a form adequate for the taxi-cab problem. So there is a presumption that anyone who does systematically ignore Bayes's theorem in his probabilistic reasoning is just not operating with a function that is mathematically definable in standard terms (e.g. in terms of Kolmogorov's axioms). Indeed, we might even have to take what such a person says more as evidence about what conception of probability he is operating with than as evidence about his ability to operate with that conception correctly.

Secondly, robust experimental data have been produced by other psychologists[21] that are difficult to reconcile with the existence of an inclination, among statistically untutored individuals, to commit the base-rate fallacy. These other data have been interpreted as showing that, where new information is integrated with old, in relation to a not wholly dissimilar type of question, people tend to pay too much attention, not too little, to the relevant prior probabilities. In the experiment subjects have to estimate the probability that a randomly chosen bag contains predominantly blue or predominantly red chips, on the

---

[21] L. D. Phillips and W. Edwards, 'Conservatism in a Simple Probability Inference Task', *Journal of Experimental Psychology*, 72, 1966, pp. 346-54; C. R. Paterson and W. M. Du Charme, 'A Primacy Effect in Subjective Probability Revision', *Journal of Experimental Psychology*, 73, 1967, pp. 61-5; D. M. Messick and F. T. Campos, 'Training and Conservatism in Subjective Probability', *Journal of Experimental Psychology*, 94, 1972, pp. 335-7; M. L. Donmell and W. M. Du Charme, 'The Effect of Bayesian Feedback on Learning in an Odds Estimation Task', *Organizational Behavior and Human Performance*, 14, 1975, pp. 305-13.

evidence obtained by drawing (blindly) a chip at a time from the bag and replacing it. The subjects are told that each of the set of bags contains either predominantly blue or predominantly red chips; they are told the numbers of chips of the majority and minority colours, which are the same in each bag; and they are also told the ratio of bags of the one type to bags of the other, which is assumed to afford them a prior probability for their task. They are then shown a sequence of twenty chips, drawn one at a time from the chosen bag and each replaced immediately after being shown, and they are asked to revise their previous estimate (of the probability that a certain type of bag has been chosen) after each new chip is shown. In the event subjects tend to revise their estimate less than psychologists calculate that they should do according to Bayes's law. At each revision the prior probability seems to have too much influence on the estimate. Subjects are therefore accused of being excessively conservative in the integration of new information. And the difficulty of explaining subjects' responses in the taxi-cab case is thus compounded. Reasons have apparently to be found that will explain why people have a genetically or culturally induced way of judging probabilities whereby, on the one hand, prior probabilities are intuitively ignored in favour of more immediate evidence when the probability of a particular taxi-cab's being blue is at issue, and, on the other, prior probabilities are intuitively allowed to dominate over more immediate evidence when the probability of a particular bag's containing predominantly blue chips is at issue. What kind of computational procedure, information-processing mechanism, or biological need could possibly explain the persistent occurrence of such disparate errors in the treatment of relatively similar issues?

These two considerations count strongly against the psychologists' treatment of the taxi-cab problem. But, unless that treatment is replaced by a more satisfactory one, there will still be room for doubt here about the assumption of rationality on which the practice of analytical philosophy depends. What is required, in order to allay such doubt, is a coherent interpretation of the experimental results that does not impute a flawed capacity for reasoning to most people and also has substantial independent support.

§ 17 THE DOMINANCE OF COUNTERFACTUALIZABLE
PROBABILITIES OVER NON-COUNTERFACTUALIZABLE ONES

Summary. To think of a probability as counterfactualizable is to think of it as applying not only to the entities that are actually members of the reference-class, but also to any others. To think of a probability as non-counterfactualizable is to think of it as applying only to the actual members of the reference-class. People are naturally inclined to think in terms of counterfactualizable probabilities, rather than in terms of non-counterfactualizable ones, wherever it seems reasonable to do so. In these terms it is easy to construct an interpretation of recent experimental data that avoids the elements of paradox and incoherence which are present in the accounts given by the investigators themselves. This interpretation has the further merit of resolving the fallacy of alleged conservatism and the so-called 'gambler's fallacy'.

The key to the issue about the so-called 'base-rate fallacy' is to distinguish between two relevantly different conceptions of probability. Both satisfy standard mathematical principles, but one will be termed 'counterfactualizable' and the other 'non-counterfactualizable'. The psychological hypothesis will then be that normal adults in our culture have both conceptions at their disposal, as well as non-mathematical causal reasoning, though they tend to employ the counterfactualizable conception rather than the non-counterfactualizable one when both are applicable. When the experimental data are interpreted in these terms, the case for the 'base-rate fallacy' collapses and so does the case for the alleged fallacy of conservatism. But to fortify that conclusion a philosophical argument for the validity of this popular, if usually unselfconscious, dualism will also be needed. And it will then turn out that counterfactualizability can be regarded as a matter of degree, with non-counterfactualizability as the zero-point on the scale.

A probability is being conceived counterfactualizably if and only if it is thought of as applying not only to entities that are actually members of the reference-class but also to those that are not. It is thus a probability with counterfactual implications. For example, to accept that, on the assumption that he is a 50-year-old asbestos worker, a man has a 0.8 probability of death before the age of 70, is to accept a generalized conditional probability that applies not only to any person in the history of the universe who is actually a 50-year-old asbestos worker but also to any individual who is not. So such a probability can guide a person's decisions and lead him to act otherwise than he might have done. It can tell a young man about a probable consequence of his continuing to work in an asbestos factory, without any risk of being refuted by the deterrent efficacy of the warnings thus delivered. If the reference-class (50-year-old asbestos workers) had come to have either more or fewer members than it in fact has, the probability of any member's dying before the age of 70 would have remained the same. Indeed, even if we did not already have such a way of judging probabilities, we should do well to develop one because of the important uses to which it can be put.

In contrast with this a probability is being conceived non-counter-factualizably if and only if it is thought of as applying only to those entities that are actually members of the reference-class. A non-counterfactualizable probability is an accidental property of its reference-class and has no counterfactual implications. For example, in the currect climate of educational politics to accept a 0.4 probability of studying science for any 1983 freshman at Oxford University is not to accept a probability that could be relied on to have held good if more students had been admitted that year: perhaps the additional places would all have been reserved for science. Similarly to accept a 0.25 probability of being green for any stopping-place on a particular roulette-dial, because it happens to have 8 green and 24 blue stopping-places, is not to accept a probability that could be relied on to apply if further stopping-places were inserted. Moreover, because such a non-counterfactualizable probability has no counterfactual implications—because its range of application does not extend beyond the actual membership of its reference-class—it is correspondingly much less valuable as a guide to the making of decisions. It affords no basis for advice that is intended to change people's attitudes towards per-forming actions that add new members to the reference-class. One should hardly be surprised therefore if, as the psychological hypo-thesis under consideration asserts, ordinary people tend to let the counterfactualizable conception of probability displace or override the non-counterfactualizable one whenever both are employable. To do otherwise would obviously be imprudent.

One can see quite easily that the dominance of counterfactualizable over non-counterfactualizable conceptions of probability, as a hypo-thesis in the psychology of everyday, unsophisticated, pre-theoretical judgement, readily accounts for the experimental data that we have been considering, without any need to suppose the existence of a base-rate fallacy, or of a fallacy of conservatism, in the integration of new information.

Consider the taxi-cab data first. Here the subjects who are told only the cab-colour base-rate may be taken to evaluate a non-counterfactualizable probability in most of their responses, since they are given no reason to suppose that the ratio of cab-colours, or of cab-colour appearances at the scene of the accident, would remain the same if more cabs were introduced into Smithville. But the subjects who are told also the facts about the witness's reliability have the opportunity to evaluate the likelihood of the witness's reporting the cab to be green, given that it is in fact blue, as a counterfactualizable probability, since the witness's reliability would presumably remain approximately the same even if he testified in other cases. So in this situation, on the hypothesis that a counterfactualizable conception of probability dominates a non-counterfactualizable one wherever possible, the subjects may be expected to concentrate their attention on calculating a counterfactualizable posterior probability. The relevant prior probability also would then have to be a counterfactualizable one, such as the probability that a cab involved in the kind of accident in question is a blue one; and that probability, because there is as much (or as little) stated for it as against it, could reasonably be put equal to 0.5. Hence the probability of the cab's being blue, on the available information, would quite reasonably be put at 0.2 by anyone who operates in accordance with Bayes's theorem and assumes, consciously or unconsciously, that his task is to state, if he can, a counterfactualizable rather than a non-counterfactualizable probability. If, instead, he took the specified base-rate–the ratio of cab-colours in the town–as the relevant prior probability for his calculations, he would be committing the fallacy of equivocation, because he would be arguing from a non-counterfactualizable probability in order to determine a counterfactualizable one. Of course, if a subject were sufficiently sophisticated he would ask the experimenter 'Do you want me to state a counterfactualizable, or a non-counterfactualizable probability?' But if the experimenter were sufficiently sophisticated he would pose an unambiguous question, rather than leave it to the subjects to presume that he must prefer an answer in terms of a counterfactualizable rather than a non-counterfactualizable probability when such an answer is possible.

It is superficially tempting to object that, if the base-rate for blue cabs in the town were 100%, the relevant prior probability would certainly be determined by the base-rate and that therefore this base-rate should also be taken into account when the ratio of blue cabs is less than 100%. But the relevant counterfactualizable prior probability is the probability that the cab involved in a particular accident is blue. Obviously this probability is 100% if the ratio of blue cabs in the town is 100%. But it need not be 99% if the ratio of blue cabs in the town is 99%: the single green cab might be highly accident-prone. Of course, some legal systems allow a proportionate distribution of legal liability in some such cases. But this possibility is a special feature of the legal situation, and concerns what is to be done about the practical issue of compensation. One can see that the epistemic question about probability is an independent issue if one considers the situation where a medical patient has symptoms that in 85% of cases are associated with disease A and in 15% with disease B, and a discriminatory test that has 80% reliability indicates disease B: to mix the medicines in corresponding proportions might well be fatal!

The dominance of counterfactualizable over non-counterfactualizable probability provides an analogous explanation, which need not be detailed here, for the standard intuitive responses in regard to the problem about lawyers and engineers. And it can also be shown to account satisfactorily for the experimental data that are supposed to reveal conservatism in integrating new information about the colour of the majority of the chips in a bag. In applying Bayes's theorem to this task of bag identification a subject has to assume initially three different kinds of premises: a prior probability, $p(E)$, for the evidential fact of drawing, say, a red chip (if that is the colour that he has in fact drawn); a prior probability, $p(H)$, for the hypothesis of drawing, say, a predominantly red bag; and a conditional probability, $p(E/H)$, for drawing, let us say, a red chip on the hypothesis that a predominantly red bag is drawn. These probabilities would all be properly thought of as counterfactualizable ones, since they are concerned with outcomes of drawings, whether these drawings be of chips from a bag or of bags from an ensemble of bags. Because replacement is supposed to take place, the value estimated in each case applies not only to the actual drawing of a bag, or red chip, but also to any others that might have been made under the same conditions. But it is easy to confuse these three counterfactualizable probabilities about certain indefinitely repeatable events with three non-counterfactualizable ones about certain definite objects. There is the known prior probability, $p(E')$, that any one chip, within the total population of chips, is a red one;

there is the known prior probability, $p(H')$, that any one bag, within the population of bags, is a predominantly red one; and there is the known conditional probability $p(E'/H')$, which is the probability that any one chip is a red one given that it is in a bag which predominantly contains red chips. These probabilities are all non-counterfactualizable ones because they apply only to those objects that are members of the relevant populations. They imply nothing about what any additional bags or chips would be like.

Now it is reasonable to equate $p(E)$–the initial overall probability of *drawing* a red chip–with $p(E')$, since the effect of any bias in how chips lie in, or are drawable from, a particular bag might be expected to be cancelled out by other biases in other bags. Again it is reasonable to equate $p(H)$–the initial probability of *drawing* a predominantly red bag–with $p(H')$ because the drawing of the bag is stated to have been done at random. But it would also be reasonable to regard $p(E/H)$ as not being equal to $p(E'/H')$ but rather as being somewhere between $p(E')$ and $p(E'/H')$, in order to allow for the effect of any bias in how chips lie, or are drawable from, a particular bag. It will then follow that $p(E/H)/p(E)$ will be nearer to 1 than $p(E'/H')/p(E')$ is, and so by Bayes's theorem $p(H/E)$ will be closer to $p(H)$ than $p(H'/E')$ is to $p(H')$. And analogous results will be appropriate for later drawings.

Let us suppose that the subjects take their task to be concerned with the value of, say, $p(H/E)$ rather than with that of $p(H'/E')$. If interpreted thus, the subjects' reported responses are not fallacious or unreasonably conservative. They accord with Bayes's theorem and, in their predictable preference for counterfactualizable over non-counterfactualizable probability, reflect a healthy disinclination to accept without evidence that the outcome of each draw from a particular bag is a matter of pure chance. Moreover, if this interpretation is correct, one would expect an appropriate change in subjects' responses if they are encouraged to think that the outcome of each draw from a particular bag is indeed a matter of pure chance. As subjects bring the value of the counterfactualizable probability $p(E/H)$ into line with that of the non-counterfactualizable one $p(E'/H')$, 'conservatism' should diminish or disappear. And experiments show that such an expectation is justified. 'Conservatism' disappears when sequences of estimates are calibrated against actual frequencies of the relevant outcomes that reveal a genuinely chance set-up.[22]

The same dualistic psychology of probability-judgement serves to

[22] Messick and Campos, op. cit.

transform the so-called 'gambler's fallacy' into a valid conclusion from a trio of premises each of which is inherently reasonable in the situation concerned. So the hypothesis that was initially proposed in order to provide a coherent interpretation of the data about base-rate problems acquires further confirmation from its successful application to quite a different kind of problem.

Of course, if we think of coin-tossing, for example, as a game of pure chance, it is absurd to suppose that the outcome of a particular toss is in any way affected by previous outcomes. However long a run of heads has occurred with a particular coin, the probability of the coin's falling tails on the next toss will still be 0.5. But that is because, in the very act of regarding the coin-tossing as a game of pure chance, we have put the value of the relevant counterfactualizable probability equal to the value of the relevant non-counterfactualizable one. The general principle is that, within what is assumed to be a game of pure chance, we measure the probability of any single outcome by the reciprocal of the number of mutually co-ordinate and jointly exhaustive outcome-types. More specifically, we measure the counterfactualizable probability of achieving heads, say, on a particular toss of a coin, however often we play the game or fail to play it, by the non-counterfactualizable probability of heads within the population of two outcome-types, heads and tails.

But the situation is quite different for a person who does not just assume (even though he thinks it highly probable) that the game is one of pure chance and therefore does not just measure the counter-factualizable probability of each outcome by its associated non-counterfactualizable one. For such a person it becomes reasonable to base his estimates on all the relevant premises that he has available, such as past experience of coin-tossing or the present long run of heads, and each of the following three propositions then becomes inherently plausible:

(1) It is counterfactualizably much more probable than not that every toss's outcome is a matter of pure chance (i.e. there is a presumption that the counterfactualizable probability of each outcome is equal to its associated non-counterfactualizable probability).

(2) If it is counterfactualizably much more probable than not that every toss's outcome is a matter of pure chance, then, in the case of each toss's outcome, that outcome will (counterfactualizably) probably not increase the present low counterfactualizable probability that not every toss's outcome is a matter of pure chance (which is like

saying that, if there's strong evidential support for p, then there's some evidential support for believing of each as yet unknown piece of evidence that it will support p).

(3) If the next outcome, after the present long run of heads, is heads yet again, that outcome will increase the present low counterfactualizable probability that not every toss's outcome is a matter of pure chance (which is like saying that only a born sucker—or a dupe of the sorites paradox—never suspects a rigged wheel or a stacked deck).

And from these three propositions it follows by a short sequence of elementary logical or mathematical steps[23] that it is counterfactualizably more probable than not that the next outcome, after the present long run of heads, will not be heads yet again.

There may also be other ways of rationalizing the 'gambler's fallacy',[24] and no doubt many people get sufficiently muddled about probability to make genuine mistakes about it. In order to find out exactly what goes on, and why, we need more experimental data, and in particular more subjects' protocols. But the simplest available explanation of the prevalence of the 'gambler's fallacy' is that it stems from a quite legitimate use of the counterfactualizable conception of probability in contexts where it is not assumed, or not taken as established, that pure chance is operating.

That is certainly a more satisfactory explanation than the claim that subjects are influenced by the so-called heuristic of representativeness to predict an outcome which helps the sequence of outcomes to represent the chance process at work. For, if such a heuristic were operative, one would expect after a run of n heads that subjects would predict not just one outcome of tails but a run of n tails. (But the theory that posits a heuristic of representativeness is infinitely adaptable. When subjects think that a sample of 100 people is more likely to contain 53 men and 47 women than 50 of each, they are said to think of the composition of the sample as representing the randomness of the sample's selection, and when they stay far closer to 0.5 than the mathematics of chance predicts in estimating the proportion of times that a coin falls heads they are said to think of this as representing the fairness of the coin.[25] How convenient that the fairness of the sample's

[23] Cohen, 'Are People Programmed to Commit Fallacies?', pp. 261-2.

[24] Cohen, 'Can Human Irrationality be Experimentally Demonstrated?', pp. 327-8.

[25] See A. Tversky and D. Kahneman, 'Judgements of and by Representativeness', in D. Kahneman, P. Slovic, and A. Tversky (eds.), *Judgement under Uncertainty: Heuristics and Biases*, Cambridge: CUP, 1982, p. 87, and id., 'Belief in the Law of Small Numbers', ibid., p. 24.

selection is not represented rather than its randomness, and that the randomness of the coin-tossing is not represented rather than its fairness! Indeed, even in the taxi-cab case one can still ask why, if a heuristic of representativeness is being used, the subjects' answer tends to represent the evidence afforded by the witness's testimony rather than the evidence afforded by the distribution of cab-colours in the town.)

Moreover, if the interpretation proposed here is correct, one would expect that encouragement to think of every outcome as a matter of pure chance would diminish or eliminate the kind of response that psychologists commonly take to be fallacious. And this does indeed turn out to be the case. When the number of trials with a well-constructed gambling device has been increased sufficiently to achieve calibration of probability estimates against actual frequencies, the 'gambler's fallacy' no longer recurs.[26] The counterfactualizable probability has been equated with the relevant non-counterfactualizable one. In terms of the proposed interpretation we can say that proposition (3) has then become unacceptable and that correspondingly the prediction of a change in the sequence of toss-outcomes, which follows from the conjunction of (1), (2), and (3), no longer has an adequate function.

The point here, it should be emphasized, is not that in each of the experiments discussed there is, under all consistent assumptions, a uniquely correct answer, namely the answer given by the majority of the subjects. Rather, in each case the answer that is actually given by the majority is a reasonable one on the facts stated, but under admissible alternative assumptions the answers that the psychological experimenters think correct would not be unreasonable either. If, for example, your experience gives you reason to assume that the two different cab-fleets' relative frequency of appearance at the scene of the accident would be kept constant by a municipal licensing authority, you would be right to take the base-rate as a counterfactualizable prior probability. Similarly, if your experience gives you reason to assume that each act of coin-tossing is evenly balanced, you would be right to suppose a 0.5 counterfactualizable probability of heads on each toss. But, because this issue about cab-licensing or the mechanics of coin-tossing is not settled by the information actually given to the subjects, it is reasonable for them to supply their own, more natural assump-

---

[26] H. Lindman and W. Edwards, 'Unlearning the Gambler's Fallacy', *Journal of Experimental Psychology*, 62, 1961, p. 630.

tions, namely that the cab-colour ratio is accidental (i.e. not upheld by any continuing causal process) and that the even balance of the coin-tossing is presumptive but not certain.

§ 18 THE FOUNDATIONS OF COUNTERFACTUALIZABLE PROBABILITY

Summary. The dominance of counterfactualizable over non-counterfactualizable probability needs to be defended in a way that is not exposed to the charge of circularity. It must be shown to stand or fall with a systematic body of ideas that critics will be reluctant to sacrifice. This body of ideas is not to be found within any of the familiar theories of probability, but rather in association with the analogous difference between law-stating generalizations, from which ampliative counterfactuals are derivable, and accidentally true generalizations, from which they are not. Variational induction is what establishes degree of counterfactualizability or of proximity to natural law: enumerative induction is what establishes non-counterfactualizable statements of probability or accidentally true generalizations.

The psychological hypothesis proposed in § 17 obviously provides a much smoother interpretation of the data than can any interpretation that assumes a unitary conception of probability. We need no longer infer, for example, that people strangely reverse their attitudes to base-rates when they move from integrating new information about the colour of a cab in an accident to integrating new information about the predominant colour of chips in a bag. We need no longer suppose two distinct kinds of fallacy here, and a third in the case of the 'gambler's fallacy'. Instead the commonest responses in such situations are not fallacious at all, if it is reasonable for counterfactualizable probabilities to dominate non-counterfactualizable ones.

But there is a possible challenge to the reasonableness of this dominance that has to be met. The challenge might run as follows. 'The claim that the concept of probability has both a counter-factualizable and a non-counterfactualizable form, and that it is prudent to prefer the former to the latter wherever possible, was defended by an appeal to examples. Such examples are presumably intended to evoke relevant intuitions. But surely that defence must be circular? What is focally at issue is whether singular intuitive judge-ments afford appropriate premises for philosophical induction. And what is charged is that, at least in regard to probability, they cannot be relied on to do so if the psychologists' interpretations of relevant experimental data are correct. So, in the present context, such interpretations can hardly be overthrown by a rival theory that relies on premisses of the very same kind as those that are at issue, namely singular intuitive judgements, while you have yourself argued (in § 9) that general intuitions afford even weaker premisses than singular ones.'

This is a powerful challenge. The only way to meet it is to show how the thesis about counterfactualizability stands or falls with a systematic body of ideas that critics will be reluctant to sacrifice. In other words, a hypothetical mode of argument has to be adopted since, in the nature of the case, any apposite categorical argument would beg the question.

But where is such a connected body of ideas to be found? Not, unfortunately, within any of the standard theories about the nature of probability.[27] In particular, the distinction between counterfactualizable and non-counterfactualizable probability cuts right across the familiar division between subjectivist and objectivist theories. The same distinction can be drawn on both sides of that division, even though particular versions of subjectivism, or of objectivism, may be more interested in counterfactualizable than in non-counterfactualizable probability.

According to the standard subjectivist account probability is to be explicated as an evaluation of the strength of the speaker's own belief, or of the strength of belief that is appropriate, where strength of belief that p is true may be measured by the odds acceptable on p within a system of odds on related issues that is not inherently loss-making. Probabilities thus explicated are counterfactualizable when the bet relates to, say, the performance of a particular horse in virtue of its past record and present competition, since presumably the same odds would have been acceptable in relation to any other horse that was similarly circumstanced. But such betting-odds are non-counterfactualizable when they apply to, say, the professional characterization of a particular man in a group about which nothing is known except that it happens accidentally to contain 70 lawyers and 30 engineers at the time in question.

According to the most defensible objectivist account a probability is to be thought of either as the relative frequency of relevant events or

---

[27] My earlier treatment of the taxi-cabs paradox was rather misleading in this respect: e.g. 'Can Irrationality be Discussed Accurately?', p. 736.

entities in the finite class specified, or as a causal propensity, or as a logical relation of partial entailment. Clearly some of the probabilities so conceived are counterfactualizable, such as the long-run relative frequency with which 50-year-old asbestos workers die before the age of 70. Others are clearly non-counterfactualizable, such as the relative frequency of lawyers in the group that I have just mentioned. Only the propensity and logical relation theories seem tied exclusively to counterfactualizable probabilities. But so much the worse for any claim to comprehensiveness that may be advanced on their behalf.

We need, therefore, to seek arguments in this matter within a wider framework–a framework that transcends the whole problem of probability. Specifically we need to begin by relating the distinction between counterfactualizable and non-counterfactualizable probabilities to another, and better known, distinction that is also based on the derivability or non-derivability of counterfactual judgements. I have in mind here the philosophically familiar distinction between statements of natural laws, like

Where there's fire there is heat,

and statements of accidental uniformities, like

All the men in this room on 1 January 1983 were bald.

Admittedly, even from such an accidentally true generalization a certain kind of counterfactual conditional is derivable, like

If Mr X had been one of those in this room on 1 January 1983 he would have been bald,

where the point of the assertion would normally be that evidence already exists for the falsity of the consequent and any such evidence is also evidence for the falsity of the antecedent. This kind of assertion does not contemplate any addition to the class of entities denoted by the predicate of the antecedent clause. But, if instead the antecedent of a derivable counterfactual posits the existence of at least one more entity satisfying a specified condition than the world contains, as might be the case with an assertion of

If there had been a fire in this room it would have been warm,

then the generalization instantiated by the counterfactual conditional is being treated as the statement of a law. Let us call such counterfactuals 'ampliative' in order to distinguish them from those that even accidentally true generalizations entail.

Of course, there is a difference between describing a generalization like

Where there's fire there is heat

as the statement of a law, and incorporating some modal expression into the generalization so that it intrinsically purports to state a law, as does

Where there's fire there *must* be heat.

In the former case the description of the generalization functions as a tacit additional premiss when an ampliative counterfactual is derived; in the latter case no such additional premiss is needed. But for most purposes this difference is an unimportant one, as is the analogous difference between describing a particular statement of probability as counterfactualizable and including that counterfactualizability within the meaning of the statement. What *is* important in all four cases is whether or not propositions are being asserted (or implied) that can function as premisses from which a certain kind of counterfactual conditional is derivable.

Nor should it be surprising that the familiar distinction between laws and accidental uniformities is thus mirrored by an analogously marked distinction between counterfactualizable and non-counter-factualizable probabilities. Every generalization is equivalent to an assertion of the corresponding rule of inference or demonstration. For example, the generalization 'Where there's fire there's heat' is equivalent to the rule 'From the presence of fire one may infer or demonstrate the presence of heat' (though in the case of a general-ization for which accidental truth is claimed the applicability of the rule of inference is correspondingly restricted to cases in which the premisses are true). And inferability or demonstrability is just the limiting-case of probability; or, to put it the other way, a probability may be viewed as a degree of inferability or demonstrability. This connection between probability and demonstrability was clearly recognized by John Locke,[28] as by several other philosophers subse-quently. Moreover, the fundamental differences between familiar theories of probability correspond, as I have shown elsewhere,[29] to accepted differences between different kinds of system for inference or demonstration. Consequently we should expect probability to

---

[28] John Locke, *An Essay Concerning Human Understanding*, bk. 4, ch. xv, § 1, (London: Dent, 1974, vol. 2, p. 249).

[29] L. Jonathan Cohen, *The Probable and the Provable*, Oxford: OUP, 1977, pp. 12-32.

bifurcate in the same directions as generalizations do. The existence of both counterfactualizable and non-counterfactualizable conceptions of probability is predictable from the existence of both law-stating and accident-stating generalizations, once we recognize both the equivalence of generalizations and rules of inference (or demonstration) and also the connections between inferability (or demonstrability) and probability.

Admittedly some philosophers have held that only law-stating generalizations are equivalent to rules of inference or demonstration. But this thesis cannot be defended unless some rather *ad hoc* restriction is placed on what is to count as a rule of inference or demonstration. In default of such a restriction it is quite legitimate to state our entitlement to infer, say, that a particular person is bald from the statement that he was present in a certain room at a certain date: the entitlement is generated by the uniformity that accidentally prevailed in that room on that date. It is true that in the case of such an accidental uniformity the corresponding rule of inference applies only to inferences about persons who were in fact in the room on the date in question. But to point this out is merely to direct attention to the fact that rules of inference, just like generalizations, may be divided into those that have the ampliative kind of counterfactual applications and those that do not.

Clearly then the concepts of counterfactualizable and non-counterfactualizable probability are closely linked with those of law-bound and accidental uniformity. It would be inconsistent to repudiate the former distinction without also repudiating the latter. But this inconsistency is all that a strategy of semantic ascent can reveal here. And on its own it will not suffice to substantiate the validity of the distinction between counterfactualizable and non-counterfactualizable probability upon which the resolution of the taxi-cab paradox, and related issues, depends. The inconsistency shows how deeply that distinction is entrenched in our conceptual system, but not how necessary the distinction is for the correct assessment of actual judgements of probability on particular occasions. For the latter purpose we need to employ a strategy of semantic descent also. We need to look at the facts that characteristically underlie the relevant assertions. We need to know how it is possible to have reasons for accepting one particular judgement as an evaluation of counterfactualizable but not of non-counterfactualizable probability, and another as an evaluation of non-counterfactualizable but not of counterfactualizable probability. It is

this kind of decision about acceptability that the proposed psychological hypothesis attributes to people who make the normal response
to the taxi-cab riddle. And the question that remains to be answered
here is how such a decision can be justified.

The key to that question's answer is to be found by examining the
analogous problem about generalizations. How do the characteristic
evidential reasons for accepting a generalization from which ampliative counterfactuals are derivable differ from the characteristic evidential reasons for accepting a generalization from which ampliative
counterfactuals are not derivable? An answer to this question was
given in § 2: in order to give evidential reasons of the former type, one
engages in the variational form of induction that is best typified in
controlled experiment, while to give evidential reasons of the latter
type one engages in what is traditionally called 'enumerative' induction. But the point needs to be expanded a little here.

In enumerative induction we look only to the number of instances
in which a generalization has been favourably satisfied and to the
absence of counter-instances. The ideal outcome is reached when we
have run through all the relevant individual instances. An exhaustive
enumeration of all the actual instances, if favourable, establishes the
truth of the generalization. And, since our mode of reasoning has then
been to infer from the evidence that the generalization applies to such-
and-such individuals, the only counterfactuals legitimately derivable
from the generalization are non-ampliative ones. We have no evidence
about other individuals, such as the men *not* in a certain room on 1
January 1983. Consequently we cannot draw conclusions about them,
such as that, if one of them had been in the room then, he would have
been bald.

In order to be entitled to derive ampliative counterfactuals from a
generalization, we need instead to have reasons for inferring that the
generalization applies to whole kinds of instances, not just to
individuals. For then it applies to any individual of such a kind,
whether actual or merely possible, and not just to the actual individuals that have been examined or ought ideally to have been so. And
this is indeed what emerges in controlled experiment.[30] By varying the
experimental circumstances we test their relevance to the phenomenon under investigation. The wider the range and combination of
suitably selected variations of circumstances that fail to falsify a hypo-

[30] Ibid., pp. 129-66; and L. Jonathan Cohen, *The Implications of Induction*, London:
Methuen, 1970, pp. 95-105.

thesis, the more highly we esteem it, i.e. the more nearly a law we hold it to be. Ultimately, if a generalization resists falsification under every variation of circumstance that we believe appropriate, we have as good a reason as we can then expect for calling it a law. If necessary, indeed, we can tailor the wording or meaning of a generalization (or add a *ceteris paribus* proviso) so as to maintain this resistance.[31] And then, because our mode of reasoning here is always to infer that a generalization applies to such-and-such combinations of circumstance, not to such-and-such individuals, we can take ourselves to have obtained a generalization from which ampliative counterfactuals are derivable. So far as the relevant surrounding circumstances of the counterfactual instances are appropriate (i.e. are among those to which the covering generalization is taken to apply), the conditional must be true. After all, if there are experimental results that genuinely testify to the reliability of the generalization, they *should* be replicable again and again, whether or not the experiment is actually replicated.

Now, if this is a correct account of the different types of reasoning that support statements of accidential uniformities and of laws, respectively, we should expect an analogous explication for correspondingly different types of reasoning that support judgements of non-counterfactualizable and counterfactualizable probability, respectively. Moreover, just as nearness to law or legisimilitude, as I have termed it elsewhere,[32] is a matter of evidentially certifiable degree, so too we should expect counterfactualizability to be. Just as generalizations (and their substitution-instances) may be partially ordered, within a particular field of enquiry, by their legisimilitude, so too we should expect generalized probability-judgements (and their substitution-instances) to be partially ordered within a particular field by their degree of counterfactualizability. The wider the range of relevant circumstances within which either a generalization or an estimate of probability fails to be falsified, the wider the range of possible surrounding circumstance for the counterfactual instances about which we should be entitled to derive conclusions. And in fact these expectations can easily be shown to be justified.

If we look at the way in which judgements of non-counterfactualizable probability are established, there is an obvious analogy with the way in which enumerative induction is used to establish statements about accidental uniformities. Ideally each member of the

---

[31] *The Probable and the Provable*, pp. 182-7.
[32] In 'What has Science to do with Truth?', *Synthese*, 45, 1980, pp. 489-510.

reference-class is enumerated and its relevant characteristic recorded. For example, if we suppose that the probability of a 1983 freshman's studying science at Oxford University is a wholly accidental fact, we are rejecting the view that there are causal factors working to sustain this level of probability. So we have no reason to think that any mere sample of the population might be sufficiently representative for the purpose of evaluating this probability. Instead, in order to know that there is a 0.4 probability of studying science for any 1983 freshman at Oxford University, we should normally need a record of the total number of 1983 freshmen alongside a record of the number studying science. The same kind of enumeration is needed also in order to know that the prior probability of a particular Smithville cab's being blue is 0.85, or that the probability of a particular stopping-place's being green, on a given roulette wheel, is 0.25. And because each member of the reference-class has thus to be enumerated and classified, in order to evaluate the probability at issue, there is no reason to suppose that this probability will also hold good for entities or items that are not actually members of that reference-class. Hence, the only counterfactuals that are derivable from judgements of non-counter-factualizable probability are non-ampliative ones.

Now compare a typical estimate of counterfactualizable probability. It may well be based on some procedure for sampling and associated with some value for a parameter that is related to the size of the sample, such as a coefficient of confidence. But, if the population is not appropriately homogeneous, the sample selected may be severely biased and the estimate correspondingly unreliable, as further sampling will show. For a more reliable estimate we shall then need to take an appropriate sub-population as the reference-class. As Keynes put it, 'the weight [of the estimated conditional probability] is increased if we are able to employ as the class of reference a class which is contained in the original class of reference'.[33] And this partitioning of the population for the purpose of estimating probabilities is in principle the same kind of move as that made when the wording or meaning of a generalization is tailored in such a way as to maintain or increase its degree of legisimilitude–i.e. its range of non-falsifying circumstances–in the face of otherwise falsificatory evidence.

[33] J. M. Keynes, *A Treatise on Probability*, London: Macmillan, 1957, p. 77. Cf. L. Jonathan Cohen, 'Twelve Questions about Keynes's Concept of Weight', forthcoming in *The British Journal for the Philosophy of Science*, 1986, and 'The Role of Evidential Weight in Criminal Proof', forthcoming.

Many issues arise about the details of this procedure, not least about the best strategy for selecting lines of relevant partition. But these details need not concern us here.[34] What is important in the present context is that an ampliative counterfactual which is derived from a generalized judgement of conditional probability—i.e. from an evaluation of the probability in question for any member of the given reference-class—is reliable only so far as the combination of causally relevant circumstances in which the counterfactual instance is supposed to be situated is a combination to which the generalized judgement of probability can be restricted without altering its value. If that value is affected, then, as the reference-class that is achieved by appropriate partitioning becomes more specific in relevant respects, any counterfactual judgement of probability that is derivable may be said to become correspondingly more reliable.

It should be noted too that the same pattern of gradation affects the derivability of singular statements of unconditional probability—i.e. of probability on all possible evidence—as when an 80% probability that the cab in the accident is blue is inferred from two premisses: the premiss of an 80% conditional probability that the cab is blue given that the witness says it is and the premiss that the witness did in fact say this. The strength or reliability of such an inference depends on the extent to which the value of the appropriately generalized judgement of conditional probability—a judgement that applies not just to a particular, specified cab, like the cab in the accident, but to any cab—is unaffected by restricting membership of its reference-class to possessors of such-and-such causally relevant characteristics that the cab in the accident happens to possess. An insurance company would soon go out of business if it paid no attention to this type of consideration in regard to an individual client's probability of survival to a particular age. It may need to determine the relevant reference class not just by the client's occupation, but also by his medical history, spare-time activities, etc. In short, the counterfactualizability of a generalized judgement of conditional probability determines the derivability of the corresponding judgement of unconditional probability about a specified individual, because that counterfactualizability is identical with the legisimilitude of the proposition that, if the individual satisfies the condition predicated in the former judgement, then the latter judgement is true.

Once counterfactualizability is thought of as a matter of degree, it is

[34] Cf. Cohen, *The Implications of Induction*, pp. 106-24.

obviously convenient to think of non-counterfactualizability as the occupier of the zero position on the scale. Similarly accidentally true generalizations are generalizations that hold good despite having zero legisimilitude. But this reduction of a difference of kind to a difference of degree does nothing to restore the credibility of those interpretations of the psychological data which take most normal adults to be prone to systematic fallacies about base-rates, conservatism, etc. What has been shown is rather that most of the subjects providing such data must be attributed a more coherent intuitive grasp of the relevant concepts than most of the psychologists conducting the experiments appear to have. For it has been shown not only that these subjects exhibit an implicit appreciation of the importance of counterfactualizability, but also that, like level of legisimilitude in the appraisal of generalizations, level of counterfactualizability must always be a crucial issue in appraisals of the evidential backing for judgements of probability. To put the point in other words, appreciation of what Keynes called 'weight' is a hidden variable in the experiments, and most subjects rightly seek to maximize the weight of the conditional probabilities that they estimate—and thereby the reliability of their inferences to the required unconditional probabilities. And not only is appreciation of weight a hidden variable in the psychological experiments. We can also say that in any categorical philosophical reasoning about such problems we have another example of the kind of situation described in § 11 where we make progress by breaking down a familiar species of confused intuition into two species of relatively clear and distinct intuitions. In the present type of case one such intuition is about the size of a probability, and the other about its weight or counterfactualizability. But the confused intuition that has to be discounted is not that of the majority of subjects, who are wrongly supposed by the psychologists to be in error, but that of the psychologists themselves.

In general, the way to avoid erroneous imputations of fallacy in this area is to recognize that, whenever a judgement of probability that has relatively high counterfactualizability is compounded with one that has relatively low counterfactualizability, the outcome of the calculation is necessarily infected by the low counterfactualizability of the latter judgement, because it is exposed to at least as wide a range of invalidating circumstances. Hence in the interest of maximizing counterfactualizability for the outcome of a Bayesian calculation, the right procedure may often be not to use base-rates as prior probabilities if they afford only a zero-level or rather low counterfactualizability. The taxi-cab problem is an obvious example of how this issue can arise in the case of zero-level counterfactualizability. And the diagnosis of a rare disease can afford a similar example in regard to low counterfactualizability. In the interest of obtaining a reliable estimate for the probability that his patient has a certain rare disease it may be cognitively correct for a clinician to ignore the very low rate of occurrence of the disease in the world at large when he considers the more highly counterfactualizable posterior probability that is afforded by positive test-results. Instead, the clinician needs to choose a value for his prior probability that is appropriate to the patient's own relevant circumstances, so far as these are known. The frequency of the disease among people relevantly similar to the patient in domicile, occupation, etc. not its frequency in the world at large, is the appropriate prior probability to invoke.[35] A correct approach to the type of problem exhibited in the taxi-cab paradox may thus be a matter of life or death for any of us.

There is, of course, a temptation to suppose that, as the counterfactualizability of a base-rate increases, the level of the prior probability should be taken to get closer and closer to the base-rate and thus to have an increasing impact on the calculation of the correct posterior probability. But this would be just to confuse two different parameters, namely, the size of the posterior probability and the weight or counterfactualizability of the posterior probability. It would thus confuse the proper value to be assigned to n in the generalized judgement that the conditional probability of an unspecified thing's being H given that it's E is n, with the proper measure for the reliability of an inference from a specified individual's being E to the unconditional singular judgement that the probability of its being H is n.

§ 19 RATIONALITY VINDICATED

Summary. Psychologists have not succeeded in demonstrating that ordinary adults in our culture tend to have incorrect principles for deductive or probabilistic reasoning, or that they tend to lack correct ones, but at most that they can sometimes be led astray in the application of their principles. No acceptable psychological findings, therefore, conflict with the presuppositions

---

[35] J. J. J. Christensen-Szalanski and J. B. Buckyhead, 'Physicians' Use of Probabilistic Information in a Real Clinical Setting', *Journal of Experimental Psychology: Human Perception and Performance*, 7, 1981, pp. 928-35.

of inductive reasoning in analytical philosophy. And a system of lay juries and universal suffrage remains rationally justifiable.

The hypothesis that in normal people's minds counterfactualizable probabilities dominate non-counterfactualizable ones will not suffice to explain away all the apparent evidence of deep-seated proneness to fallacy in lay reasoning about probabilities. But other alleged fallacies are equally spurious. For example, some experimental data have been interpreted as showing that statistically untutored people are unaware of the principle that larger samples of a given population show less variance. Subjects are questioned as follows:

A certain town is served by two hospitals. In the larger hospital about 45 babies are born each day, and in the smaller hospital about 15 babies are born each day. As you know about 50% of all babies are boys. However, the exact percentage varies from day to day. Sometimes it may be higher than 50%, sometimes lower. For a period of one year, each hospital recorded the days on which more than 60% of the babies born were boys. Which hospital do you think recorded more such days?

Because the majority of subjects replied that both hospitals recorded about the same number of relevant days (and the rest were evenly divided between the larger hospital and the smaller), Tversky and Kahneman concluded that most of their subjects were in error.[36] They took this and similar results to demonstrate that the principle that sampling variance decreases in proportion to sample size 'is evidently not part of people's repertoire of intuitions'.[37] But it turns out in other experiments that even children can be cued to exhibit awareness of this principle.[38] So, when most subjects ignore the significance of sample-size, the preferable explanation is that they have not been cued by the formulation of the question, or the context in which it is asked, to view the problem in terms of mathematical probability. Instead, these subjects may be construed as asking themselves whether the relative sizes of the two hospitals can be causally relevant to fluctuations in the boy-girl birth ratio, and as reaching a negative conclusion. The appropriate hypothesis therefore is that, under

---

[36] 'Judgement under Uncertainty: Heuristics and Biases', *Science*, 125, pp. 1124-31.
[37] Ibid., p. 1125.
[38] C. J. Jones and P. L. Harris, 'Insight into the Law of Large Numbers: a Comparison of Piagetian and Judgement Theory', *Quarterly Journal of Experimental Psychology*, 34A, 1982, pp. 479-88. See also J. St. B. T. Evans and A. E. Dusoir, 'Proportionality and Sample Size as Factors in Intuitive Statistical Judgement', *Acta Psychologica*, 41, 1977, pp. 129-37.

conditions of uncertainty, just as in normal people's minds counter-factualizable probability dominates non-counterfactualizable proba-bility, so too judgements in terms of causality dominate those in terms of mathematical probability. But a judgement in terms of mathe-matical probability can be cued by the subject's interest in statistical reasoning, by the experimenter's statement of particularly salient variations, by calibration exercises, and so on.

It is as if ordinary people desert causal reasoning with great reluctance. They prefer it to probabilistic reasoning wherever possible, and even within probabilistic reasoning they prefer to get as near to a causal law as they can—by maximizing counterfactualiza-bility. We may need a lot more experimental enquiry into the range of factors that affect a person's choice of which information-processing strategy to apply to a given task. But experimenters should always be wary of supposing without confirmation that a subject interprets a task precisely as they intend him to do, rather than that his interpretation of the task is affected by the factors that control his choice of strategy for dealing with it. Indeed, what has to be learned from the experi-mental data is not only how subjects respond to the questions posed them, but also how they interpret these questions. And attempts to get subjects to understand precisely what logical or mathematical task they are being asked to perform may require submitting them to educational procedures that are grounds for treating their eventual responses as evidence about the efficacy of those procedures rather than as results of naive and unsophisticated intuition.

Nor are there some rules of reasoning (e.g. mathematical ones) that always operate successfully and others—labellable as 'heuristics'—that sometimes operate successfully and sometimes do not. Even reliance on applying the law of large numbers may give you a wrong answer in practice if your sampling method is biased: your calculations may be quite correct, but the conditions inappropriate for applying them.

Again, experimenters have argued that statistically untutored subjects tend to overestimate the probabilities of conjunctive out-comes and to underestimate the probabilities of disjunctive ones. In particular, subjects often estimate the probability of a conjunction to be greater than that of one of the conjuncts,[39] which it can't be.

[39] J. Cohen and C. M. Hansel, 'The Nature of Decision in Gambling: Equivalence of Single and Compound Subjective Probabilities', *Acta Psychologica*, 13, 1957, pp. 357-70; M. Bar-Hillel, 'On the Subjective Probability of Compound Events', *Organizational Behavior and Human Performance*, 9, 1973, pp. 396-406; R. Nisbett and L. Ross, *Human*

Presented with the profile of a certain type of person, they may judge it moderately probable that such a person is a Republican lawyer, yet rather improbable that he is a lawyer. But here too the relevant experimental data turn out to be open to alternative interpretations that fit well with the hypothesis of an intuitive tendency for interest in causality to dominate interest in relative frequency.[40] The mistake that most subjects make, on this view, is not an error in calculating the answer to a correctly understood question, but an error in their understanding of the question. They carelessly jump to the conclusion that they have been asked to estimate the causal coherence of a story. So when they admit afterwards that they have given an incorrect answer, what they are to be interpreted as admitting is not, *pace* Tversky and Kahneman,[41] that they grasped exactly what the questioner meant and nevertheless miscalculated the answer, but that they failed to grasp properly what the questioner meant and therefore applied an inappropriate algorithm. For, if we define probability by its fundamental laws, they cannot have understood that probability was at issue, since it is the 'most fundamental qualitative law of probability'[42] to which most subjects' answers do not conform. Moreover, it is quite clear that, when a question about probability is presented in terms that have no causal suggestiveness, most lay subjects are quite capable of responding in accordance with correct mathematical principles in regard to the probability both of a conjunction and of a disjunction.[43]

In sum, ordinary people have not been demonstrated either to possess incorrect programs for deductive or probabilistic reasoning, or to lack correct ones. But, in a variety of ways, they can clearly make mistakes or be led astray in the application of their programs, as in the four-card trick; or the principles actually guiding their singular intuitive judgements can be wrongly interpreted or inadequately appreciated, as in suppositions about a fallacy of the converse, a base-

Inference: Strategies and Shortcomings of Social Judgement, Englewood Cliffs, NJ: Prentice Hall, 1980, p. 147.

[40] Cohen, 'Are People Programmed to Commit Fallacies?', pp. 263-5.

[41] A. Tversky and D. Kahneman, 'Extensional Versus Inductive Reasoning: The Conjunction Fallacy in Probability Judgement', *Psychological Review*, 90, 1983, pp. 293-315.

[42] Ibid., p. 294.

[43] L. R. Beach, 'Accuracy and Consistency in the Revision of Subjective Probabilities', *IEEE Transactions in Human Factors in Electronics*, HFE-7, 1966, pp. 29-37; L. R. Beach and C. R. Peterson, 'Subjective Probabilities for Unions of Events', *Psychonomic Science*, 5, 1966, pp. 307-8.

rate fallacy, a gambler's fallacy, a sample-size fallacy, a conjunction-fallacy, and so on.

Thus in answering the question 'How is analytical philosophy possible?' we cannot avoid engaging with some issues about rationality that require experimental investigation. We need to know at least whether there are reasons to suppose it unsafe for an ordinary person to build up a coherent reconstruction of his own tacit principles on the basis of his own singular intuitions. Some psychologists have implied that this would be unsafe because they have claimed that some of those singular intuitions are regularly and demonstrably incorrect. But fortunately it turns out, as we have seen, that the facts do not support this sytematic discrediting of ordinary people's intuitive judgements as a source of premises for analytical philosophy. Either the psychologists' data—for example, those derived from experiments on deductive competence—are inherently closed to interpretation as evidence of systematic fallacies. Or such an interpretation is excluded by there being an alternative and scientifically more satisfactory explanation of the data, as in the case of the experiments on probabilistic reasoning.

Indeed, one might well turn the argument back against the psychologists who impute these fallacies to most of their fellow human beings. If the methodology of analytical philosophy is taken to have been discredited by such experimental research, how else are the correct principles of deductive and probabilistic reasoning to be established? If intuition cannot normally be trusted to supply the premises for this task, what can? And, if certain people's intuitions are exceptionally trustworthy, what certifies them as such?

One response that is sometimes made[44] to this challenge is that there is indeed an objective, independent criterion by reference to which some, or even all, of an ordinary person's singular intuitions may be shown to be erroneous (or shown to be correct, if they are so). That criterion is said to be constituted by the consensus of relevant experts.

But, first, it is by no means always clear which body of élite opinion is to count as the consensus of relevant experts. This is obviously the case in regard to ethical intuitions, where priests and pundits express such a notorious variety of opinions. But many issues in the foundations of probability are scarcely less controversial. Secondly, even if

[44] e.g. S. Stich and R. Nisbett, 'Justification and the Psychology of Human Reasoning', *Philosophy of Science*, 47, 1980, pp. 188-202.

as a spectator one could see that most people, including all who might count as experts, are agreed that p, this need not count as a dominant consideration–from within one's own point of view–why one should accept that p. One might be a person who thought that there were good reasons why this majority ought to be persuaded to reform their opinion. Fortunately Galileo, for example, was that kind of person. And in fact, thirdly, just such a majority has often come to believe at a later date that certain propositions believed by a similar majority at an earlier date were incorrect. So élitism is an inconclusive strategy even by its own standards. Finally, and most importantly, since the experts presumably deliberate rationally with one another in order to arrive at whatever consensus they achieve, they must invoke among themselves some other criteria of acceptability than their own consensus or expertise. But the defence of those criteria must then fall back ultimately on the evidence of immediate, unreflective, and untutored intuitions–evidence of the very kind that the consensus theory was trying to make superfluous.

Another proposal for an objective, independent criterion some-times surfaces. This is the pragmatist claim that an intuition is correct if and only if it survives in the long run. But not only is such a criterion useless for all practical purposes, because these always have to be achieved in the short run. It is also exposed to the criticism that survival is as poor a guarantee of truth as is the consensus of experts. A belief may survive just because it has never been seriously evaluated. But, if evaluation occurs, some independent criterion has always to be invoked in order to justify letting one belief survive rather than another.

A different kind of objection is also foreseeable. 'You yourself have shown (in § 4)', it may be said, 'how mistaken a priori arguments about thought and language-learning were used to prop up the linguistic thesis about analytical philosophy. Is it not equally risky to employ empirical findings about human rationality as a prop for the inductivist element in your own account? Surely the feasibility of analytical philosophy should not be made to stand or fall with the outcome of an empirical enquiry, let alone of a current and highly controversial one? Even if there were no other reasons against this, it would introduce an obvious circularity into the epistemology of empirical enquiry. Perhaps, instead, you mean to argue in the opposite direction, treating the accepted possibility of analytical philosophy as the main premiss of a transcendental argument for human rationality–

roughly, the possibility of analytical philosophy requires human rationality, analytical philosophy exists, therefore people are rational? But, even if this is your meaning, you imply that the possibility of analytical philosophy is vulnerable to empirical disproof, since by contraposition of your argument any experimental data that count against human rationality will also count against the possibility of analytical philosophy.'

This objection conflates two different kinds of threat to analytical philosophy. One of these is a threat to its intellectual integrity, the other to its popularity.

The former kind of threat is that experimental data about rationality might turn out to be in danger of conflict with a proposition that every analytical philosopher's inductive reasoning presupposes–specifically, with the proposition that all his replicable singular intuitions are normally correct. If a threat of this kind exists, an analytical philosopher cannot derive much comfort from the fact that existing experimental data need not be interpreted as being in conflict with his presuppositions. It would certainly weaken the independent, critical standing of his analyses if the experimental refutation of analytical methodology remained even a conceptual possibility. But fortunately this conceptual possibility does not arise, since a psychologist would have to appeal in the end to his own intuitions in order to defend a claim that certain intuitions, which his experiments reveal most others to have, are fallacious. That is, he would have to adopt the reasoning-patterns of analytical philosophy, not reject them, but he would do this (as very many analytical philosophers have done on other issues–see § 11) to show that certain common opinions were mistaken.

The other threat, however, is undeniably a real one. Any psychologist who thinks that he has empirical evidence of widespread error in human intuitions, can legitimately argue that, on his own premises, few peopl are intellectually qualified to practise analytical philosophy, or at least that there are considerably fewer universally shared intuitions to provide a foundation for analytical philosophy than may have been supposed. Such a psychologist is therefore set on a collision course with the aspiration of analytical philosophy to remain an open dialogue with self-recruiting participants. Yet the empirical evidence is in fact against him, as we have seen. Of course, the proposition that people sometimes make errors of performance in the application of valid principles is a truism that anyone can afford to grant (§ 11). And another such truism is that people often *assert* wrong principles, either to themselves or to others. As already remarked, (§ 9), analytical philosophy is far from being committed to the correctness of people's intuitive assertions on general matters. But the important issue is a different one. It is whether most people regularly employ faulty principles to direct their reasonings about particular logical or mathematical issues. And, fortunately, no known experiments in fact elicit singular intuitions that show this.

Perhaps someone will now object that, even if there is empirical evidence for the hypothesis that normal people have coherent norms for deductive reasoning, for probabilistic reasoning, etc. there are also good reasons for supposing the existence of contradictions at a deeper level. 'For example', the objector may say, 'Thomas Nagel[45] has stressed the importance of conflicts between objective and subjective points of view over a wide range of other philosophical issues, such as determinism and free-will, body and mind, etc.'

But this objection refutes itself. The introduction of modifying prefixes like 'objectively' and 'subjectively', should have the effect of averting contradiction, not of fostering it. Such modifications instantiate a familiar pattern of philosopical reconciliation for superficially conflicting claims, which was mentioned in § 11 above. Indeed, because the purpose of the categorical mode of procedure in analytical philosophy is to determine what should, or should not, count as a reason for what, it can never rest content anywhere with the conclusion that some particular pair of mutually contradictory assertions about inferability are both well-founded, since each member of such a pair must also count as a powerful reason for rejecting the other. To be content with such an irrational conclusion is to give up analytical philosophy for some favoured form of obscurantism. So most of those who are prepared to tolerate a few local contradictions within a theory that has counterbalancing virtues would still regard consistency as an ultimate ideal. And, though some analytical logicians think that inconsistent worlds are possible–i.e. worlds in which some particular proposition both obtains and does not obtain–even they still insist that in order to reason cogently and coherently about such a world, or about any other kind of world, one should aim not to assert any self-contradictory statement.[46]

In short, conflicts that may be inescapable in analytical philosophy

[45] T. Nagel, *Mortal Questions*, Cambridge: CUP, 1979, pp. 196-213.
[46] N. Rescher and R. Brandom, *The Logic of Inconsistency*, Oxford: Blackwell, 1980, pp. 4, 25, 138-41.

are not between different intuitions in the same mind (§ 11), but between different people's formulations of coherent philosophical analyses to take account of their intuitions (§ 12). Hence, because the analysis of analytical philosophy has to allow for the intellectual respectability of there being so many divergent and conflicting theories in everyday philosophy, it has to be constructed from a point of view that is external to most of that philosophy. Of course, every analytical philosopher should think that he himself is in search of truth. He may be seeking it as a conclusion of categorical reasoning, even if only as a conclusion about what is the best available theory. Or he may be seeking a true connection between assumptions and conclusions in hypothetical reasoning. To think of himself as not seeking truth in either form would be frivolous or irrational. But he also has to credit that others too, holding divergent views, think of themselves in the very same way. So, at the metaphilosophical level he must accept that ultimate consensus is not to be counted on, even after very long discussion, at the level of ordinary philosophy. Then at this metaphilosophical level, by excluding themselves from discussion of most ordinary issues, analytical philosophers may get a little nearer to consensus on metaphilosophical issues. And if, even at this level, they continue to disagree, there is still hope at the metametaphilosophical level.

Finally, it is worth noting that, just as analytical philosophy, as remarked in § 6, tends to promote a tolerant and democratic culture, the psychological doctrine that ordinary people are innately programmed to commit fallacies in logical or probabilistic reasoning has an opposite potential. Already some lawyers have been persuaded by it to propose that lay juries should be either abolished, or so closely regulated in their decisions that in effect they cease to use their own powers of judgement.[47] Popular errors about factual matters, such as about the accuracy of eye-witness testimony, can easily be corrected in the courtroom. Emotional prejudices, though perhaps with greater difficulty, can be discounted. A judge, or even an expert witness, can warn the jury in a way that is appropriate to the special circumstances of the case. But a judge can hardly be expected, at each trial, to conduct a course in logic and statistics for the benefit of the jury. So, if in the normal course of events lay jurors or assessors cannot otherwise be expected to be roughly correct in their intuitive judgements of logic or probability (because their reasonings are structured by incorrect

---

[47] M. J. Saks and R. F. Kidd, 'Human Information-Processing and Adjudication: Trial by Heuristics', *Law and Society Review*, 15, 1980-1, pp. 123-60, esp. p. 134.

rules), the interests of justice require a radical reform of present ways
of using jurors or lay assessors for juridical fact-finding. We should
need to move backwards towards the medieval idea that forensic
proofs must be weighed and measured in accordance with explicit
rules (the supposedly 'correct' rules).[48] Moreover, if jurors and
assessors must accordingly either belong to a logically and statistically
trained élite, or have their deliberations closely controlled via the
incorporation of permissible logical and statistical proof-procedures
into the law of evidence, it is scarcely possible to avoid the conclusion
that voters should be treated similarly, because they too, if they are to
act rationally in pursuit of their several ends, need to draw inferences
from facts. Nobody, it will be said, should have the right to vote unless
he is either certified to have discarded his various innate strategies of
fallacious reasoning or is prepared to submit his electoral decisions to
the guidance of those who have. Thus, so far as universal suffrage
assumes universal rationality, an attack on universal rationality is an
attack on universal suffrage. And of course, once the principle of universal, independent suffrage is given up on the ground that many
people are programmed with faulty systems for deductive or
probabilistic reasoning, there is room for further restrictions on the
right to vote in the light of other intellectual inadequacies, such as
factual ignorance. But analytical philosophy, with its characteristic
methodology, is a strong ally for any society that wishes to resist such
attacks, just because anyone who propagates analytical philosophy is
propagating—among other things—a form of inductive reasoning that is
ready to fit normal, replicable intuitions into a rationally coherent
system within which they may be taken to corroborate one another.[49]

   This is not to say that one reason for esteeming the principles and
presuppositions of analytical philosophy is that they help to sustain
democratic institutions like universal suffrage and the jury system.
That kind of argument would confuse the truth of those principles
with the social value of accepting them. Rather, the case for analytical
philosophy is an independent, intellectual issue, but the social implications of endorsing it are important enough to deserve a more explicit
statement than they commonly receive.

---

[48] See L. Jonathan Cohen, 'Freedom of Proof', in W. Twining (ed.), *Facts in Law*
(*Archiv für Rechts- und Sozialphilosophie*, Beiheft 16), Wiesbaden: Franz Steiner, 1983,
pp. 1-21, esp. pp. 6-7.
[49] On conditions for the consilience of inductively supported generalizations see
Cohen, *The Implications of Induction*, pp. 86-8, and id., *The Probable and the Provable*,
pp. 157-61.

IV

Analysis and Computation

§ 20 COMPUTERIZATION AS AN ANALYTICAL TECHNIQUE

Summary. Contemporary psychology assumes that human thought processes are characterizable in computational terms. This suggests support for the thesis that analytical philosophy, if occupied with the analysis of human reasoning, is concerned at bottom with the structure of computational competence in each major area of intellectual activity. Computational analogues can in fact be developed both for semantic ascent and for semantic descent. Computerization is thus comparable with logical formalization as a technique of analysis that may be useful in the treatment of certain problems. But there are important reasons why this fact does not afford any general characterization of analytical philosophy.

THIRTY or forty years ago, when computers were a novelty and much less seemed to be known about them than about human thinking, it was natural for the question 'Can computers think?' to be among those in the forefront of discussion. This question soon dissolved very fruitfully, under the pressure of enquiry, into a vast number of more specific issues in the various sciences of computer hardware and software. As a result we have eventually come to have rather more extensive and accurate knowledge–knowledge that is still growing rapidly–about what computers can do and how they can do it than we have ever had about the actual mechanisms of human thinking. For the last decade or two, therefore, the guiding question in the science of thought has tended to point in the opposite direction. The question raised has not been so much 'Can computers think?' but rather 'Do humans compute?'

The computational hypothesis, which has come to dominate cognitive psychology, assumes an affirmative answer to this question, not in the sense of a metaphysical claim that the essence of mind is computation but in the sense of a scientific methodology. It expects the computational analogy to be more successful than any other in generating a variety of theories that are not only testable, but also worth while testing, about how particular mental processes operate. Memory, perception, visual imagery, concept formation, problem solving, speech comprehension, etc. are treated as fields of research in which experiments may be used to test theories that such-and-such a combination of iteration, recursion, chunking, pushdown storage, horizontal searching, vertical searching, geometrical coding, linguistic coding, or other mode of information processing is at least part of what is at work. Various different computational methodologies have been proposed. Perhaps the simplest, and the one most relevant to the issues discussed in the present chapter, is as follows. Ideally the researcher first constructs, or sketches, or surveys a suitably wide range of computer-programs (implementable on a suitably wide range of computer-architectures) that, when compared with a preliminary characterization of the mental process in question, would be descriptively adequate, in the sense of generating analogous outputs for analogous inputs. He then devises experiments on the performance of human subjects in order to determine which of these descriptively adequate computer-simulations has greatest explanatory adequacy, in the sense of closeness to the kind of explanatory mechanism required by the results of the experiments. For example, differences in reaction-time may be used as prima-facie evidence about relative complexity in explanatory mechanisms or subjects' verbal protocols may be taken as prima-facie evidence for the structure of the computational routines that they prefer.

This is not to say that the computational hypothesis, when thus understood, is capable of resolving all or most of those problems about mental states that have exercised philosophers from Descartes's time onward. Such problems are principally about states of conciouness that are characterized by perceptual or imaginative experience, or by familiar feelings of conviction, joy, sorrow, fear, amusement, etc. But most of the information-processing that the computational hypothesis offers a strategy for modelling is supposed to be subconscious or unconscious. The hypothesis thus directs its attention away from those aspects of mind that are paramount in the Cartesian conception and looks instead towards hidden processes that may be supposed to play a part in causing them. It certainly has nothing to say about whether the raw feelings of consciousness are identical with, emergent from, or parallel to bodily events.

The merits of the computational hypothesis are therefore a matter for psychologists, not philosophers, to determine. But at present, despite the fact that the variety of alternative computational models which are currently available to explain some particular mental operation often seems much wider than the variety of corresponding differences in human behaviour or neuronal activity that current experimental techniques are fine-grained enough to detect, the computational hypothesis has no serious rival as a methodology for cognitive psychology. So it deserves at least as much attention today among philosophers as has been given at various times in the past to the view that every unit of human thought is a copy of some previous experience, or to the view that the process of thought is not distinct from its expression. In particular, it clearly allows no room for the view that the process of a person's thought is always identifiable with its vocal or sub-vocal expression in some particular natural language that he is using at the time. Even where people do put their thoughts into words we have to suppose that the computational programs for doing this, as for learning to do it, are somehow prior to, and explanatory of, their linguistic output. And a great deal of thought that takes place in the world may now be treated as non-verbal, because there are ways to describe and explain its occurrence independently of the acquisition of natural language–both in the minds of infants and animals, and also in many adult human information-processing activities. So the linguistic thesis about analytical philosophy has altogether lost whatever support it had from psychological doctrine. Not only are there experimental facts (especially about infants' apparent development of the concept of a physical object, as discussed in § 4) which undermine this support. But also there is a widely accepted new theoretical framework–the computational hypothesis–which allows no room for it. One day this computational hypothesis may itself be displaced from its current position of esteem. But at the present moment it is undeniably the best, if not the only, overall hypothesis that cognitive psychologists have at their disposal.

The natural temptation, therefore, is to infer that, since the computational hypothesis must be supposed to have supplanted the view that the process of thought is identical with its linguistic expression, so too some computational account of analytical philosophy should replace the linguistic thesis. This temptation is bound to be reinforced by recognition of the fact that, implicitly or explicitly, analytical philosophy is engaged in the study of reasons. Is not computation the best available model with which human reasoning may be compared? If we want to sidestep Wittgensteinian objections to the existence of a private language when we assume (§ 8) that a person's intuitions about rationality reflect the content of his own tacit norms for reasoning, must we not be conceiving of these norms as if they are computational programs rather than conventions of linguistic practice?

The copy theory about thinking–i.e. Hume's theory that simple ideas are copies of previous impressions–placed paradoxically tight empiricist restrictions on *what* could be thought about. The linguistic theory of thinking implicitly lifted these restrictions (*pace* Schlick, Ayer, etc.), because it allows for the creation of new concepts by analogy and metaphor, as well as by compounding of simples. But the linguistic theory places unjustifiably tight restrictions on *who* can be supposed to think: babies, cats, dogs, and others who know no language are excluded and are thereby attributed a discontinuity with adult human behaviour that runs counter to the empirical evidence. The computational hypothesis now lifts those restrictions in their turn, though only at the cost of placing new restrictions on *how* people must be supposed to think in their tacit processing of acquired data. But the limits thus imposed are as yet scientifically unprobed, and may be for ever unprobeable. So they do not irk. The temptation, therefore, to give a computational account of analytical philosophy is quite a strong one. Nevertheless, though such an account might take various forms, each of them runs eventually into serious difficulties.

Sloman has claimed that the computational hypothesis should–if not now, then at least eventually–promote answers to very many philosophical questions of the form 'How is knowledge possible?', 'How is it possible to know truths of logic and mathematics?', 'How is it possible to think about the past or the future?', 'How is it possible for a social system to be just?', 'How is it possible for there to be anything at all?', and so on.[1] But many of Sloman's questions have their most obvious interpretation as problems for cognitive psychology. To explain successfully, in this sense, how such-and-such a cognitive process is possible for human beings, what one needs is a computational model of the process that has a sufficiently high level of explanatory adequacy, in the light of appropriate experimental data about human performance. If, therefore, we set all these psychological questions on one side, as being of no immediate concern for analytical philosophy, what are left in Sloman's list are questions for which the computational models that are suggestible as answers need have only

[1] A. Sloman, *The Computer Revolution in Philosophy: Philosophy, Science and Models of Mind*, Hassocks: Harvester Press, 1978, p. 65 ff.

descriptive adequacy. In each case they are questions about the structure of a human competence, not about its mode of acquisition or about the mechanisms by which it is executed in normal performance. They call for an investigation of the product, not of the producer. What are viewed as being at issue are such questions as: how can we best articulate the several competences actualized in thinking that *p*, in recognizing the shape of *q*, in operating with the concept *r*, and so on.

It has been argued, for example, that any set of beliefs may be analysed, and their tacit assumptions made explicit, by being simulated in a computer program. Stich claims

Philosophical analysis, when done well, is continuous with the project of the cognitive simulator. The philosophical analyst can be viewed as giving a discursive characterization, a sort of sketchy flow chart, for the program the simulator is trying to write.[2]

Similarly Todd claims, in effect, that a descriptively adequate program for accepting things as instances of a particular concept constitutes a useful new format for the philosophical analysis of that concept.[3] He, like Sloman (and like Sayre and Crosson also[4]), does not always distinguish clearly enough in such matters between the analytical and perhaps idealized description of a cognitive competence and the psychological explanation of actual performance. But we need concern ourselves here only with the more modest claim, namely that the correct answer to philosophical requests for definitions, like Plato's query 'What is a sophist?' may be set out in a flow chart that could be rewritten as a computational program. Such a chart will outline a program for questioning that aims to simulate an ideal procedure for examining whether or not the evidence about a given object justifies ascribing it the attribute in question. As in playing the children's game of 'Twenty questions', each answer that is obtained, prior to the very last one, operates as a guide to choosing the next question to be answered. For example, each stage of the procedure prior to the last may present a binary branching, where each of the two branches leads to a further branching: is the person under

---

[2] S. P. Stich, 'On the Ascription of Content', in A. Woodfield (ed.), *Thought and Object*, Oxford: OUP, 1982, p. 154.

[3] W. Todd, 'The Use of Simulations in Analytic Philosophy', *Metaphilosophy*, 8, 1977, pp. 272-97.

[4] In K. M. Sayre and F. J. Crosson (eds.), *The Modelling of Mind*, Notre Dame, Ind.: Notre Dame UP, 1963, pp. vii-x and 3-24.

examination skilled or unskilled? If skilled, is he acquisitive or creative? If acquisitive, does he acquire by purchase or by conquest? If by conquest, does he acquire by fighting or by hunting? And so on. When, and only when, the input answers trace the preferred route through successive branchings, the final output asserts that the entity thus describable is a sophist.[5]

Again, in accordance with the view that all thinking is a form of information-processing, Simon has argued that scientific discovery may be simulated in artificial intelligence by programs similar to those for theorem-proving, chess-playing, etc.[6] Such programs operate via a highly selective, trial-and-error search of solution possibilities. A good chess-playing program, for example, uses appropriate heuristic strategies to sidestep the combinatorial explosion that would be entailed by the exhaustive exploration and evaluation of possible moves, counter-moves, counter-counter-moves, etc. A good scientist, says Simon, does the same. No doubt it is easier to understand how this can happen when a space of possible solutions is determined by some accepted framework or dominant paradigm. But Simon claims that 'there are no qualitative differences between the *processes* of revolutionary science and of normal science, between work of high creativity and journeyman work'.[7] In his view this is because both the creation of new problems and the creation of new representations are incidental to the operation of any sufficiently sophisticated, and sufficiently exercised, problem-solving system. Such a system generates new problems for itself by the discovery of anomalies–facts that cannot be reconciled with existing solutions. Similarly, new representations are never completely novel but arise by the modification and development of previous ones. Just as the experience and expertise of chess-masters supplies the computer scientist with useful heuristic strategies to incorporate into his chess-playing program, so the experience and expertise of leading scientists help others to search in the right directions for appropriate developments of their problems and representations.

Simon is, of course, aware that great discoveries in science are rather rare, and seeks to turn that fact to advantage in support of his own theory. He argues from it that a system which is to explain human problem-solving and scientific discovery does not need to incorporate

[5] Cf. Plato, *Sophistes*.
[6] H. A. Simon, *Models of Discovery*, Dordrecht: Reidel, 1977, pp. 263-341.
[7] Ibid., p. 283.

a highly powerful mechanism for inventing completely novel representations. 'If it did contain such a mechanism', he says, 'it would be a poor theory, for it would predict far more novelty than occurs.'[8] Indeed, real discoveries are so rare that a theory to explain them 'must predict innumerable failures for every success'.[9] But Simon seems to overlook the fact that this would be a psychological theory, explaining a familiar form of weakness in human performance. A philosophical theory needs to concern itself rather with the underlying competence. And unless some element of bootstrapping–i.e. of self-derived self-improvement–is obtainable from the computational reconstruction of such a competence it is not of much philosophical interest.

Simon goes on to propose a psychological explanation, in computational terms, of the fact that unconscious incubation of a scientific problem is so often reported to have prepared the way for awareness of its solution. But again we need not concern ourselves here with this psychological aspect of the matter. Simon's philosophical claim is, in effect, just that computational models could be used by philosophers (or anyone else) to reconstruct the best available methods of scientific discovery. If he is right, therefore, the computationalist thesis would not only be capable of amplifying or clarifying those philosophical analyses that involve semantic ascent, as in Todd's flow-chart for a procedure defining the concept of sophistry. The computationalist thesis would also be able to amplify or clarify those philosophical analyses that involve semantic descent, as must any account of an ideal procedure for acquiring scientific knowledge.

In its claim to show the possibility of a methodology for scientific discovery, Simon's theory certainly runs into some serious practical difficulties, though recognition of these difficulties in no way belies the enormous benefits that may be derived in science from the use of computers as tools of research wherever the multiplicity or complexity of the data defeats other human resources.

The rules of chess are constant from player to player and from situation to situation. It is therefore possible to take moves as legitimate units in terms of which to measure depth or width of search, and to compute appropriate comparisons between different players or different types of chess-situations. On the basis of such measurements and comparisons, programs for chess-playing may come to include powerful strategies and advantageous criteria for evaluating alternative

---

[8] Ibid., p. 302.
[9] Ibid., p. 288.

attainable positions. But similar measurements and computations are scarcely possible for scientific discovery, except perhaps within those very narrowly determined frameworks within which computer-controlled experiments are actually carried out under current conditions. The terminology of one field of scientific enquiry is seldom sufficiently analogous to that of another for any well-defined units of analysis to be evident in both. Yet without our being able to draw explicit comparisons on the basis of such units–comparisons between what happens in one subject or circumstance of research and what happens in another–there seems little prospect of building up a sufficient store of experience and expertise for writing widely-applicable programs that would generate genuinely novel discoveries.

Moreover, the difficulties here pertain not just to horizontal comparisons between different problem-areas (which might conceivably be attainable in some cases, especially with the use of probabilistic rather than deterministic criteria for satisfying relevant concepts), but also to vertical comparisons between different stages of development within any one problem-area. The rules of chess define the space of possible moves from which at any one stage of the game an appropriate selection is to be made. But there are no fixed determinants for the space of possible hypotheses that needs investigation at a particular stage of scientific enquiry.

Again, the chess-player's problem is a constant one. The rules of the game are invariant and the player's object is to find a way, in conformity with the rules, to checkmate his opponent. Hence chess-playing programs can be gradually improved (though they still have a long way to go) by incorporating strategies and criteria that are distilled from the experience and expertise of great chess-masters. But the problems of science, and the frameworks within which solutions are to be found, are continuously changing as the horizons of enquiry retreat. So the experience and expertise of great scientists cannot be relied on to constitute a source of general heuristic maxims that would be as useful for discovering patterns in nature as are the dicta and recorded games of great chess-masters for discovering good moves or tactics in chess. Rather, a worthwhile pattern-discovery program for a particular set of scientific problems could best be put together only when major contributions to solving these problems had already been independently made by the pioneering efforts of individual scientists. Indeed, something very like this is already achieved in contemporary science whenever a series of tests or experiments is controlled and monitored by a computer and the resultant readings are digested into some visually displayed pattern or print-out. Moreover, in each such case the overall objective is to find an explanation for the patterns that have thus been revealed; and there cannot be any general guidance for programming the computer to perform this task. We may, for example, have a program that will assist the diagnosis of heart conditions from electrocardiograms by discovering the complex combination of arrhythmias that a patient manifests.[10] But the physiological cause of each kind of arrhythmia has to have been discovered independently.

So, if a relevant analogy between science and chess is to be maintained, one would have to suppose that the rules of chess, or at least the definition of a win, were changed every time a program had been constructed that could play as well as a grand-master. Even then such changes in the rules of the game might be governed by humanly designed, and therefore humanly knowable, higher-order rules. But Nature does not reveal in advance the various ways in which new discoveries about her will come to pose yet further problems. So, though we have no reason to say that a great scientist does not have a tacit methodology of discovery, we do have good reason to doubt whether we shall ever have enough evidence to reconstruct this expertise in a form that has useful applications to major new problems. At best we might one day be justified in taking the failure of existing programs to resolve a problem as a measure of that problem's novelty.

Nevertheless, these difficulties affect Simon's theory only so far as it argues the possibility of a general methodology for future scientific discovery, rather than just of a methodology for reconstructing patterns of research expertise that have proved fruitful in particular areas of scientific research in the past and may do so elsewhere in the future. In the latter role Simon's theory, like Todd's flow-chart analysis of the concept of sophistry, does undoubtedly illustrate how the computational approach may be used to sharpen up the treatment of certain problems with which analytical philosophy has long been concerned. What we have here is certainly a new weapon in the armoury of techniques with which analytical philosophy may approach its problems. In this respect the technique of computerization—i.e. the substitution of relevant implementable programs for discursive accounts in

---

[10] See D. Michie and R. Johnston, *The Creative Computer: Machine Intelligence and Human Knowledge*, Harmondsworth: Viking Press, 1984, p. 127.

ordinary language–is appropriately compared with that of logical formalization.

As a result of Frege's and Russell's work on the foundations of mathematics, logical formalization has long had a widely accepted part to play in certain areas of analytical philosophy. For example, it may be suspected that a scientist's judgements of the evidential support for his hypotheses impose certain constraints on one another, in the sense that the level of support for a particular proposition may constrain the level possible for its negation in a certain way, and may constrain other logical functions of it in other ways. Is each of the logical consequences of a hypothesis at least as well supported as the hypothesis itself? How does the support for a conjunction of hypotheses relate to that for the hypotheses on their own? And so on. But when we have prepared a provisional list of principles to answer such questions, several further problems arise. Are our principles consistent with one another? Do they corroborate one another at all? Are any additional principles derivable from them? If our discussion of evidential support is not to be relatively superficial, we must attempt to resolve these further problems. And for that purpose we need to achieve a suitable axiomatization for our provisional list of principles, setting up this axiomatization as a formal system in terms of which the problems admit of rigorously demonstrable solutions. It is in this light that Carnap's theory of symmetrical c-functions[11] may be viewed or my own logical syntax for Baconian induction.[12] Similar formalizations have proved useful in many other areas of philosophical analysis–in studies of time and tense (Prior), of knowledge and belief (Hintikka), of obligation and permission (von Wright), and so on.[13] The tracking and tracing of commitments is crucial to responsible philosophy.

What I am suggesting here is that in appropriate problem-areas analogous objectives of rigour, system, coherence, and comprehensiveness may be achievable by computerization. Wherever a philosophical analysis has to be constructed in terms of a relatively intricate sequence of instructions, the possibility is open that computerization,

---

[11] R. Carnap, *Logical Foundations of Probability*, Chicago: Chicago UP, 1950, pp. 489-92.
[12] L. Jonathan Cohen, *The Implications of Induction*, London: Methuen, 1970, pp. 216-37.
[13] A. N. Prior, *Time and Modality*, Oxford: OUP, 1957; J. Hintikka, *Knowledge and Belief: An Introduction to the Logic of the Two Notions*, Ithaca, NY: Cornell UP, 1962; G. H. von Wright, *An Essay in Modal Logic*, Amsterdam: North-Holland, 1951, pp. 36-41.

or at least a sketch for it, may be useful. For example, Todd has argued a case for this in regard to the definitions of certain complex concepts, like that of sophistry. And I have elsewhere suggested its utility in regard to certain questions that arise about inductive learning.[14] In many such cases enquiry into how an appropriate kind of artificial intelligence can be validly programmed may force the discovery of otherwise undetected presuppositions, assumptions, and implications, or it may confirm that there are none of these to be discovered.

But, however useful this new technique may be, its utility does not in any way define the analytical conception of philosophy. Indeed, it is a sound metaphilosophical principle that when a new technique is introduced to help deal with certain analytical problems, one must be careful not to let the technique arrogate to itself the privilege of defining what is to count as a philosophical problem. In the past there have been those who thought that if a certain category of human discourse was not amenable to formal-logical analysis it did not warrant philosophical interest, and also those who thought that, if an issue was not resoluble by analysis in terms of ordinary language, it was not a genuinely philosophical problem. We have seen earlier (§§ 2-6) that these ideas have to be rejected: the problems of analytical philosophy should be taken to determine its methods, not vice versa. And there are at least three interconnected reasons why we should put computationalist claims into the same perspective.

The first reason is that the distinctive procedures involved in setting out a sequence of rules as an implementable program are not in any way peculiar to the rules that need to be stated in setting out philosophical analyses. Whatever the level of the programming-language employed, the basic procedures that may need to be adopted in computerizing a philosophical analysis—the loops, iterations, recursions, list-searchings, etc.—are no different from those used in other programs for artificial intelligence. And this does not make that kind of philosophical analysis just a species of research in artificial intelligence, any more than the employment of mathematical techniques in formalizing the provisional conclusions of another kind of philosophical analysis makes the latter just a species of mathematical enquiry. But, in both cases, the unwary can get so fascinated by the technicalities involved in carrying through the enterprise that they come to treat these as its central purpose, as if the purpose of a

---

[14] L. Jonathan Cohen, *The Probable and the Provable*, Oxford: OUP, 1977, pp. 145 and 207.

person's making a journey were the construction of the vehicle needed to transport him. Or, to use a different metaphor, we could say that, unless the programming language that is used is particularly well adapted to its task, the fineness of weave in the analysis tends to direct attention away from the somewhat coarser lines of structure that determine whether or not the analysis is actually satisfactory.

Secondly, to the extent that analytical philosophy is a rational dialogue the arguments for or against an analysis are at least as important as the analysis itself (see § 14 above). Very often indeed, perhaps more often than not, the arguments are what is novel and interesting while the conclusion that they support or undermine–the analysis itself–is in substance familiar, traditional, or unexciting. This holds good whatever form the analysis takes–whether it be a statement of principle, a critique of usage, a systematic formalization, an idealized reconstruction, a recommendation for conceptual reform, or even just a claim that such-and-such an assembly of reminders is relevant to such-and-such a problem. So philosophers who start into the logical technicalities of their formal axiomatic analysis after a few short introductory sentences are engaged in a kind of low-grade mathematical monologue rather than in a characteristically philosophical enterprise. They have omitted the arguments that are needed to connect analysans with analysandum. And something analogous is true for any philosopher who puts forward his analyses as implementable programs but does not take seriously the need to give reasons why these analyses are correct (or better than their familiar rivals, or at any rate feasible), or does not treat those reasons as a primary issue for his research. In resolving Zeno's paradoxes about motion, for example, it would not be enough for him to write a program for measuring the distance and velocity of an object's movement. He would also need to justify the claim that there is something to measure thus, and to explain where and why Zeno's arguments for the impossibility of this or that movement break down.

Thirdly, in formulating a philosophical analysis the possibility of computerization, like that of formalization, is normally dependent on the existence of a prior linguistic formulation, whether this is achieved by semantic ascent or by semantic descent. The object of the computerization is to improve on the rigour and thoroughness of this linguistic formulation. But if the prior linguistic formulation were not available the computerization or formalization could not get off the ground and achieve some intelligible connection with the philosophical question at issue. So one can hardly regard the problems of analytical philosophy as being intrinsically computational, any more than they are intrinsically mathematical. This point is connected with an important distinction that needs to be drawn between two different kinds of artificial intelligence, but it will take a short digression to establish the distinction.

§ 21 SIMULATED PARROTING AND SIMULATED UNDERSTANDING

Summary. Most artificial intelligence programs combine elements of simulated parroting with elements of simulated understanding. At present they have to contain so much larger a proportion of the former than of the latter that any computerized philosophical analysis is largely parasitical on a formulation of the analysis in some particular natural language. But it might be suggested that eventually such analysis could perhaps be carried out in the universal language that is supposed by some to be the tacit vehicle of people's inner thoughts.

In the writing of programs for artificial intelligence considerable use is often made of a certain ambivalent category of expression-type. An expression-type E of this kind is characterized by having both of two mutually exclusive sets of properties. On the one hand there are the properties that E has in virtue of its belonging to a high-level computer-programming language where E has no meaning or function other than as a name (or quasi-name) of itself or as part of an expression that names (or quasi-names) it by including it within the scope of quotation-marks or a quote-function. On the other hand there are the semantic properties that the same expression-type E has in virtue of its also belonging to the ordinary vocabulary of a natural language. Thus in running Shortliffe's interactive program MYCIN,[15] which is written in Interlisp, the machine may output: 'ANY OTHER SIGNIFICANT EARLIER CULTURES FROM WHICH PATHOGENS WERE ISOLATED?' But this output has no reference in Interlisp to events in the outside world. It merely serves to invite a response-input of a kind that the computer has been programmed to register and process whenever this output occurs. In English the expression asks whether there were any

[15] E. H. Shortliffe, *Computer-Based Medical Consultations: MYCIN*, New York: Elsevier, 1976.

other significant earlier cultures from which pathogens were isolated. But in Interlisp it has no such meaning, because expressions like 'CULTURES' and 'PATHOGENS' have only formal, syntactic properties, one might say, in Interlisp. And, if computer programs had only expressions of this kind as their inputs or outputs, they might accordingly be described as operating solely on formal properties, not on semantic ones. The expressions would be subject to formation rules and computational transformations, but no semantical properties would be assigned them either by the program MYCIN or by its programming language, Interlisp. Whenever such programs were put forward as models of actual human reasoning, the modelling–we might call it 'simulated parroting'–would always be a kind of formalization. Indeed, the claim has been advanced by Turing and many others that a computer understands a natural language just so far as it can thus formally participate in dialogue in that language.[16] And, on the other side, it is to this kind of claim that Searle seems rightly to be objecting when he argues that computer programs *cannot* serve as adequate models of human understanding.[17] Simulated parroting is not to be identified with simulated understanding.

But it is a mistake to suppose that the computational hypothesis directs us only towards such formal simulations. In fact it makes available a distinction evident in familiar, higher-level programming languages, which is closely analogous to the difference between operating on forms and operating on meanings in relation to natural language.

For example, the Basic formula 'PRINT X, Y, Z' orders a procedure that does operate solely on the formal properties of whatever 'X', 'Y', and 'Z' stand in for, though not on the formal properties of 'X', 'Y' and 'Z'. Basic instructions such as 'READ' or 'RESTORE' are like 'PRINT' in this respect. To anyone running through a program in his head they would appear as requiring him to mention, rather than to use, the expressions concerned. But the formula 'PRINT X + Y' involves both formal and non-formal properties: the numbers denoted by 'X' and 'Y' are to be added and the numerical expression denoting that sum is to be

---

[16] A. M. Turing, 'Computing Machinery and Intelligence', *Mind*, 59, 1950, pp. 433-60. Cf. D. G. Bobrow, 'Natural Language Input for a Computer Problem-Solving System', in M. Minsky (ed.), *Semantic Information Processing*, Cambridge, Mass.: MIT Press, 1968, pp. 125-213, and B. Raphael, 'SIR: Semantic Information Retrieval', ibid., pp. 33-84.
[17] J. R. Searle, 'Minds, Brains and Programs', *The Behavioural and Brain Sciences*, 3, 1980, pp. 417-57.

printed. And the formula 'IF X > 7 THEN GO TO LINE $_{30}$' instructs execution of the instruction on line 30 if the value of X is greater than 7. So the condition on which this instruction hinges concerns the size of the number denoted in the context by the expression 'x'. The semantic property of denoting that number is crucial here. Nor is it possible to understand the condition as a purely formal one by thinking of it as depending in some way on the shape of X and '7', since the very same symbol-type '7' has also to be used to trigger the operation of simulated counting that is involved in the setting-up of arrays (by what Basic calls 'DIM' statements): compare Russell's view that we can never give a purely formal characterization of arithmetical procedure because 'we want our numbers to be such as can be used for counting common objects'.[18] The expression '7' may be said to *quasi-designate* the number 7 on such occasions in a highly general sense like that which has been defined for 'designate' by Newell.[19] In this sense an expression may be said to 'quasi-designate' x to the extent that when the computer (or the person running through the program in his head) takes that expression as input the computer's (or the person's) ensuing behaviour depends in part on what x is and would be correspondingly different if the expression were different. Such a concept of quasi-designation, when applied to the particular case of numerals in a high-level programming language, helps to sustain the analogy between what is being said here about numerical expressions in such a language and what Russell said, apropos of Peano's axiom-system, about numerical expressions in ordinary use. Moreover, by using numerals to quasi-designate a set of positions in a two- or three-dimensional matrix it is possible to use the programming language to represent a geometrical structure and by programming the machine to change these positions in real time it is possible to represent movement. The peripheral graphic displays that can then be generated are a way of exploiting the sensitivity of the program to the quasi-semantic properties of expressions that are part of the data or input. These expressions may therefore be said to 'represent' the relevant geometrical structure. How else should we describe the relationship between the numerical evaluation of the matrix, on the one side, and, on the other, the structure-types of which tokens appear on the dis-

[18] B. Russell, *Introduction to Mathematical Philosophy*, London: Allen and Unwin, 1919, p. 10.
[19] A. Newell, 'Physical Symbol Systems', in D. A. Norman (ed.), *Perspectives on Cognitive Science*, Norwood, NJ: Ablex, 1981, pp. 37-85.

play-screen or print-out? Similarly the sign '>' may be attributed a quasi-predicative function in virtue of the computer's response to its occurrence in expressions like 'IF X > 7 THEN GO TO LINE 30'. And so on, for a considerable range of mathematical, logical, and syntactic properties.

We can thus distinguish between simulated parroting, as already defined, and what may conveniently be called 'simulated understanding'. So far as a computer is programmed to simulate uncomprehending participation in an exchange of linguistic utterances, for example, it may be said to display simulated parroting of dialogue in that natural language. A person taught to perform the same kind of simulation as the computer would certainly be aware of needing a good memory about which speech-sounds to utter in response to which, but might not be aware of needing any other intellectual skill. On the other hand, so far as a computer-program operates on the quasi-semantic properties of expressions in its programming language, it may be said to display simulated understanding, since it enables a machine to execute procedures (enumerating, calculating, proving, list-processing, detecting one pattern within another, etc.) which are substitutes for other human skills than textually cued memory of text. Simulated parroting deals only with formal properties, simulated understanding only with quasi-semantic ones, though in practice elements of both tend to coexist, often in an intricately interwoven pattern, in most artificial intelligence programs.

In short, a machine simulates parroting insofar as it mimes the outputs of an uncomprehending, but relevantly trained, person when confronted with a particular category of input. It simulates understanding insofar as it works things out for itself: in doing so it has to provide an artificial means of executing specified procedures that humans know how to execute in their own minds, and it thus behaves as if it understands those specifications.

There is, however, a rather strict constraint on the range of quasi-meaningful specifications expressible in a high-level programming language. Nothing can be said in such a language that is not reducible eventually to procedures executable by the logic gates, circuitry, and peripheral devices of the digital computers on which it is to be implemented. So we cannot yet quasi-designate a flower or quasi-name the parts of a rifle in one of these languages. We can only quasi-designate expression-types isomorphic with those that name such things in natural language, insofar as we can register control of a circuit that will print out tokens of the required expression-type in an exercise of simulated parroting.

Of course, if we were interested in artificial intelligence programs only for their possible use as props, aids, short-cuts, substitutes, etc. in the execution of human tasks–i.e. as extensions of human performance in science, medicine, engineering, administration, business, etc.–it would be reasonable to adopt a conception of semantics for them that allowed all their expressions to have much the same meanings as these expressions would have in natural language. After all, that is how we regularly treat read-out expressions on the dials of clocks, speedometers, scientific instruments, domestic appliances, etc. in our technological culture. But it would achieve nothing to employ such a conception of semantics for expressions in artificial intelligence programs when those programs are being used in accordance with the computational hypothesis to function as models for the detailed psychological explanation of semantic processing and other cognitive activity in the human mind or as philosophically oriented analyses of concepts and procedures in human thought. Any understanding that we had of these models or analyses would just echo our understanding of part of that which was being modelled or analysed.

There is, however, no a priori constraint on what could count as a peripheral device. So the variety of procedures executable in the implementation of a program could, in principle, be substantially extended if a robot's sensory transducers were linked to the computer's input and its output was linked to the robot's behaviour as well as to the display screen. Simulated understanding could thus be extended via the specification of procedures for, as it were, investigating and describing the computer's environment, for communicating with other similar machines, and for deliberating and deciding about actions. Simulated understanding would then not occur just in virtue of the specification of procedures for enumerating, calculating, proving, etc. but would extend considerably beyond what those procedures make possible. And, if such an extension were achieved, an expression in the programming language could come to quasi-designate, relative to the peripherally enhanced computer, a particular environmental entity or event of any desired kind, as Newell points out[20]–at least in the sense of 'quasi-designate' that applies if, when the computer takes the expression as input, the computer's

[20] Ibid., pp. 58-9.

ensuing behaviour depends on what that entity or event is and would be correspondingly different if the expression were different. We should then have available an artificial language of analysis that would be comparable with, though different from, the interpreted calculi that are used in the techniques of analysis by formalization.

But, in fact, we are still a very long way from having artefacts that exhibit anything but a very narrow range of simulated understanding. This range of understanding is rather far from measuring up to the rich variety of concepts invoked in typical philosophical analyses, such as the concept of intending that is invoked at one point in Todd's analysis of sophistry or the concept of arthritis that enters into Stich's discussion of belief. Without such an extension of simulated understanding, in a community of intercommunicating computer-robots, a computerized philosopical analysis would have to make so much use of simulated parroting that it would be largely parasitical on a formulation of the analysis in some particular natural language. Only the logical and mathematical articulations in the analysis could have a strictly computational etymology.

Moreover, even if we did manage to achieve a very extensive range of simulated understanding, within a community of appropriately programmed computer-robots, any computerized analysis would still need to be defended by arguments that would have to be thought up independently and expressed in natural language. And it is these arguments that would normally be the primary focus of philosophical interest (as already pointed out in § 20). Of course, a computationally-minded philosopher might seek to construct a program for discovering arguments of the appropriate kind, and in any expert systems analysis a computer can be programmed to justify–on demand–the particular set of procedures that it has just executed. But, about any such program in this context, the question on which philosophical interest would now focus would be: what reasons are there to suppose that the arguments or justifications which it supplies will be valid?

'You are assuming', it may be objected, 'that in the computerization of philosophy the language of analysis should be an invented system that is regarded as an analogue of the learned, outwardly spoken language of a human speech-community. On this approach computerization is just a technique that may be useful in handling certain problems although it is not integral to the nature of those problems that they be resolved in computational terms. But there is another approach that goes deeper. If analytical philosophers are engaged in the study of rationality, their ultimate objects of analysis are judgements in the tacit universal programming language of inner thought, since this is the language in which, according to modern cognitive psychology's computational hypothesis, all human information-processing must be supposed to take place. Correspondingly the objectives of analytical philosophy are most closely pursued by constructing a depth grammar of the human mind in computational terms, revealing both its innate potential and its innate limitations. In sum, whatever the current shortcomings of computationalism as a philosophical technique, it nevertheless reveals what analytical philosophy must ultimately aim to accomplish.'

This is certainly a bold idea and, at least at first sight, a rather attractive one. It holds out the hope of eventually putting every philosophical analysis, plus supporting arguments, into computational uniform and of parading such computational formulations under a traditionalist Kantian banner as the mind's articulation of its own powers. But the plausibility of the idea depends on supposing that psychology's computational hypothesis implies the existence of a basic, inner language of thought, since analysis of our competence in that tacit language is offered as the ultimate source of resolution for any philosophical problems that arise about features of our competence in verbally explicit thought. We therefore need to investigate whether the computational hypothesis does indeed have such an implication. And this investigation, which will occupy §§ 22-4, will necessarily be a rather intricate one.

§ 22 INFORMATION-PROCESSING ARGUMENTS FOR A LANGUAGE OF THOUGHT

Summary. The computational hypothesis has been supposed to imply the existence of a universal internal language, on the ground that the computational processes of the mind must be supposed to operate on the formal properties of internal representations (in a sense in which 'formal' means 'non-semantical') and that, if internal representations have formal as well as semantical properties, they must be open to being treated as sentences of an internal language. But this formalist theory of mental computations is neither supported nor refuted by current psychological investigations into the question whether human deductive reasoning is processed on syntactic or semantic lines. Nor is such a theory supported by any need for referential opacity in regard to how a person must be supposed to represent his own beliefs, wants, etc. to himself.

An important new scientific theory often provokes a tangle of philosophical accretions. Implications are imputed that go well beyond the original, experimentally oriented scope of the hypothesis. Notoriously evolution, relativity, and quantum mechanics, for example, have in turn all suffered in that way. And the computational hypothesis has also been attributed some rather specific philosophical implications, irrespective of any particular experimental outcomes. Foremost among these supposed implications is the existence of a universal inner language of thought. The best line of argument in favour of such an implication would run roughly as follows.[21]

Considered action, concept learning, and perceptual integration are now accepted achievements of pre-verbal children and of certain infrahuman organisms. So, if these cognitive achievements are to be explained computationally, their authors must be attributed representational systems that are not natural languages. Moreover, humans cannot learn a language whose terms express types of meanings not expressed by the elements of some representational system that they are already able to use. Hence the innate, non-conventional system of representation, which has in any case to be postulated in order to account for non-verbal and pre-verbal thought, must be supposed to have a vocabulary that suffices to express anything expressible in any natural language. And the computational programs of tacit human reasoning must be supposed capable of operating on representations constructed from this private vocabulary. Indeed, it is only in these terms that we can even make sense of statements which attribute non-verbal beliefs or other mental attitudes to children or animals. Such statements have to be taken as asserting the existence of a corresponding relationship between the possessor of the mental attitude and an appropriate internal representation. Note too that

---

[21] J. A. Fodor, *The Language of Thought*, New York: Crewell, 1975; id., 'Methodological Solipsism Considered as a Research Strategy in Cognitive Psychology', *The Behavioural and Brain Sciences*, 3, 1980, pp. 63-109; id., *Representations: Philosophical Essays on the Foundations of Cognitive Science*, Brighton: Harvester Press, 1981; Z. W. Pylyshyn, 'Computation and Cognition: Issues in the Foundations of Cognitive Science', *The Behavioural and Brain Sciences*, 3, 1980, pp. 111-69; id., *Computation and Cognition: Toward a Foundation for Cognitive Science*, Cambridge, Mass.: MIT Press, 2nd edn., 1985; and J. Haugeland, 'Semantic Engines: An Introduction to Mind Design', in J. Haugeland (ed.), *Mind Design: Philosophy, Psychology, Artificial Intelligence*, Cambridge, Mass.: MIT Press, 1981, pp. 1-34.

these internal representations, even if subverbal, must be taken to be linguistic in character, rather than pictorial or imitative, in order to allow for the distinction that is necessary between their form and their meaning. Oedipus's courtship behaviour, for example, may be said to depend on which form of designation he (literally) has in mind for the object of his affection, since, though in fact the two forms 'Jocasta' and 'my mother' have the same reference, he does not know it. Because of this referential opacity—i.e. this resistance to the substitutivity of identically referring terms and even of logically equivalent ones—within a person's own internal representations of what he believes, wants, etc., we have to suppose that his mental processes operate on the formal properties of his internal representations, not on their semantic or representational properties. It is not the actual reference that counts, but the form of the referential expression. Nor, we are told, is such a dependence on formal properties at all surprising here: it is exactly what the computational model of the mind should lead us to expect, since all computers are formal systems.

If this line of argument were successful we should have to accept that the computational hypothesis, which is currently the best available scientific hypothesis about the nature of human reasoning, implies the existence of a universal inner language of thought, and that therefore, so far as we can tell, the ultimate subject-matter of analytical philosophy is the structure of this universal inner language and of the procedures, principles, plans, etc. that may be formulated in it. But in fact that account of analytical philosophy is without foundation because the computational hypothesis, as I shall shortly argue, does not have the implication which is needed to support it.

Of course, not every one of the arguments for a universal inner language of thought rests on the computational hypothesis. But it is easy enough to spot the weakness in the argument that humans cannot acquire a language whose terms express types of meaning not expressed by the elements of some representational system that they are already able to use. For, if—in order to stop an infinite regress—the internal language must be supposed capable of representation without acquiring this capacity by reference to a yet more fundamental language, then why should not such be the case with ordinary natural language? And another obvious point to be made here is in regard to the nature of the thing to which a possessor of a mental attitude is said to be related by a statement about his possession of the attitude. We are certainly not compelled to interpret such a statement as asserting that this thing is an actually existing token of a sentence in some internal language. For example, if George believes tacitly that it is raining, then the relation in question may be construed as being between George and a saying-type,[22] instead of between George and a saying-token, since a token of the saying-type 'that it is raining' would occur consciously in George's mind *if* his belief were not a tacit one. But this point in any case concerns only the *meaning* of statements about beliefs and other mental attitudes. Perhaps it would have been surprising if the prehistoric culture in which such meanings originated had already anticipated thereby a certain contemporary doctrine about what events actually occur in the unconscious mind.

We have to take rather more seriously, however, the claim that these events themselves, if computational in nature, must involve operations which bear on formal properties of internal representations. For we can hardly refuse to grant that anything which goes to establish a distinguishable difference between formal and semantic properties of internal representations goes to establish the reality of an inner language of thought. If a distinction between the formal and the semantical can be used to classify different properties of certain internal representations, then it would be only a terminological quibble to refuse to classify those internal representations as elements of a language. That is because they would at least be radically different from pictorial representations, where a distinction between formal and semantic properties is largely inapplicable. A picture has to be isomorphic, in some recognizable way, with what it pictures, but the structural description of a sentence tells us nothing about what the sentence asserts.

The formalist claim is not as easy to defeat as it is tempting to suppose. For example, Stich has argued[23] that mental states cannot be classified by their form rather than their content without serious paradoxes arising about look-alike worlds on remote planets. If Hither-Fodor believes that Jimmy Carter is from Georgia, he would, as Stich points out, entertain a representation that is of just the same *formal* type as Yon-Fodor (who has a corresponding belief about Yon-Carter and Yon-Georgia), despite the fact that the two beliefs are actually about different men and different places of origin. To avoid such a

---

[22] On sayings cf. L. Jonathan Cohen, *The Diversity of Meaning*, London: Methuen, 2nd edn., 1966, pp. 162-72.

[23] S. Stich, 'Paying the Price for Methodological Solipsism', *The Behavioural and Brain Sciences*, 3, 1980, pp. 97-8.

possibility, argues Stich, we should need to classify mental representations by their contents rather than their forms. But, from the fact that Stich's type of example provides a reason for one person not to classify another person's internal representations by form alone, it does not follow that this is how each person should be supposed by psychologists to treat his or her own internal representations. And that is what is at issue here, since we are concerned with the question whether or not a person's mental operations have access only to the formal properties of *such* representations.

More promisingly, perhaps, the formalist claim might be attacked on the ground that it seems to restrict human logical performance unduly. Due mainly to the work of Tarski and Carnap[24] modern logicians distinguish between a syntactical and a semantical characterization of logical relations. But apparently the formalist doctrine allows only the former to be a basis for mental performance.

It will help here to review briefly the prototypical operation on purely formal properties that was invented by Aristotle. His theory of syllogistic reasoning exploited, in effect, the possibility of stating rules that permit or forbid certain transformations of specified sequences of symbols in an object-language so as to treat those rules as metalinguistic criteria for the correctness or incorrectness, respectively, of corresponding inferences in the object language. Similarly, it is possible to formulate a criterion of provability from given axioms as a set of rules for transforming the corresponding well-formed formulas in a specific symbolism. Standardly, such a symbolism is a listed set of types of visually recognizable objects, such as two-dimensional lettertypes, numeral-types, punctuation-types, etc. Types of tangible objects would serve as well, at least for those logicians who have welldeveloped tactile discrimination. Other sensory modalities too could be used. But they are less convenient to invoke here, because smells, tastes, and sounds cannot be so easily arranged as shapes in checkable and recheckable sequences of tokens. So what is crucial to the idea of logical formalization is just that a specified procedure of sensory verification stands guarantor for any intuitive intellectual operations that are involved in inference proof. This procedure, stipulated in a syntactic metalanguage, pays no attention to any meanings, or truthconditions, or translational equivalences that may be independently assigned to well-formed formulas of the object-language.

[24] See R. Carnap, *Introduction to Semantics*, Cambridge, Mass.: Harvard UP, 1948, preface, pp. vi-vii.

In the logical context, therefore, formalization consists in a deliberate and self-conscious substitution of manipulative procedures dependent on the perception of forms (in general, on the visual recognition of shapes) for intellectual procedures apparently dependent on an intuitive grasp of semantic properties such as the meanings of the words 'some', 'any', 'if', 'not', etc. According to the computational hypothesis, however, those intellectual procedures are themselves to be understood by analogy with the operation of appropriate computer programs. How then can these programs be construed as operating solely on formal, *non*-semantic properties? The formalist doctrine seems to assert the paradoxical claim that the very same intellectual operations that logicians, over more than two thousand years, have sought to replace by formalized proxies are already intrinsically formal. Nor do exponents of the formalist doctrine offer any explanation why those operations have appeared, and still appear, to so many as dependent on intuitions of semantic properties.

Perhaps, however, formalists who come to consider the matter will be inclined to object that the apparent dependence of logical operations on semantic properties of the object-language is an artefact of linguistic processing. Meaning seems to enter into the situation, they may say, only when we formulate our inferences in natural language, because we then have to connect up pivotal elements in our derivational structure with particular linguistic morphemes, such as 'some', 'any', 'if', or 'not'. The apparent meanings of these morphemes are thus explained away as being parasitic on an underlying system of operations on purely formal properties,[25] and so the formalist doctrine is not refuted by the fact that intuitive judgements of inferential accuracy appear to depend on knowledge about the meanings of key words.

But such a defence of formalism makes the crucial assumption that pre-verbal and subverbal reasoning follows a syntactical rather than a semantical pattern. And this assumption is by no means implicit in the computational hypothesis. Admittedly, some psychologists have proposed accounts of deductive reasoning that construe it as operating in accordance with syntactical procedures. Thus Rips has constructed a model ANDS which works rather like a person struggling systematically to solve textbook exercises in propositional calculus natural deduction by searching dilligently through what conclusions can be derived from relevant premisses, and what premisses can serve

---

[25] See N. D. Belnap, Jr., 'Tonk, Plonk and Plink', *Analysis*, 22:6, 1962, pp. 130-4.

for the derivation of relevant conclusions, where the legitimacy of derivations is governed solely by rules for permissible transformations.[26] But semantical accounts are also current. For example, Johnson-Laird has constructed a model of deductive inference that relies, not on conformity with stipulated rules of derivation, but on knowledge of the truth-tables for propositional connectives in order to process inferences involving relations between propositions and on an interpretational decision procedure in order to process inferences involving quantification with monadic predicates.[27] Both Rips and Johnson-Laird claim that their respective computational programs are consistent with the kinds of error that actually occur in human reasoning. And no crucial experiments have yet been proposed that might help to determine whether tacit human reasoning operates on a syntactical or a semantical basis, or sometimes on one and sometimes on the other. Perhaps one day we shall have such experiments. But this issue, whatever its eventual outcome, is at any rate best taken as an open empirical issue. It is an issue of the kind that the computational hypothesis indicates a general strategy for resolving–by means of computer-simulation and experiment. So philosophers risk obstructing the path of enquiry if they try to anticipate such a resolution by reading some partisan implication into the computational hypothesis itself. Indeed one inherent disadvantage of the formalist doctrine is that it appears to impoverish computational methodology by thus closing it off from certain otherwise respectable avenues of psychological research involving semantic considerations. Nor should the contrast between a syntactical and a semantical psychology of reasoning be seen as one between a theory that postulates rules of mental inference and a theory that dispenses with them, since the construction and utilization of mental models must also be controlled by appropriate computational rules.

It may well be objected now, however, that the formalist doctrine should not be construed as excluding the possibility that human reasoning operates in terms of what logicians call semantical properties. For example, a mechanism that executes a truth-table

---

[26] L. J. Rips, 'Reasoning as a Central Intellective Ability', in R. J. Sternberg (ed.), *Advances in the Study of Human Intelligence*, vol. 2, Hillsdale, NJ: Erlbaum, 1984, pp. 105–47, and id., 'Mental Muddles', forthcoming in M. Brand and R. M. Harnish (eds.), *Problems in the Representation of Knowledge and Belief*, Tucson: Arizona UP.

[27] P. N. Johnson-Laird, 'Mental Models in Cognitive Science', in D. A. Norman (ed.), *Perspectives on Cognitive Science*, Norwood, NJ: Ablex, 1981, pp. 147–91.

decision procedure on given sentences of a particular language, in order to determine whether or not they are truth-functional tautologies, need not be attributed any knowledge of their meanings, despite the fact that it could be described as operating a semantical procedure. It may be described instead as just manipulating symbols according to predetermined rules. So the formal properties on which the mind operates may be taken to include those within the domain of what Carnap once called 'pure semantics'[28] (and many people now call 'formal semantics') as well as those within the domain of logical syntax. What the formalist doctrine does exclude, it will now be claimed, is mental operation on semantical properties of a different kind. It excludes the possibility that human computational operations may sometimes be concerned with those meanings that a person cannot specify without making some reference to features of his own environment. But *such* knowledge is certainly not needed for executing the procedures of pure semantics.

All right. Let us grant then that the formalist doctrine, in an appropriately restricted version, is not committed to an assumption that pre-verbal or subverbal reasoning follows what logicians would call a syntactical rather than a semantical pattern. So the doctrine is not to be ruled out *ab initio* on this score, any more than by Stich's argument. But does the doctrine have any positive merit?

Fodor has claimed that it is supported by the existence of referential opacity within a person's own internal representations of what he believes, wants, etc.[29] But no such referential opacity exists. The semantic structure of belief-ascriptions in natural language is not necessarily indicative of the actual state of affairs that exists privately in a person's mind when he believes something. More specifically, we can see that Oedipus's behaviour must depend, not on which description he has in mind for the object of his affection, but on what he believes about this object. For, even though he had had the name 'Jocasta' in mind for the object of his affection, because he liked the sound of the word, he might have believed also (would that he had!) that Jocasta was his mother and he would then have been in a position to infer, without any difficulty from resistance to substitution, that the object of his affection was his mother. Thus the concept of referential opacity has no part to play in characterizing how a rationally coherent

---

[28] *Introduction to Semantics*, p. 12.
[29] 'Methodological Solipsism Considered as a Research Strategy in Cognitive Psychology', p. 66. Cf. id., *Representations*, p. 159.

thinker should regard the representations embraced within his own current mental state. In a statement made by Tiresias, whether publicly or privately, the sentence 'Oedipus wants to marry Jocasta' may contain a referentially opaque occurrence of 'Jocasta', since whatever belief Tiresias has about Jocasta's identity he may wish not to impute that belief to Oedipus. But, in a statement made privately by Oedipus to himself, the sentence 'I want to marry Jocasta' ought to contain a referentially transparent occurrence of 'Jocasta', since Oedipus would not be a rationally coherent thinker if he had said anything thereby to exclude himself from exploiting, in his *own* reasoning, whatever beliefs he may hold about Jocasta's identity. A representation towards which a rationally coherent thinker is privately ascribed a certain current mental attitude can be characterized as referentially opaque only if we are out to articulate the logical constraints that operate when the person using that ascription of it as a premiss for his reasoning is not also the person to whom it is ascribed.

In other words, an ascription of belief normally generates referential opacity because any speaker or hearer of the ascription might well accept some identity-statements to which the believer does not himself subscribe, and it would therefore risk turning a true ascription into a false one if any substitution on the basis of these statements were carried out within the formulation of the belief. But in the special cases when the speaker, the hearer, and the believer are all just one and the same person at one and the same moment no such risk arises. So if you currently adopt a certain mental attitude towards a particular representation of your own, you would be irrational if you do not, at least in your private reasoning, treat it as referentially transparent. Consequently any computational processing to which your self-ascription of this attitude is subjected is not necessarily anchored to a particular form of reference at any one point: to the extent that there is such an anchoring, your thoughts lack rational coherence. It is not the form of your self-ascription that will normally determine its computational liaisons at any one moment, but rather the total, interlocking system of your mental attitudes at that moment.

What all this helps to demonstrate, however, is not so much a categorical point about the *meaning* of the computational hypothesis, but rather a hypothetical point about its *truth*. What has been shown is that, if the computational hypothesis does indeed have formalist implications, then it does not fit well with the referential transparency that a person attaches to his own mental attitudes at any one moment.

So if you want to maintain the hypothesis you need to give it a sense in which it does not have formalist implications. But what about the argument that, since computers are essentially formal systems, the computational hypothesis cannot but have formalist implications? Do we not thus need to base our interpretation of the hypothesis on the nature of the model rather than on that of the modelled?

§ 23 REALISM VERSUS ANTI-REALISM IN THE COMPUTATIONAL ANALOGY

Summary. The computational hypothesis might be supposed to entail a formalist theory of mental information-processing on the ground that, while tokens of Mentalese may be supposed to occur in the running of a mental program, just as tokens of a high-level programming language may occur in the running of a computer program, the mind has as little need to understand the semantic, or non-formal, properties of Mentalese tokens as a computer has to understand such properties of programming language formula-tokens. But it is more economical to treat such formula-tokens as belonging to the negative part of the analogy between minds and computers. Mental processes do need to be characterized by the psychologist in software terms, but this software characterization is part of the psychologist's theory, not part of the processes under investigation.

Every explanatory or heuristic model in natural science has both positive and negative analogies with that which it models. If it had no positive analogy, it would be irrelevant, and if it had no negative analogy it would be just another instance of the puzzling process that needs instead to be modelled. But the precise extent of the positive analogy, as against the negative one, is often open to discussion. And in the case of the computational hypothesis it is worth while raising this issue with reference to the programming language that is implemented in the articulation of any model generated by the hypothesis. More specifically, since formula-tokens of an appropriate programming language normally play an integral role in programming a computer, in supplying inputs for programs, and in the formulation of outputs, do such tokens of software formula-types belong to the model's positive analogy? If they do, then it is easy enough to see a sense in which tacit mental processes may be said to be operations on formal properties, since the analogous computer operations may be said to latch on to (or be triggered by) the formal, or non-semantic, properties of these programming-language formula-tokens.

Admittedly the people who design or use programming languages have to attach meanings to their formulas. When a programmer tries out a short program, executing it consciously in his imagination, he exploits these meanings. But we need no more suppose that a computer is responsive to the meanings of formulas tapped out on its keyboard than that an electric kettle understands the meaning of the word 'off' when the switch is depressed which bears that label. In the case of the kettle it suffices for the off-switch to be the one that is depressed. Similarly in the case of the computer it suffices for the '7' and '4' levers, say, to be depressed in succession. The computer does not need actually to understand the meaning of the numerical expression '74', let alone the semantic force of utterances in which that expression plays a part. The computer does sufficiently well if it behaves as if it understands. It may thus be said to operate on the formal, non-semantic properties of its input. And, if the human mind does indeed work analogously, the human mind too must operate on the formal properties of appropriate pieces of what has been called 'brainwriting'.[30]

Such a conclusion would not be at odds with the distinction already drawn between simulated parroting and simulated understanding. That distinction depends essentially on an analysis of programming-language formula-types, since it differentiates between those computer operations that correspond to the mention, and those that correspond to the use, of expressions in the construction of such formula-types. It is a distinction that remains valid even when programs are executed on paper or consciously—in a writer's imagination—rather than in a suitable machine. It is thus a distinction that runs quite across the distinction between what a machine responds to and what such a programmer does. On the other hand the present distinction between formal and non-formal properties is more or less parallel with the differences between what a machine responds to and what a programmer does. It certainly makes every machine computation an operation on formal properties; and as a consequence it makes the computational hypothesis imply that every tacit mental process which is analogous to a machine computation will also be an operation on formal properties.

[30] D. C. Dennett, *Brainstorms: Philosophical Essays in Mind and Psychology*, Hassocks: Harvester Press, 1979, pp. 39-50.

But the formalist doctrine is successfully propounded in this sense only if programming-language formula-tokens do indeed belong to the positive analogy. If, instead, they have no counterparts in the mind and should therefore be taken to belong to the negative analogy, the formalist doctrine gets no purchase on the situation. If the computational model's positive analogy does not include these formula-tokens, then it no more includes their formal properties than their semantical ones. So let us examine how far, and for what reasons, such tokens should be regarded as part of the positive analogy.

They certainly have an obvious role in that analogy where the mental process under investigation involves the use of actual or subvocal speech. But this is not important in the present connection, since the formalist doctrine is fundamentally about pre-verbal and subverbal thought. And there it is not at all so obvious that programming-language formula-tokens have a part to play in the positive analogy. Perhaps a person is programmed, as it were, with the help of natural-language sentence-tokens, when he is taught a foreign language. But the intellectual skills that gradually mature in a child are like programs that, in default of positive evidence to the contrary, do not need to be written in any language. So long as they come to be there, and are stored available for execution when an appropriate occasion arises, they may well be hard-wired: they do not need to exist at any time in a quasi-written form as well. Of course, the experimental psychologist is encouraged (by the computational hypothesis) to write a program in some suitable high-level programming language that will match the infant's apparent program as closely as possible. But the sequence of programming-language formulas that the psychologist writes down forms part of his explanatory theory. By stating that the infant behaves as if programmed in this way, he describes what kind of a mechanism he imputes to the child's mind. And the same is true for the study of tacit mental mechanisms at any later stage of human life also. The psychologist does not need also to impute to his subjects a counterpart of his own written program.

Indeed the great virtue of information-programs as explanatory mechanisms is the catholicity with which they admit of embodiment. They can be embodied in many different kinds of hardware (in computers of different architecture or different manufacture); in written-out memoranda (sometimes a list of formulas, sometimes a flow-diagram) for consciously obedient execution by human readers (whether orally, manipulatively, or in imagination); and also, according to the computational hypothesis, in our neuronal networks. Why then should we have to suppose that, whenever they are embodied in our neuronal networks, they must always be embodied in *both* of two quite different ways–one a counterpart of the way in which they are embodied in a computer and the other a counterpart of the way in which they are embodied in written-out memoranda for consciously obedient human execution? Just as an artificial computer may be hard-wired, so too the brain may be.

Precisely the same point can be made about the representations that may constitute the input or output of pre-verbal or subverbal programs in the human mind. Such inputs or outputs are in any case to be conceived as being immanent in the functioning of a person's neuronal network, as in the functioning of a factory-made computer. What is called an internal representation may thus be stored, retrieved, or operated upon. But we do not need to postulate the occurrence also of some mental counterpart of the programming-language utterance-token, or of the print-out or graphic display, which occurs peripherally when an analogous representation is processed by a computer. Such an occurrence triggers, or is triggered by, the information-processing operations of the computer. But in the human being the analogous information-processing operations may be supposed (when not triggered by other information-processing operations) to be triggered directly by the sensory transducers and also to trigger directly any effector nerves that are to come into play.

The issue at stake here may be further clarified by bearing in mind a distinction that is familiar in other fields within the philosophy of science. We often need to distinguish between an instrumentalist and a realist interpretation of certain expressions in scientific theories. Are these expressions just convenient instruments for use in constructing informative descriptions of the behaviour of relatively familiar entities, or do they denote the existence of quite unfamiliar–and normally unobservable–entities? Thus in the philosophy of physics Berkeley was a pioneer of instrumentalism as Locke had been of realism. And in the present issue the expressions open to either an instrumentalist or a realist disambiguation are those constructed in accordance with the computational hypothesis and ascribing internal representations to a person in the metaphorical terms of formulas in a high-level programming language. Are these ascriptions just a convenient way to characterize the information-processing aspect of the person's neuronal system at a particular moment, or do they assert the real existence of tacit sentence-tokens in Mentalese–bits of physically salient brainwriting–every time the person's neuronal computer receives the corresponding input or delivers the corresponding output? Is the psychologist claiming merely that a person's neuronal computer behaves *as if* it has received an appropriate software input or is he claiming that it *actually* has received this in some form?

Both the instrumentalist and the realist mode of interpretation allow the possibility of conscious representations in natural language or mental imagery. Both modes of interpretation are compatible with all sorts of differing theories about the richness of our innate conceptual apparatus and about how our various intellectual activities are possible. Indeed, an overwhelmingly cogent reason exists why there does not seem to be any possible *psychological* evidence[31] that is explicable on the realist assumption and not on the instrumentalist one. The reason is that every computationally relevant feature of the alleged sentence-tokens in natural language or Mentalese has in any case to be got into, or out of, the neuronal hardware. Admittedly, the realist interpretation carries over more positive analogy from any computational model when it imports these extra elements into what is postulated by psychological explanations. But it does so at the cost of greater ontological extravagance. So, in default of any relevant *neurological* evidence, considerations of ontological economy favour rejection of the realist interpretation here. The computational hypothesis makes bold enough assumptions already about the working of the brain as an information-processing system, without our saddling it with yet further, and speculative, assumptions about the existence of tacit programming-language counterparts. By dissociating the computational hypothesis from these further assumptions we make it clear that when phenomenologists or behaviourists criticize the thesis of brainwriting they are not thereby saying anything to weaken the computational hypothesis itself.

The realist in particle physics posits a domain of invisible entities that can cause effects in the visible world (scratchmarks on photographic plates, vapour trails in cloud-chambers, etc.). So the opposing instrumentalist may fairly be accused of placing anthropocentric limits on the horizon of explanation. But in computational psychology the instrumentalist is not open to any comparable accusation, because he leaves open the possibility of basing explanations on the neuronal

---

[31] Such as that cited by Fodor, *Representations*, pp. 28-9.

hardware, and it is the realist who verges on anthropocentrism through his belief in the reality of brainwriting.

It has in fact been pointed out[32] that there are many biological phenomena which can usefully be characterized in terms of a software representation, such as a set of generative rules, but can nevertheless be understood solely as the activity of a structure-determined system, with no mechanism constituting a software representation. And the psychological controversy about visual imagery has certainly to be regarded in this light. Those who doubt the reality of Mentalese sentence-tokens will also be inclined to doubt the reality both of the visual buffer proposed by one side[33] in the controversy and also of the propositional entities proposed by the other.[34] For such an instru-mentalist the choice here is just between the neuronal process charac-terizable by a software representation of a picture and the neuronal process characterizable by a software representation of a proposition (with appropriate time differences between the two processes), however difficult it may be to resolve that issue on the basis of behavioural data.[35] Here too it is conceivable that neurophysiological evidence might support the realist point of view. But in default of such evidence the instrumentalist has a stronger case: it is quite un-necessarily extravagant to suppose actual pictures in the head as well as the necessary neuronal mechanism—let alone to suppose actual sounds in the head whenever we have auditory imagery.

What follows is that the formalist doctrine is on rather weak ground if propounded in the sense currently under consideration. Since the mental reality of tacit programming-language counterparts is an unnecessary and extravagant assumption, there is no reason to suppose that mental representations have any formal properties analogous to those software ones on which computers or their pro-grams may be said to operate. So there is no reason here to suppose that mental processes operate *characteristically* on the formal proper-ties of internal representations, and no reason also, therefore, to suppose that such representations must be attributed formal as well as

[32] By H. R. Maturana, 'The Biology of Language: The Epistemology of Reality', in G. A. Miller and E. Lenneberg (eds.), *Psychology and Biology of Language and Thought: Essays in Honor of Eric Lenneberg*, New York: Academic Press, 1978, pp. 27-63.

[33] S. M. Kosslyn, 'The Medium and the Message in Mental Imagery: A Theory', *Psychological Review*, 88, 1981, pp. 48-66.

[34] Pylyshyn, 'Computation and Cognition: Issues in the Foundations of Cognitive Science', pp. 111-69.

[35] J. R. Anderson, 'Arguments Concerning Representations for Mental Imagery', *Psychological Review*, 85, 1978, pp. 249-77.

representational properties, as if they consisted of sentences in an inner language.

§ 24 SHOULD TOKENS OF MENTALESE BE SUPPOSED TO OCCUR IN THE NEURONAL HARDWARE?

Summary. It may be tempting to regard the hardware of a computer as being itself a system of language, conducting operations on the formal properties of its elements. But this would imply that in order to know best how computational operations occur one needs to know how linguistic ones do, whereas the computational hypothesis implies that in order to know best how mental processes, including linguistic ones, work, one needs to know how computational operations occur. Nor are those operations any different when a programmer executes them in his own head on the basis of his understanding of relevant formulas in his programming language. In effect, the distinction between formal and semantic properties is inapplicable to the subject-matter of computational operations. So the computational hypothesis lends no support to the existence of an internal language that might constitute the ultimate instrument of resolution for the problems of analytical philosophy.

A determined formalist might perhaps claim that, even if we suppose screened or printed tokens of program software, or of input or output formulas, to belong to the computational model's negative analogy, there is still a sense in which formal properties have an indispensable part to play in its positive analogy. When a computer is programmed, or a program is executed, the form or structure of the hardware is altered. Certain logic gates are opened, and others shut, in an appropriate sequence or sequences. So the state of the hardware is to be regarded—the formalist might claim—as being itself a translation or encoding of the written program. Indeed the computer might then be said to show its understanding of program-tokens or input-tokens by virtue of its ability to produce such translations. And, though the computer's user may think in terms of the meanings of these tokens if he executes the program in his conscious imagination, the machine has regard only for the state of its own physical structure. In other words, the machine operates on formal properties, not semantic ones. Analogously, the formalist's claim might be that the human brain-state undergoes a physical transformation whenever it registers a representation of anything, and it is this transformation that may be supposed to trigger the execution of any appropriate programs. Mentalese is thus not a programming language that stands to the brain's computing circuitry as software to hardware. Instead its tokens, according to the formalist, are identical with relevantly transformed states of people's brains: the registering of a subverbal representation consists in such a transformation, and no more. So tacit mental computations are on this view just as much concerned with formal properties, and just as little with semantic ones, as are the operations of programmed artefacts.

This version of the formalist position has the virtue of not multiplying entities beyond necessity. Its extravagance is conceptual rather than ontological. The trouble now is that a metaphor is being used to explicate a metaphor. The original metaphor to be explicated was the computational conception of the mind. But now the computationally relevant properties of computer hardware are being viewed as linguistic forms that have the same meanings as relevant programming-language formulas. Instead of treating the input and output of programming-language tokens in the usual manner as a two-way flow of information between human user on the one side and computer hardware on the other, we are now being asked to treat the states of this hardware as being themselves the sentences of a language, albeit a language that has no communicative role. And this highly strained and metaphorical conception of how a computer functions puts a serious restriction on the extent to which the computational hypothesis can be regarded as supplying a directly apposite model of the mind. Apparently one has first to conceive the functioning of a computer by reference to the model constituted by the functioning of a language and then conceive mental processes on the model of corresponding computational ones. Instead of a suggestion how familiar but puzzling mental events such as language-processing may be explained in terms that belong to a different and better understood category of description—the terminology of computing—we are offered an interpretation of the computational hypothesis that seeks to explain one kind of language in terms of another.

It looked like being a very promising feature of the computational analogy that it could lead us to see how information that is familiarly processed in linguistic form can also be processed by a machine. It looked as though the neuronal transformations that underlie speech and rational behaviour could, in principle, all be described in an independent terminology of computational operations. It looked thus as though psychology had achieved a breakthrough into the classical pattern of scientific explanation whereby familiar kinds of events are economically explicable in terms of others that, though less famimliar, are nevertheless arguably real. But our great expectations are doomed to disappointment if computers are just languages in disguise. Indeed, if this is how computers are to be regarded, it now becomes natural to suppose that in the computational analogy the human mind is being regarded as a model for understanding how a computer works, rather than the other way about. And at least one formalist, Fodor,[36] has explicitly recognized this to be a consequence of his own view, though without explaining how such a conception may be reconciled with the currently accepted aims and methods of cognitive psychology.

Moreover, even if one were prepared to stomach this blurring of the model's direction in order to be able to talk about formality in the required sense, the computational hypothesis could still not be construed as implying that all mental processes are formal in that sense. The reason is that even if we now think of the typical computer's execution of a program as semantically blind, a programmer's conscious execution of the same program in his own imagination may just as much require awareness of semantic properties, if anything ever does. Such a person has to have mastered the functions of the various expressions in the software version of the program, quite as much as anyone who understands instructions about how to calculate square roots, say, must know the meanings of the sentences that formulate those instructions or that list the number to be so treated. Moreover, the computerized and the consciously humanized versions of the program must be precisely similar to one another in structure. Precisely the same sequence of iterations, recursions, chunkings, horizontal searches, vertical searches, etc. must occur in each. Insofar as a model is to be provided for a particular kind of tacit explanatory mechanism in the mind, it does not matter which version of the program is invoked. Hence the computational hypothesis is certainly not to be taken as implying that all mental processes are formal in the sense under examination. But neither does it imply that they are all semantical.

It should be noted too that, as soon as brain-states are treated as formulas of an internal language, a deep and important philosophical problem seems to open up. Specifically, such a language, like any other, ought to have a semantics as well as a syntax. So what would constitute that semantics? Fodor has even claimed that 'this problem is now the main content of the philosophy of mind'.[37] But Fodor's

[36] *Representations*, p. 203.   [37] Ibid.

awesomely blown-up problem is conveniently deflated, if theories about human information-processing are constructed in accordance with the interpretation of the computational model that was proposed in § 23. We do not then treat brain-states as representational formulas of a real internal language but suppose instead that, by referring as our paradigm to the linguistic (software) articulation of an appropriate program that can be run on factory-made computers, we have a tool for describing the programmed brain-processes that are responsible for certain experimentally detectable results. As we extend the range of simulated understanding that is operative in such computational models, we may hope thereby to extend the range of behaviour for which such an explanation is available. Thus internal representations do exist, just so far as the brain-processes exist that are describable with the help of representational formulas in a program that models the computational activity of such processes. But no internal *language* needs to be postulated, and *a fortiori* we do not need to be puzzled by the problem of what would count as a semantics for such a language.

Perhaps someone may be tempted to object: surely any move towards extending the range of simulated understanding that is operative in a computational model is *ipso facto* a move towards building up a semantics for the language of neuronal machine states? Not at all. In such a model simulated understanding is the appropriate machine response to certain types of software input. A machine which exhibits this kind of response is not a language, nor are its states sentences, any more than a human being who understands written instructions is himself a language. In applying the computational hypothesis to tacit mental processes we should treat simulated understanding as a model for a certain type of intelligence or conceptual competence–e.g. the ability to take account of numbers or shapes in a sensory input or the ability to learn a natural language–rather than for a certain type of internal semantics.

The upshot of all this is that the formalist doctrine is quite unfounded. There is no relevant sense in which the computational hypothesis implies that all mental processes operate on formal properties. Indeed, because the modern concept of computation is a highly fruitful, new idea, linked closely with the development of new technology, we should perhaps not be altogether surprised that it turns out to resist capture within the framework of old distinctions, drawn from other fields, like the distinction between form and content or between syntax and semantics. If we insist on applying those rather trite descriptive frameworks, what we find is that either both terms of the antithesis may be said to be applicable or neither. On the one hand, the computational hypothesis should be capable of generating both syntactic and semantic accounts of deductive reasoning, and it should also be able to exploit models that exhibit both simulated parroting and simulated understanding. On the other hand, if the instrumentalist interpretation of the computational hypothesis is correct and there is no internal language or 'brain-writing', there are then no relevant sentences to have either form or meaning in the sense in which these two kinds of feature may be contrasted with one another, and so tacit mental computations cannot properly be said either to operate on forms or to operate on meanings. One can certainly distinguish, at least in principle, between the physiological form, and the computational function, of neuronal transformations, and also between those computational functionings for which simulated parroting provides analogues and those, including internal representings, for which simulated understanding does. But there is no case to regard such internal representings as linguistic entities that themselves have both forms and meanings. What may have both form and meaning is a representational formula in the software version of a computational model. What we may say of the relevant neuronal transformations is that they are analogous in structure–i.e. in computational structure–to the transformations of the computer hardware that register, recall, or operate on this representational formula.

In sum, the computational hypothesis gives no support to the doctrine of a tacit, universal language of thought. So the hypothesis affords no reason to hold that a psychologically sophisticated conception of human thought should lead us to treat philosophy as being concerned, at bottom, with the analysis of such a language. Instead, by adopting the instrumentalist viewpoint, we may at best hope to derive some philosophical insights from any program that psychologists conclude to be the most suitable model, in artificial intelligence, for use in describing the actual process of human computation within some particular field of mental activity. But such a model would tell us *how* thinking happens there, not *what* is the optimal pattern of thought. The computational metaphor does make it possible–in principle–for a psychologist to devise models of performance for the various competences in reasoning that an analytical philosopher may discover himself (and others) to possess. Cognitive psychologists may thus be able one day to give an account of what is going on when a person, on the evidence of his singular intuitive judgements, may be said to have, or to operate with, or to be capable of applying, such-and-such a tacit general principle, like the contraposability of conditionals or the decrease of statistical variance with sample size. But even then a great deal of progress in constructing programs for simulated understanding will be necessary before a useful account of this kind can be given in regard to tacit norms that are substantive (e.g. ethical) rather than logical or mathematical.

Computational analysis and artificial intelligence programs are useful new additions to the analytical philosopher's stock of technical resources. But they cannot provide an adequate characterization of the general nature of his problems and purposes. The new psychology of thinking does not promise a foundation for metaphilosophy that can fill the gap left by rejection of the older imagist and linguistic theories. Rather, we have to say again (compare § 19) that analytical metaphilosophy–as normative reasoning about the normative study of reasoning–does not require any kind of foundation in psychological theory. The validity of its account of analytical philosophy no more depends on the validity of the computational metaphor than it depends on the validity of imagist or linguistic theories, or on the invalidity of the view, held by certain psychologists, that human beings commonly employ several fallacious principles in their reasonings.

Index

CONTRACTED
TO HER
GREEK ENEMY